LEABHARLANN CHONTAE ROSCOMAIN

This book should be returned not later than the last date shown below. It may be renewed if not requested by another borrower.

Books are on loan for 14 days from the date of issue.

383397 (0)

640

DATE DUE	DATE DUE	DATE DUE	DATE DUE
23. 10. 04	29. JAN 08		
06 MAY 05	2. JUN 08		
10. OCT 06.	18. NOV 08		
03. FEB 07	31. MAR 09.		
30. AUG 07			
01. NOV 07			

HOME TIME

HOME TIME

JOCASTA INNES

EBURY PRESS
LONDON

To Angeles, Marta, Eva, Jana, Isabel, Katrin, Doris, Radka I and Radka II, Zdenka, Victoria, Istvan, Fatma, Natalia; all the au pairs conscripted into what I tend to think of as Mum's Army. A varied and picturesque crowd, remembered by my entire household with reminiscent laughter and real affection. You expanded our horizons. I wonder if we expanded yours?

First published in Great Britain in 2002

1 3 5 7 9 10 8 6 4 2

Text © Jocasta Innes 2002

Jocasta Innes has asserted her right to be identified as the author of this work under the Copyright, Designs and Patents Act 1988.

First published by
Ebury Press
Random House, 20 Vauxhall Bridge Road, London SW1V 2SA

Random House Australia (Pty) Limited
20 Alfred Street, Milsons Point, Sydney, New South Wales 2061, Australia

Random House New Zealand Limited
18 Poland Road, Glenfield, Auckland 10, New Zealand

Random House South Africa (Pty) Limited
Endulini, 5A Jubilee Road, Parktown 2193, South Africa

The Random House Group Limited Reg. No. 954009

www.randomhouse.co.uk

A CIP catalogue record for this book is available from the British Library.

Editing and layout: Margot Richardson   Design: Chris Smith   Illustrations: Tim Mayer
Proofreading: Cathie Gill   Index: Ingrid Lock

ISBN 0091879353

Papers used by Ebury are natural, recyclable products made from wood grown in sustainable forests.
Printed and bound in Scotland by Scotprint

CONTENTS

MY STATEMENT

One word you will not find in this book, except in quotation marks (as in 'housewife's dermatitis', see page 140) is 'housewife'. Although many women, and an increasing number of men, still spend a great deal of their time keeping their homes up to scratch – cleaning, organising and generally making nice – they no longer see this as a lifelong vocation or a sufficient *raison d'être* as it undoubtedly was as recently as the 1950s and '60s.

Then, clever advertisers beamed their seductive copy at those women, millions of them, who had not yet woken up to the brave new world of washing machines and vacuum cleaners and – wait for it – detergents. In contrast to the real-life housewives, emerging from a world war and a decade of austerity (make do and mend, sheets sides to middle, etc) these guys dreamed up a new iconic 'housewife': a wasp-waisted cutie who raced through the household chores in high heels wearing a frilly pinny and a radiant lipsticked smile, thanks to a plethora of wondrous new appliances which took the slog out of housework. I don't suppose her real-life counterparts, in their shabby overalls, hair tied up in scarves, identified with the ad man's fantasy, but they cottoned on fast to the labour-saving appliances.

And rightly so! The vacuum cleaner and the washing machine remain epochal inventions of the twentieth century, freeing up countless women from exhausting tasks that could now be expedited at the press of a button, or the flick of a switch. My mother's generation fairly scrambled to get in on the act.

The irony is that this astonishing liberation of female energy killed the frilly, cutie household icon stone dead. Women got uppity, joined the Women's Liberation Movement, discarded their frilly pinnies, burned their bras, refused to be 'cabbages', got political and angry. (My younger sister signed up for a carpentry course and constructed a leviathan of a sofa bed out of marine ply, with giant drawers beneath for bedding. Sensible thinking, except the drawers were so heavy that it took two people to wrench them open. Meanwhile dust accumulated on the display shelves of state-of-the-art Scandinavian glasses, and cat litter spilled over on to the rubber industrial flooring – cutting edge back then in the '70s.)

The mood was edgy and confrontational, the women (bright, talented and often graduates) intent on breaking out of the domestic mould of 'housewife', mum and 'cabbage', left their menfolk puzzled, resentful, uncomprehending and darkly suspicious. Marriages broke up, women flocked back to work desperate for independence and determined to realise their talents in careers such as journalism, publishing and the media, and to distance themselves from the whole notion of housewifery which they saw as demeaning, unpaid servitude. The word 'housewife' quietly dropped out of common parlance.

That was then. Since that time a new generation has grown up, the children of the women who quoted Germaine Greer, Betty Friedan and Marilyn French. As often happens, they have reacted against what were burning issues to their parents' generation. Most young women today take their careers seriously, and expect to combine work with marriage (or partnership), having children, and running a home. This is a tough and demanding remit, as they are finding. They certainly don't regard themselves as 'housewives' (though oddly 'househusband' seems to be an acceptable definition of the man who takes domestic charge while his partner carries on with the 8 to 5 routine).

The difference is that they don't think of housework as degrading per se; in fact, many women find it surprisingly therapeutic, enjoying the change of rhythm from day job to homework, even finding it creative. Where they have a problem is inexperience. Those fiery feminists were not about to fall over themselves teaching their offspring the domestic skills they were so hot to abandon for the world of 'proper' – regular and paid – work. So now we have this quaint situation: a post-feminist generation without ideological hang-ups about housework as such, but all adrift about how to begin, what is entailed, how to get the best results in the least time and with the least effort.

My evidence is anecdotal, admittedly, but I think it is fairly representative of how many of the 20-something generation goes about household tasks:

Washing up: Fill the sink, add a squirt of detergent, and then shove everything in from glasses to greasy roasting pans, all at once! Leave for 10 minutes (for the detergent to get to work) while you catch up on your texting. This is followed by some halfhearted work with a brush in the now cooling water. Surprise – a broken glass or two. Greasy plates pack the rack and pots and pans are 'left to soak'. Mugs retain a dark splodge and forks may hold tiny food particles within their tines.

An alternative approach, hygienically preferable, but costly on hot water, is to wash each item individually under a running tap. In both cases, debris such as rice, tea leaves and coffee grains are washed down the plughole, storing up future drainage problems.

(See page 137 for further thoughts on washing up.)

Washing: Thank goodness there is a machine here; no donkey work. Washing powder or liquid is added generously (who reads those boring instructions?) and everything from designer items to smelly socks gets bunged in pell-mell. Colours run,

woollies shrink. *C'est la vie!* Left overnight in the machine, the garments cook into interestingly abstract shapes, which are then flung hurriedly, without pegs, over the washing line. A bit of tut-tutting if the weather misbehaves, but the odd sock blown into a puddle gets the punishment it deserves: it is stepped over and left to rot.

(See Laundry, page 171.)

Brooms and mops: The generation I am addressing – 20-somethings – are baffled by these antiquated implements. Raised in a push-button world, they have a touching faith that the tool will sort of lead the way and do the work if they push it in front of them and hang on to the handle. If mopping, they flood the floor, add enough detergent or Flash to raise suds, dab with the mop then 'leave to dry naturally'. If you remonstrate, that is their comeback; it sounds sort of green and caring.

(See Cleaning Tools on page 113.)

OK, these are worst-case scenarios, but I suggest they are not uncommon.

Housework is by no means rocket science, but if your mum didn't stand over you at some point and convince you that there is a right (fast and effective) way to wash up, sweep, sort the wash, or deal with any of the manifold jobs involved in running a *decent* home, how do you find out?

Somewhere along the communication chain of domestic knowledge passed from mother to daughters and sons, a link went missing. Whether you ascribe this ignorance to feminism, reliance on appliances, more demanding jobs, later motherhood – the fact remains that an astonishing number of youngish people are clueless, to put it bluntly, when it comes to the necessary disciplines, routines and priorities that structure housework and deliver a home that is a good place to return to, and live in. The latter is important, an urgent need even, as the world out there becomes more threatening and confusing.

MY PITCH

This book grew out of the foregoing. I enjoy writing out of personal hands-on knowledge and experience. I don't claim to be a Superwoman, or a Mrs Wonderful (I tend to see her as suffering from an obsessive compulsive disorder), but I think I can modestly say that when it comes to housework, I have been there, done that and know it inside out. I have lived in bedsits, artisan dwellings and big houses, combined with raising a family and running a home, usually on a tight budget, following a career, pushed for time and aiming higher than I could realistically achieve.

I came to housework late (mid-20s), uninstructed and no more enthusiastic than the average girl-about-town today. It didn't bother me that my tiny, sunless bolthole in Walton Street (not the chic address that it is now) was by any standards a tip, or that my most sophisticated boyfriend rushed straight out to the nearest hardware store to equip me with household basics: Vim, Fairy Liquid, a mop, brush and pan, dish rack and tea towels. This was my Sally Bowles period.

What put an end to this blithe sluttishness was less marriage than motherhood. I had not expected this; in fact I remember assuring myself that no baby was going to turn me into one of those mumsy types I met at natural childbirth classes prattling on about layettes, push chairs, Dr Spock, and what colour to paint the nursery. I was definitely unsentimental; today it would be called 'in denial'. No sooner was the sloe-eyed infant attached to the engorged footballs (I no longer recognised my breasts), denial gave way to affirmation. The game was up for Sally Bowles. This tiny creature was *mine*, and her blind need and dependency awoke a protective passion which is nothing amazing (we share it with most female creatures), but it stood all my egotistical preconceptions on their head. My copy of Dr Spock fell apart as I consulted our guru about nappy contents, stertorous breathing, weight gain, and establishing a routine – he was quite laid back about that.

Hygiene – or possible lack of it – became a preoccupation. I mean how clean was clean? How sterile was sterile? Did I need to boil the water before adding a carefully measured dose of Milton, and the container too? The good Dr was suddenly too laid back for me. From carefree slattern to frantic mum was a short, irrevocable step. There is nothing new about this; it goes with the territory. It eases with each new birth – three in my case – but the old insouciance never quite returned.

Nowadays, I get itchy when I see overflowing sinks or laundry baskets; red wine slopped on my scrubbed table; greasy worktops splattered with crumbs, onion peelings and empty glasses; and sofas deep in discarded newspapers. In order to relax and enjoy my home, I simply have to deal with it. NOW! Even returning – groggy – from a long-haul flight, I get into the clean-up routine before checking my mail. I suspect this is a normal householder's compulsion, whether male or female. The acerbic author of *Biting the Dust*, Margaret Horsfield, notes an identical response in herself in the same situation. Where we differ, I think, is that she feels apologetic, or diffident, about this urgent need to restore order and get things straight. I sense she imagines a feminist jury – Betty, Germaine and Marilyn et al – raising their eyebrows in disapproval, sneering and voting her an unreconstructed 'cabbage'.

Too bad. The way I see it (while much admiring feminist achievement in the workplace) is that I like my home a certain way – important to me but incomprehensible to others – and getting it that way is a task I acquit myself of more efficiently and thoroughly than anyone else. Furthermore, if I am honest, I quite soon find myself enjoying putting things to rights: squeaky-clean crocks, scrubbed table and all that. Domestic rituals, however banal, add a certain structure to daily life, most often appreciated in its absence. Enforced idleness can also be a strain. For this reason, I mostly opt for self-catering holidays. Shopping abroad is an adventure and cooking with exotic new ingredients provides a creative challenge and the trifling washing up routine offers a small, but stimulating, sense of accomplishment – after that *dolce far niente*.

THE CLASSIC COMPLAINT

Repetitiveness, the job no sooner done than needing to be done all over again. This is the most common complaint about housework, and there is no denying that cleaning, vacuuming, tidying and ironing are as ongoing as life itself. At moments of low energy, or depression, it reads like a monstrous imposition and one feels resentful and trapped. Contrariwise, during a 'high', it all seems tediously trivial, a drag on ones *joie de vivre* or creativity. I think that everyone goes through these moods. They are part of our emotional weather, and as such, they change and pass. However, the plain truth is that housework *needs* doing or things quickly slide into squalor and chaos. The disintegration of your private home is a dismal and threatening sight. We can usually live with a reasonable amount of mess and disorder, but dirt is another matter altogether. I have a vivid memory of Hagia Sofia in Istanbul, one of the world's great buildings, its huge dome and spectacular mosaics and marbles sadly marred by a coating of grime lying thickly wherever one looked and giving once proud Sofia an air of wretchedness. Dirt is sad, end of story.

When the chips are down, it is the person who cares most who has to deal with it and dealing with dirt requires physical effort – the famous elbow grease. Think yourself lucky that vacuum cleaners, washing machines, dishwashers – and I would add a steam cleaner (see page 116) – have taken the real heavy-duty effort out of cleaning. These are great twentieth-century inventions, helping to fill the gap left when the servant problem became the no-servant problem. Hiring muscle, if you can afford it,

in the shape of cleaners or au pairs, helps spread the load, though inevitably it will create new people-type problems (see page 234). It is a fact of twenty-first-century life that all solutions create new and different problems: tradesmen don't turn up, cleaners skimp or au pairs do a runner.

Outside of these gadgets and problematic helpers, you are on your own, frankly, making do with elbow grease. There are few miracle products that will do the job for you effortlessly. The hype may tell you differently. If you listen to the hype, you will end up with all your shelves and cupboards filled to bursting with bottles, sprays, cans, jars and tins that eat into your weekly budget and, with few exceptions, don't deliver. One detergent, one abrasive cleaner and one powerful grease buster or de-blocker (see page 106) equip you for most domestic contingencies.

Spraying your kitchen worktops with anti-bacterial spray is no substitute for a good scrub down and rinse-off effort. At best it is a lazy compromise, at worst it is a pitiful attempt to turn your kitchen into an operating theatre (see page 150 for thoughts and facts about The Hygiene Hypothesis). Nor is it 'green', and we should all be concerned about that.

> Our mistake is to imagine that technology can provide an alternative and effortless solution.

The more people I talked to while compiling this book, from globe-trotting hygiene experts to ordinary people with long experience and high standards, the clearer it became that cleaning, as in truly sweetly clean, does not come out of a spray bottle or a packet of 'wipes'. There is no escaping the fact that cleaning usually means rolling up your sleeves, grabbing a scrubbing brush, a sponge or cloth and getting down to it. Use your loaf and apply common sense about where to put your effort on a regular basis. *Plus ça change, plus c'est la même chose*, this is as true of housework as fashion, politics, sex, relationships, poverty.

One thing which struck me, researching this book, is how little is new about housework. There are the invaluable appliances I have mentioned, some new products, but what has changed most seems to be our attitudes. Maybe 'new man' hasn't fully emerged yet but there are signs of a new spirit of co-operation from the sex. Speaking of which, sex I mean, I kept finding that people are as coy about their little domestic manias and foibles as they used to be about their sexual habits. It takes patient questioning to get them to admit to being fussy about sticky door handles, or

obsessive about the order in which their CDs are stacked, but once the truth is out – that yes, they do really care about clean floors, scrubbed tables, nicely ironed shirts – it's as if a taboo has been lifted. They feel free to talk about domestic stuff without worrying about looking silly and trivial minded. This includes both men and women. Gay people are in a category of their own here, often exceptionally house proud, and not in the least embarrassed to say so.

It turns out, when you scratch beneath the surface, that most people seriously care about their homes, the way they look, how clean or tidy they are, that they dependably provide an oasis of peace and order in a tumultuous and stressful world. This is where domestic management comes in, which I happen to think is as complex as any other form of management, and requires much the same skills. (Talk about multi-tasking!) These usually have to be learned too. But there are models to follow here. With housework, we tap into centuries of honed, modest, hands-on routines whose main purposes have always been the same: to protect the young, safeguard health, reinforce family intimacy and pride, sweeten, comfort and order our daily lives. I rest my case.

GETTING A GRIP: THE ROUTINE

When it comes to running your home, large or small, your best ally is a routine. If you find the word repugnant, think of it as a blueprint, a checklist or an infrastructure. As everyone's circumstances are different, it can never be cast in stone, but it provides a guideline to refer to; broken down into daily, weekly, monthly, even bi-annual actions whose sole aim is to make your home a pleasure to live in and return to. We are not talking about perfection: housework for housework's sake, or Mrs Wonderful's home, so immaculate that a cup of tea needs a little coaster just in case.

My definition of a well run home (what my neighbour, Polly Hope, calls 'a civilised home') is rather modest. It should look comely, smell nice and feel welcoming, not solely to impress visitors, but to provide you and your family with a nurturing environment, comfort and repose. This aspiration can accommodate some mess: dusty shelving, basketfuls of washing in the kitchen en route to the ironing board, baby buggies in the hall or a scatter of toys. The important thing is that one senses the mainspring of domestic life is in good working order, on the move, under control. This beneficent atmosphere is immediately recognised in its absence: rooms where mess is sliding into squalor, sinks piled high with crocks and pans, unopened mail, cat litter due for a change and grubby sheets on unmade beds. In this case, I don't think slut, but I do think depression. As Yeats wrote (admittedly in a rather different context) 'the centre cannot hold'.

I have been there, too wiped out to even start on the daily routine and indifferent to the mounting chaos. I suspect many women go through similar states of domestic apathy for many reasons: post-natal blues, post 'flu exhaustion, marital discord, tiredness, boredom and hormonal change. In this grey mood, the whole edifice of domestic family life seems an intolerable burden; all take and no give. You could cry on a good friend's shoulder or consider seeing a shrink. You could step out to the shops and reward yourself with an extravagant treat. Or you could – I suggest this diffidently, not wishing to sound facile or gung-ho – set yourself a small domestic hurdle to clamber over. For instance, clear and scrub the kitchen table to perfection or empty and clean out your fridge. Getting started is always the problematic bit. Have the radio ready, cups of tea/coffee or a slurp of Chardonnay nearby. It is an odd, surprising discovery – atavistic need, genetic programming – that absorbing yourself in a simple household task can really get the adrenalin flowing, endorphins kicking in, defeated spirit and sluggish muscles roused to action. A limited exercise, perhaps, but I feel it taps into something profound in the psyche. Action is what is needed to shift that great lump of depression: you start feeling better as you warm to the task and see results. What is so therapeutic about housework is that you do see results immediately – instant gratification. Simplistic? Try it.

An interesting fact about household routines, as spelt out by the oldest written evidence down to your modern cleaner's checklist, is that the essentials hardly vary. We are talking here about a body of pragmatic experience not to be sniffed at. Roughly speaking it goes like this: sort, clean, tidy up.

Sort and/or tidy (let's not split hairs) is first priority: it clears away inessentials so you can see what the cleaning tasks are about. To make things easier for yourself, your cleaner or au pair, try to do a quick whip round before going to bed. Collect up crockery, mugs or glasses, empty ashtrays, throw crisp packets and other debris into a binbag, clear the decks of toys, newspapers, open windows a crack to allow clean air to blow through. This should be a nightly routine, even if you have to push yourself, because this few minutes the night before alleviates morning-after blues, the dismay of confronting a stale-smelling, littered, grungy lair when you are at your most vulnerable, nerve ends twitching.

Mornings tend to be rushed, especially if you have to sort kids out as well as make a start on the housework – loading the dishwasher, clearing the breakfast table, chucking dirty clothes into the laundry basket or washing machine, airing beds, opening windows. If you have help – cleaner, au pair – you may be able to skip these actions, though most women I spoke to felt compelled to put on a bit of a show for a cleaner, and au pairs will respect you more if you set standards for them to match up to. It is different if you have a full time job yourself or a school run, or both. All the same, anything you can crack, get started on, before you make a dash for the tube, bus, car, is meritorious. Some women I spoke to, whose jobs started around 10 am, tried to fit in some vacuuming before leaving home – but they had no domestic help. Anything that can be dealt with first thing, when one is feeling fresher, is a step nearer to the orderly home you want to come back to.

Working women need to be more organised because they don't have the reassurance of time in which to catch up later in the day, or week, though they can afford more help as a rule. You may not be able to do more than token housework but you have other priorities, such as checking your bag or briefcase the night before: keys,

'Among the extracurricular activities our grandmothers of that era [mid-nineteenth century in the USA] could be expected to face up to … the making of wine; preparing diets for invalids; wage war against rodents, insects and other vermin; bake bread twice a week; turn out the Monday wash, the Tuesday folding and the Wednesday ironing; prepare and serve three meals a day; keep the well pure; make its water soft and run a vegetable patch; keep the house sparkling clean, paint a bedroom, whitewash the kitchen … make her own soap, mix her own paint, compound her own cosmetics; grow her own medicinal and kitchen herbs or collect them in woods and fields; bottle a barrel of cider and put up preserves and bring up a family; care for a milch cow, make butter and cheese; dye wool and cotton; mix furniture, shoe, floor and razor strap polish .'

Grandmother's Household Hints: As good today as yesterday,
Helen Lyon Adamson (F Muller Ltd, 1965)

wallet, mobile, filofax all present and correct. It is exasperatingly easy to forget that you left your keys in another jacket the night before, or your wallet on your desk because you were catching up on the household bills on the net. I still freeze when this happens, jumping to the worst case scenario at once – maybe I left the keys in the door, or the wallet dropped out of my bag as I fumbled about looking for my tube fare? This is, of course, the downside of multi-tasking: one's mind is overcrowded, one does things in a daze where forgetting keys, dropping a wallet, seem only too possible. Result – a panic attack which feels as if it takes years off ones life.

MOVING ON – THE WEEKEND

The weekend has to be the time when working people catch up on the chores the household needs to deal with over a week. Therefore, yet more pressure. This is not helped by the fact that workers understandably feel that the weekend should be holiday time: reward time, an opportunity to lie in, loaf, read the papers and generally potter about. Alas, time and tide (in this case, laundry, shopping and cleaning) wait for no man or woman. It should be possible, in between the self-indulgent bits, to get one load of washing on the go, hung out or tumble dried. Maybe there is time to stuff in a load, blacks or coloured, before you set off on your Big Shop. It isn't desperate if your washing gets all creased up, but it will make ironing it more time consuming (see page 181 on laundering tips). You might feel up to ironing on Sunday?

THE BIG SHOP

Meanwhile, the Big Shop is unavoidable. Some people prefer to leave it till the last half hour before the store closes, when they can pick up the best bargains, but the majority feel more comfortable getting it out of the way earlier, thus freeing up the remainder of the weekend. Furthermore, it does take time to unload your shopping and dispose of the contents in the appointed places (see page 65 for wheezes you should be primed with to make it taste better, fresher, last longer, add flavour and interest). Leaving bags of food in the car is never wise, especially in hot weather. You will be asking for trouble.

Try to allow some time on returning from the Big Shop for the sorting and disposing of goods (fridge, freezer, etc) and maybe longer term preparation, such as marinading of fish, meat, etc (see page 65 for ideas). If you have children, they might be of help here, under supervision?

CLEANING

This leaves cleaning. If you have help during the week, the basic minimum for household maintenance should be in place: carpets vacuumed, floors mopped, work surfaces cleaned up and tables scrubbed. In other words, the necessary background for Polly Hope's 'civilised home' (see page 100); nothing extraordinary or exceptional, but restored to order, friendly and habitable.

However, if you are pernickety, a bit of a control freak, or have no paid help on the domestic front, you may feel inspired to add your own gloss on things, or in the latter case, do just enough in the cleaning line to restore your pleasure and faith in the home as the best place to be. To some people this spells 'tidy', to others 'clean'; these are not mutually exclusive activities, of course, but I find myself siding with the 'clean' bunch, because a tidy room which smells stale, or manky, never makes up for superficial tidiness. However, I know people differ here in their priorities. Most men (see Nick Curtis, page 60) feel tidiness and order is the paramount requirement, whereas many women pick up on skimpy cleaning: cobwebs, dust along the bookshelves, sticky light switches, door handles and rails.

Sunday morning – after reading the papers and before the afternoon walk or gallery visit – seems psychologically the moment to have a go at the cleaning. By this point you are a bit more rested and still have the afternoon ahead of you. If you are the sole cleaner, the routine is basic: dust, mop, vacuum, etc (see page 104). If the place is reasonably maintained, you might feel up to an in-depth project; a first stab at de-cluttering (see page 44) or the annual Deep Clean (see page 121). Clear, clean and sort a kitchen cupboard, vacuum under the beds or clean some windows (see page 135).

There is no getting away from the fact that these are chores, but once you get stuck in, they offer real satisfaction, denote progress, and give you the warm glow that comes with ticking another duty off your list of 'things to do'. You may wake in the, night haunted by all the tedious work things you haven't got around to, but then the recollection steals in: I did tackle the bookcase and the kitchen corner cupboard; that's all done,and dusted. Pacified, you can drift off to sleep again. Keeping a balance between professional and domestic demands is always a struggle. The former usually wins, for the usual reasons (competition, salary and ambition, etc), but to divert your work skills to the home front, once in a while, is a healthy move, a reminder that there is a life outside work.

DO IT NOW

Where time is short, it matters all the more not to leave loose ends dangling, whether these be outstanding invoices, missing buttons or unravelling hems. Make this easier for yourself by replicating necessary equipment at key points throughout your home, to save running up and down stairs and hunting for elusive items. African jute sacks in mouth-watering colours are inexpensive and roomy enough to hold sewing kit, scissors and stamps, or all your vitamin pills, lipsalve or whatever. Try to train yourself – this requires fierce self-discipline – to pick things up and put them back: the pair of shoes you kicked off while cooking or watching television, the cheque book you took to dash off a couple of cheques.

I have a collection of old shopping baskets into which I drop things that belong elsewhere as the day goes on. I take these with me on my next trip upstairs, dropping the contents off where appropriate. Or I leave the basket on the bottom stair as a reminder. Even if you live on only one level, this system can be helpful. This isn't just a tidying or mind-clearing exercise. There is a risk that if you get soft on yourself, the right-thing-in-the-wrong-place syndrome gets somehow institutionalised; the cleaner or au pair puts it/them neatly in a corner and you lose track of it/them till the next need arises. A cheque book, as I often find, can all too easily slip into a pile of mail or newspapers, and only come to light after much hair tearing and anxiety.

A household filing cabinet (two drawers is sufficient) is a necessity, with a basket or tray on top where you can dump anything you haven't time to sort immediately. A filing cabinet doesn't have to be dull and grey: there are many colourful varieties available. But it needs to be very accessible, preferably stand alone and raised up off the ground so you don't have to stoop or kneel to access hanging files. You will also need a good over-head light, or a free-standing lamp close by.

In a busy-busy situation, the line of least resistance is always the one to go for.

REGULAR ROUTINES

LAST THING AT NIGHT

This may seem an odd place to start organising your life, but every routine is predicated on stealing a march on the next jobs, while the mood is upon you. It helps if you make these household routines habitual – like cleaning your teeth – and then you will sleep better.

● Stack dishes, crocks, pans ready for washing up (or stack the dishwasher and set it going), clear the table for breakfast.

● Nip round with a binbag into which you empty the evening's debris: beer cans, crisp packets, ashtrays or old news-papers. Add any crocks, etc, to the washing stack. Open window and doors while you do this to let fresh air blow through. A brief airing at night helps dispel that stale miasma in the morning. Then set the burglar alarm (if you have one) or lock the doors.

THE MORNING

- Open up bed, open the windows, grab up clothes to be washed, turn off lights and close doors to keep some heat in.

Assuming you are not at work:
- Get a washload going (sorted by colour, etc) while you bath or shower. Wipe up round basin, bath and brush out toilet.

- Check fridge/larder to plan the day's meals. Bin anything mouldy, slimy or 'off' smelling. Empty bin, replace liner.

- Wipe worktops, hob. Scrub table. Sweep the floor and mop if gungy.

- A quick inspection of the premises: hang up coats, jackets or dressing gowns, stash dirty washing in the laundry basket, straighten beds, thump cushions, tidy books, magazines or videos, water drooping plants. As well as clearing the decks for the new day, this allows you to check where the cleaning effort should go. Some people prefer to clean rooms in

rotation: for example, Monday living room, Tuesday bedrooms and so on. Others prefer to pack it all into one cleaning blitz and some (I am one of these) tend to put the effort where it seems most necessary on the day. For instance, a wet weekend means muddy footprints in the hall and up the stairs.

No routine is cast in stone, though it makes life easier if you have a cleaner or au pair to rough out a regular weekly cleaning plan. This becomes your 'routine'.

By my reckoning, this preliminary whip round takes about an hour and a half, bringing you to mid-morning. (The time will clearly be shorter if you have an au pair helping and longer if you do the school run or have a baby/toddler to see to.)

- **Coffee Break**. Collect and sort the mail so you can read your letters or the newspaper while you drink your coffee and also plan the day's cleaning effort.

Having re-established order throughout the home, which is the point of the daily basic routine, you are primed to forge ahead with the weekly scheme. Historically, Monday was washday, Tuesday dealt with the ironing and Wednesday you started to clean the house which spread out over the next two days, so that the weekend saw the place looking its best, not just tidy, but *clean*. That still seems a wise rhythm to aspire to because there always is more washing to be done on a Monday (the weekend's glad rags), plus this is conventionally the day for changing the bed linen; with a family this could keep the washing machine going all day.

WEEKLY ROUTINE

While a couple out at work, living in a small flat, can probably get away with a slimmed-down version of this routine, and save it all up for a Sunday morning blitz, a family house needs on-going attention over and beyond the daily maintenance I have outlined.

People and pets create mess, but they also shed an amazing amount of fallout. I don't just mean muddy footprints, cigarette ash or crisp crumbs, but actual physical debris: skin flakes and hair which settle on furniture and carpets and join in with the dust and mites to create a sort of microscopic compost layer on every surface. Unless any members of your family have allergies, I doubt this is actively harmful – families become acclimatised to their family germs – but unless it is dealt with regularly, or once a week, it looks unsightly and feels literally tacky – sticky door handles, light switches and banister rails, etc.

● Deal with family wash, hang out, iron and return to base. Only iron essentials (see page 183). At the same time, take care of urgent mending: missing buttons, split seams, unstitched hems, etc (see page 210). The washing will take two to three hours, spread over two days. It is still the heavy duty, inexorable task of the week.

● Change all beds, put out clean nightclothes and towels.

● Clean all rooms used by the family, either by rota or all in one go, whichever suits. This is more about cleaning than tidying (which is done daily in a superficial way) so takes in dusting, wiping down sticky surfaces, some polishing of furniture, thorough vacuuming (use interchangeable attachment to get beneath beds and sofas and to suck up fallout along skirtings and window sills). This weekly clean doesn't go as far as the deep clean (see page 121), but it is probably what a cleaner would deliver and what our ancestors would have called a 'good turn out'. Rooms look brighter and smell fresher for this. Once weekly might be pushing it, but it is a mark to aim for.

● Make a note as you go of light bulbs in need of replacement (replace and also check stocks), plants needing re-potting or a splash of plant food, furniture covers needing to be cleaned or washed, stains to be deal with, gadgets acting up or needing servicing.

- Collect up clothes for the dry-cleaners, shoes for the cobbler and stash them in the hall in a conspicuous spot so as to remind you to deal with them.

- Sort through mail and emails: respond and/or file.

Towards the end of the week:
- Spend a few minutes looking through cookbooks for new ideas for the week's meals.

- Start a shopping list for the Big Shop. Think seasonal.

- Clean fridge/larder, check dry goods (flour, pasta, lentils) and stocks of Marmite, jam and peanut butter; all those family faves for your shopping list. Check supplies of binbags, bin liners and cleaning materials (washing liquid or powder, Cif, bleach and detergent).

- Maybe, if you are up to it, give one thing an in-depth TLC treatment. Clean one window or mirror perfectly, handwash a few cushion covers or polish a brass door knob. When so much domestic routine is about running on the spot to catch up and

splitting your mind between so many endeavours, to do one job to perfection, for the hell of it, is somehow a treat. Even if no one else notices!

There is no question that the weekly routine is less onerous if you have help and can delegate some of the cleaning and regular jobs such as cleaning out the fridge. On the other hand, the fridge clean tells you more about what is wasted, or overstocked, than it would an au pair or cleaner. As any CEO knows – and this is what you are in domestic terms – there is a skill to delegation.

MONTHLY ROUTINE

If weekly routine is to do with taking the daily maintenance a whole step further, the monthly routine is more like a board meeting; review of performance and executive decision-making. This is a long-winded way of saying that monthly actions are mostly administrative: paying bills, booking dentist's appointments, dispatching faulty machines to be serviced or even ordering up coal/logs if winter is close. It might be a moment to consider shopping for basic household goods on the net or via mail order. If the daily/weekly routines are more or less in place, the monthly – and monthly is arbitrary here – could be two- or three-monthly depending on your lifestyle and circumstances. This should really create a pause, while you look back, get a fix on expenditure, decide whether the cleaner is shaping up or not, whether that leak needs dealing with immediately, or if it is time to replant the pots on the patio.

On the hands-on side, there are some household tasks that may need attending to:

● Oven needs a thorough clean, hobs ditto (see page 142).

● Windows could do with a clean both inside and out (see page 135).

● Paintwork, inside and out, needs a wipe down.

● One cupboard, or chest of drawers, should be cleared, sorted, vacuumed or thoroughly wiped down: serviceable clothes sent to refugee appeals; odd socks, etc, binned; outworn or worn-out clothing recycled as rags; buttons saved in your button box or jar. You might – if you are the thrifty, recycling type – start collecting knackered T-shirts: these are now being made into millennial rag rugs.

● Spend one cleaning session doing a number on any antique, polished furniture or modern oiled furniture. Clear the top, wipe off stickies, then rub over with home-made polish (see page 127) or your favourite wax or cream. Then rub, rub and rub until it comes up glowing. Do the table legs, the chair rungs, front, back and sides, as it were.

When feminists protest fiercely about the 'drudgery' involved in housework, they rarely mention the incidental satisfactions it can provide. There are moments or moods when polishing brass door furniture, or darning an exquisite linen tablecloth, can be powerfully therapeutic. Even the most creative woman can't always be writing poetry or novels, or making avant garde sculpture from cigarettes. Humdrum domestic rituals will not make you rich or famous, or express your quintessential persona; they will tap into something older and deeper in the psyche. I think it is almost a Zen thing, an absence of ego, where the very repetitiveness of the actions is soothing and lets the mind float free. The archetype here would be Homer's Penelope, busy with her weaving, repudiating her suitors, while Odysseus fought giants and monsters, extricated himself finally from the wiles of nymphs and sirens and set sail for home.

If this sets up too many gender antagonisms, perhaps another analogy might be the total absorption that young children, in that intensely imaginative pre-pubertal phase, bring to their current enthusiasms. For all adults, to lose oneself temporarily in some patient, undemanding activity which is essentially hands-on, is strangely rejuvenating to the spirit; a dip into the waters of Lethe, or should it be the Pierian Spring?

BI-ANNUAL OR ANNUAL ROUTINES

Some of this is seasonal (ie, moth-proofing, ordering firewood or calling upon a tree surgeon). Some of it is simply widely spaced – such as the deep clean – but can be tackled whenever it seems most appropriate and least disruptive. Once or twice a year, one needs to take stock of the domestic situation; it is as simple (or complex) as that. These are the sort of initiatives to think about.

● A deep clean, at least of main rooms. Set aside two, three or even four hours per room, depending on its size and condition. The deep clean is good exercise, rewards you with visible and olfactory improvements and bonds you all over again to your surroundings. This isn't sentimental crap, it is hard work, but the uplift it gives is real. To see and enjoy a room close to that elusive ideal – immaculate – lets you off the treadmill for a moment, even if it won't, cannot last because of pets, kids and life generally. What it reminds you of, even if momentarily, is that your central vision

prevails, the effort was meaningful and you remain inspired, as you must be, to carry on with the good work.

● Moth-proofing needs to be dealt with in spring and autumn, to catch the little brutes before they do untold damage to your most cherished garments. Moths have luxurious tastes (see page 161 for how to frustrate them).

● Over the year, most homes spring leaks, or exhibit other signs of faulty main-tenance: blocked gutters or drainpipes; tiles or slates gone adrift; roof lights no longer water tight. Postponing attention to these problems invariably aggravates the long-term damage, needing more repair work and thus costing more. Chase a reliable builder/handyman (see page 243) and go for closure before the bad weather sets in.

● Sign up a tree surgeon (see page 256) to deal with rioting trees and creepers in the late autumn, after leaf fall, so they have time to recuperate for a better show the following spring.

● In autumn prepare for winter by ordering fuel (coal/logs); in spring prepare for summer by sending curtains and loose furniture covers to the cleaner (although you could always wash these yourself. It was customary once to have a seasonal change of loose covers; warm-coloured for autumn/winter and paler floral chintz for the spring and summer. Still the most dramatic way to signal a seasonal change of mood and orientation. This is also practical, since one set could be 'rested' or at the cleaners in the meantime. Alas, loose covers don't come cheap, but they are cheaper than the sofas and chairs whose lives they prolong (see My Directory).

● Stock up on some long-term household necessities: light bulbs or cleaning materials through mail order or using the internet. It is preferable to do this in bulk, if you have sufficient storage space.

● If winter is upcoming, check all your hot water bottles and chuck any that look perished or leaky and then replace. If electric blankets are more your style, check that they are in good nick, wiring safe and sorted.

● If you are looking towards spring/summer, consider investing in a corn bin (see page 43) wherein to store the blankets, rug throws and winter loose covers safely away from moths and rodents.

DOING IT THEIR WAY

I am nosy about other people's domestic arrangements. I am fascinated by their different ways and degrees of coping with what is, after all, a big chunk of our shared experience, our common lot. It is not something people talk about freely as a rule, fearful of appearing obsessive; one track mind, a bore. The details of your take on a deep clean isn't likely to set a dinner table roaring with appreciative laughter, though we can all get some fun sharing anecdotes about the au pair from hell. Cleaners talk shop, young mums swap anxieties and concerns on a frankly need-to-know basis, but by and large we keep schtum about this portion of our lives, fostering the illusion that it all happens as if by magic instead of being the hard-won outcome of much thought, effort and time. Money too: I can imagine a social gathering getting off on the cost of a cleaner.

But we tend to keep quiet about our stratagems, our basic requirements, our struggles to balance home and job, the nagging dissatisfactions of never quite making it on either front. Bridget Jones might well open up a whole new topic for commiseration, empathy and laughs, if she finally took the next step: gets her man (she doesn't have to marry him), gets a home, gets pregnant, grows up.

E M Delafield's *Diary of a Provincial Lady* is one of the few books (still in print, and still funny after the best part of a century) that focuses a sharply observant eye on the absurdities and problems of a doolally 'lady' trying to get to grips with a strong, silent husband and a modestly blossoming career as an 'author'.

Do other people manage these things better? If so, what is their rule of thumb, their routine? Do they get up earlier, or stick undeviatingly to a disciplined time-sheet? Are they heroic, or are we wimps?

In an attempt to shed some light on these matters I decided to cross-question a random sample of home-owners about their priorities, preferences and comments on their priorities, and the way they run their homes. It is an interestingly mixed bag, I think, and throws up a considerable diversity of attitudes and expectations. These interviews are slotted through the book, under the generic heading 'Doing It Their Way'.

ANGELES BLASCO

Angeles is Catalan and comes from a small seaside town near Valencia. Small, sturdy, with fine Etruscan features, Angie is a life force. She has a whooping laugh, a passion for dancing and a keen business head. She entered our lives as au pair. I remember us arguing hotly whether washing-up should be done with a tiny scouring cloth ('In my town everyone does it like this!') or a washing-up brush. We would shriek at each other, close to tears, and then fall about laughing at our own absurdity.

After a Business Studies course Angie came to work as Manager for Paint Magic. She always said that she would go back to Spain if she got pregnant, because any child of hers must grow up like her in a child-centred small town society. When she fell in love with James and Sebastian was on his way, that is just what she did, missed by all.

I asked Angie to describe how her mother's generation set about their housework routine. She faxed me this: a bracing read for those of us who feel we are drowning in chores.

Angie's mother (a widow) is an 'old-fashioned housewife', her days governed by domestic and family concerns. She is also warm, dignified and authoritative. She enjoys life.

'First of all, a little bit of social background. My mother's generation have been in charge from very early age on the cleaning of the house, either for their own mothers, who were probably working at the factories or for their husbands and children when they were married. Their professional job name is *sus labores* and they take it very seriously. Their own houses are impeccable; dust free, they smell clean, the tiled floors are shiny and a visitor's first impression is that nobody actually lives there. Everything is in their place and there is a place for everything.

'Their conversations are full of housekeeping remarks. Because one is supposed to do certain things at a certain time, they have substituted the time for the particular job. For example, "I was doing the beds when my father phoned me to tell me that he wasn't feeling very well." In this instance you know that what she means is that it was around 9 o'clock and, most importantly, she has done her job.

'All the housework has to be finished by 12. After that, it is about preparations for lunch. At three o'clock the house and its contents should be back to its original clinical state. They don't like having lots of stuff on the shelves, only the minimum. They get claustrophobia otherwise.

'The schedule in chronological order:

'**Daily:** washing up, tidying up bedrooms, washing and putting things back in their place including clean clothes. They leave everything to be ironed in a pile, to be done every two days in the afternoons. Then they sweep the floors (now using the Swiffer, like a broom with a dust-attracting cloth at one end, very handy to get cobwebs off round the ceilings).

'Next, shopping for bread and anything missing for preparing lunch.

'After lunch, washing up, clean all surfaces, sweep and wash the kitchen floor. After dinner they put the rubbish outside as it is collected every day including weekends. If you live in a house you sweep the outside before you do everything else and have a chat with your neighbour.

'**Weekly:** If you live in a block of flats, once a week the whole of the stairs (eight floors sometimes) and the hall are dusted and washed. They take it in turns, or hire someone to do it. Friday is butcher's shopping day. Saturday is 'the cleaning day': all rooms, decorative objects, furniture, books, not many of these, are dusted, all floors are washed, sheets get replaced, washed and ironed. Bathrooms (including the tiled walls and floors) are deeply cleaned with bleach, *amoniaco* (ammonia), and *salfumant* (caustic) to get rid of bacteria and scale. The fridge gets emptied and washed inside and outside, cookers the same. Once everything has been done they go to the supermarket for food. After lunch they clean the kitchen as always and watch the 4 o'clock American film on TV.

'**Monthly:** Sort out clothes, get rid of some, store others. Sort out the insides of cupboards and wardrobes.

'My own schedule, I am afraid to say, has little to do with that, now that I am studying six hours a day. When Sebastian, the baby, comes back from my aunt or Mum, there is not much one can do apart from making sure he doesn't break his neck on the marble stairs, smash his face on the floor, and that he eats and goes to bed. Washing, washing up and washing the kitchen floor is every day. Saturday is cleaning day but not always – depends very much on Sebastian. Everything gets done at some point but not with the depth and consistency of Mum's generation.

'It would be interesting to mention a few tips to have clothes and wardrobes in order. Because of lack of space, people are buying an American product – a plastic bag – by mail order. You can put very bulky things like a duvet, blankets and jumpers inside and after hoovering the air out of the bag, it gets reduced to one-fifth of the original space. The other good thing about these bags is that no moths will get in and when you open them again the contents are not creased and they smell fresh.'

NOTE: The Swiffer, and alternatives, are available at Sainsbury's, and other supermarkets and DIY sheds.

ORGANISING

EUREKA? IMPOSING A SYSTEM

I am all in favour of domestic routines, best inculcated in childhood, because clearly they save time, effort and tedious thinking-it-through from scratch. They serve as a digest of household knowledge and skills – both dos and don'ts – evolved through centuries of intelligent practice. Some people pick them up quickly and instinctively; some acquire them through maternal example and instruction; and some blunder through a catalogue of errors and learn the hard way. This is me.

I was raised without training in domestic matters. My mother was a remarkable woman, beautiful, clever (Cambridge First), vigorous, up for anything a bit arduous or challenging such as planting a small forest, upholstering chairs from the frame out, pruning a five-acre apple orchard or raising free-range chickens for sale. But I don't recall ever seeing her fussing about the place with furniture polish or attacking her tiled kitchen walls with a sponge and cleaning liquid. To housework, in the sense of tended furniture or sparkling surfaces, she was grandly indifferent. More Action Woman than Mrs Wonderful. So when I fetched up running my own household, I felt parachuted into unknown territory without a map.

A longstanding addiction to old household manuals (clearly compensatory activity) left me stuffed with arcane recipes for cleaning furs (warmed bran!), kid gloves and patent leather; what quite escaped me was the logic of and necessity for a plan, a structure: in other words, a routine.

I obsessed over details that caught my fancy – restoring leather upholstery, cleaning tarnished flea-market brasses – but I was oblivious to the big picture: that living spaces require regular attention, effort and organisation if they are not to slide into squalor. Lily (see page 104) and babies jumped me out of this housework-as-play attitude, but I was so unskilled it took me a while to catch up. Years, decades, later I am pretty well there as far as cleaning, shopping, cooking and laundering are concerned. But imposing a system, so the multitudinous domestic needs are conveniently located, fully stocked up and pruned of inessentials, will always be an effort that goes against the grain.

However, whenever I see my way through the muddle and light upon something in the way of a system that works, I feel absurdly triumphant – order imposed on chaos. Eureka!

The most recent triumph, which will seem absurdly banal to anyone who absorbed domestic routine at their mother's knee, was my 'second-string' kitchen cupboard. I call it second string because it stands next to a vast pitch-pine ex-school-library bookcase. I saw my second cupboard as housing what old cookbooks call 'dry goods' or, in my vocab, 'stuff that will keep':

everything that did not require refrigeration or was too bulky to fit in the shallow wall cupboard. Confusion arose immediately when I tried to explain dry goods to my au pairs and why small jars of jam and mustard went into the wall cupboard, while larger jars of chutney, pickles and sauerkraut should be stored in the second-string cupboard. As a result, one never knew where favoured items were to be found. Marmite, for which my partner has a passion, and green peppercorn mustard proved elusive on a number of occasions! If they were hidden behind larger jars they were deemed eaten up and replacements were bought, so we often had a glut of Marmite and mustards. In the meantime, packets of dried seaweed got muddled in with packets of pasta, and bread yeast was often found lurking at the bottom of a pile.

The crashingly simple solution came to me – as it often does in such situations – while I was clearing out the cupboard. Ah! Each shelf becomes home to a different type of container: jars on shelf, tins and tubes on another and large boxes of my favourite Cipriani pasta stacked on the bottom. When I explained this system to Fatima, my au pair, I was relieved to see enlightenment spread over her face. 'That is sensible,' she said in her well-enunciated English, meaning at last here is a system she can get a handle on.

As I see it, imposing a system has to

start with the dismal chore we all put off: the big clear out. Somehow the sight of all the contents spread out around you, the newly cleaned cupboard invitingly empty, seems to float ideas and solutions into one's head. Next time I get to work on my wardrobe I shall be considering the fashionista's tip: to hang clothes by colour, a block of red and, in my case, a long section of black, etc.

Although this system takes no account of moths, I can see that it could provide a sort of visual filing system and inspire dashingly successful combinations. Another tip is to ensure that you don't add anything else to your wardrobe without getting rid of something already there. This seems to be verging on de-cluttering and on this I have ambivalent views.

STORAGE

I've lost track of the books and articles that have claimed to provide an answer to your/my storage problems. Of course, if you are a serious de-clutterer, this is not going to be a problem. However, most of us fall short of that ruthless ideal. So the nagging problem remains: how do you squeeze a pint into a half-pint pot? Colonise the loft? Damp-proof the cellar? Chuck up a wall-full of built-in cupboards in the master bedroom? Install a workbench in the garage? Convert the add-on conservatory to a utility room?

Desperate remedies? Expensive certainly. What the almost universal storage problem faithfully reflects is our uneasy position between helpless acquisitiveness and equally helpless inability to deal with a rising tide of Stuff. This is not rubbish: stuff your children hug to their chests or your spouse goes ballistic about, when you

gingerly suggest he hasn't played golf for years so why not store the kit in the loft/cellar/garage? Yes, we all tend to accumulate. Whatever happened to those 'box rooms' which used to be a welcome feature of between-the-war semis?

SOLUTIONS

Don't let yourself be seduced by those storage features in the glossies showing antique armoires with their lace-edged shelves neatly stacked with household linens in mouth-watering pastels. We all know it isn't like that in real life. Damp duvet covers fetch up stuffed round the immersion heater to dry off; unironed sheets and pillow cases refuse to fold into tidy shapes; and anyway, what is the point of doing a 'presentation' on the family towels when the next person along is going to yank impatiently at them and

Dealing with 'Stuff'

The reason why storage problems and solutions remain such a perennially fascinating topic for the glossy mags and TV home shows can be simply explained. To quote my friend Ann Maurice, C5's acerbic 'House Doctor': 'You Brits just have so much stuff!'

The first thing she does when 'staging' a house for her show is empty all the cupboards, starting in the kitchen. She says she does this to give them a thorough clean, but I suspect a touch of Schadenfreude at work here as the House Doctor casts her eye over the sorry contents. Twenty years of hoarded stuff exposed to view: teapots with chipped spouts, decanters with missing stoppers, yellowed plastic attachments to ancient mixers, stacks of patty pans and scores of glass containers in all shapes and sizes saved for a definitive jam-making session. 'I mean, some of these things haven't been moved in years! They've got this patina of dust on them,' she exclaims, rolling her eyes. 'Useless, broken and dirty junk basically taking up storage space. What is it with you guys?'

What indeed? Is it, as Ann maintains, a national trait, a muddle of sentiment, misguided thrift, foolish optimism or even a horror vacui? Nonetheless, she has lighted on a truth: stuff attracts stuff inexorably. The solution seems so easy to begin with: a few more shelves, another wall cupboard, drawers built into the bed base. But before you know it, you are opening up the loft or excavating the cellar or tacking another floor on to the garage. When your eye starts drifting over estate agents' windows (a larger house maybe, with utility room/garden studio/box room?) it is time to get a grip on yourself, do a stock take on your 'stuff' and start 'letting go' of anything you don't wear, won't read, never use, won't mend, can't be bothered to starch or otherwise maintain?

For advice on how to set about this radical surgery, see De-cluttering, page 44. As a 'stuff' addict myself (I wouldn't let Ann Maurice near my cupboards) I know how much the first cut hurts, but believe me, it gets easier as you go along, and the pay-off is that you feel freer, agreeably mature and strangely light-hearted.

leave it all sadly messed up? Along with the armoires, I would include charming stacks of fabric-covered boxes, lovingly papered box files with ribbon ties and translucent plastic containers – in fact, the bulk of the 'storage solutions' peddled at stiff prices which purport to make sense of your overflow.

I am embarrassed to admit that I have fallen for most of these appealing suggestions over the years. But the truth is that any of these 'pigeonholing' solutions needs a hawk in terms of organisation. For them to 'work' requires that they be clearly labelled, easily accessible on open shelves in your work area, and backed up by a generous worktop nearby. Stuffing them away on a shelf in a cupboard somewhere means you forget their contents, and the thrill of rediscovery is spoilt by finding them chewed to shreds by moths.

Nonetheless, there are some ingenious, cheap notions around which can seriously add to your storage space, and at the same time help you to sort matters visually.

Cupboard door backs

My favourites are made of plasticised wire. The best is a double-tier shelf design which can be screwed to the back of a cupboard door (a neglected storage space) and take a whole raft of etceteras easily lost on a deep shelf: eg, a clutch of cleaning aids, or vacuum cleaner attachments next to the power gadgets or under the sink. Equally, fixed to the back of your wardrobe door, they can store suede brushes, moth-proofing spray and sachets, shoe-cleaning stuff, even a rescue sewing kit.

The possibilities are dazzling! I suggest you order one of these for every cupboard door in your house (see My Directory).

Extra shelf

My next fave is a plasticised wire 'extra shelf', which can be slid underneath an existing shelf to add another narrow belt of storage space, brilliant for storing saucers with tea cups that crowd the shelf proper, or sponge-cloths and rubber gloves beneath the sink, or even your belts, scarves, etc, in the wardrobe. Not pretty, admittedly, but who cares once the doors are closed?

Storage bins

I am also a recent convert to translucent plastic storage bins with built-in wheels and snap-on lids, sold in many supermarkets at rock-bottom prices. The appeal of these is that they are the right height to stash under a bed with more than 30cm (1ft) of clearance. This may be under-used storage space and it merits serious consideration, though a valance will be needed to smooth and hide it all. Thereby hangs a tale.

Staying once with friends in Ireland – he an academic, she a teacher – we became aware as the night went on of a strangely complex odour, not to say stink, wafting about the guest room. Lifting up the valance, we discovered several black plastic refuse bags, tightly secured, but gently leaking a quantity of … well, methane, into our squeaky clean guest bedroom. Our hostess, a dazzling eccentric, greeted this disclosure with a shrug, and a deeply Irish shrug at that; 'But my darlings, wasn't I going to sneak it all out first thing in the morning when the rubbish men call?' This was the domestic heroine who scrubbed the top of her gas cooker last thing every night so it would look pristine for breakfast every morning!

GET SYSTEMATIC

Storage space is only as good as you are at making it work for you. For this you must have – and it has taken me years to even admit this to myself – a system or a routine. A learned response so automatic you don't stop to ask yourself 'where do I put this cellular blanket, pinking shears, mail-order catalogues, feathered wedding hat or leather restorer? Mapped in your head is a network of destination sites around the house or flat: wardrobes, cupboards, drawers, storage bins, filing cabinets and bulletin boards, all the usual storage requirements for a busy household and all carefully thought through, allocated and identified. In other words – and this is where we all chorus – 'a place for

everything and everything in its place'.

Easier said than done. I often think the intellectual rigour and creative insight to 'run a home' is grossly underestimated. Running a home smoothly seems to me as demanding of vision, tact, decisiveness and authority – all those CEO qualities – as running a successful business, except that for net profit you substitute health and happiness as the bottom line. I speak as one with fair experience of both.

But we were talking about creating and imposing a system. Mrs Wonderful seems to have no problem with this (she clearly trained at her mother's knee), but for most of us it is hard grind and we have to make up the rules as we go along and be flexible about changing them (another CEO quality) when they patently don't work. It is not sticking to the arrangement yourself that is the problem, it is drumming it into other members of the household. Training a succession of au pairs in your little ways (actually, steely ordinances) is the ultimate test both of your patience and the feasibility of your system. Finding pots, pans and implements day after day has taught me the need to keep to the simplest rules. For example, wooden implements in this jar, metal in that jar (the more stuff on show the better), shiny pots and pans in this cupboard, black ones in that cupboard and heavy casseroles in the merry-go-round unit. Sophisticated it ain't, but since one is often reduced to basic English and mime, this is no bad thing.

A system based on associative thinking is good, acting as a mnemonic. Thus packets or tins of tea are stored near the kettle, the teapot and the mugs. The latter should preferably be hung from hooks, both to give shelf space and to provide an instant check on missing items, usually to be found round the telly after a late-night movie session or on bedside tables all over the house. Au pairs are good at retrieval.

Laundry – ie, washing, drying, ironing and sorting the heaps of clothing any family sheds as freely as autumn leaves – is another major challenge to your system. This is covered under Laundry (see page 171).

Another factor to bear in mind when attempting to impose a system is that people invariably go for the shortest distance between two points, ie, the line of least resistance. Shelving too high up to reach without steps or cupboards too low or too far from the mainstream of household traffic will tend to be ignored and stuff crammed into the nearest space regardless. If this keeps happening, either you have to rethink or take on the extra effort and bother of redistribution.

If all this seems to be more about traffic flow, as it were, than parking problems, that is because – to push the analogy further – I believe the real challenge when it comes to storage isn't so much finding space as keeping the daily household functions on the move without gridlock, or indeed road rage.

'Where are those important papers I left on the hall table?' 'Where are my cuff links and trainers?' 'Get me a pozzy screwdriver, quick!' and so on; a familiar reproachful litany. Most homes today have adequate storage space, in terms of units, cupboards and shelving. If you prune the contents frequently and keep tabs on how well your system is working, you should be in control and able to cope with the heavy stuff; short of another baby coming along, your mother-in-law moving in, or a live-in nanny requiring her own bedsit. Then, yes, a larger house may be the only solution.

In the meantime, here are some quite basic suggestions for extending the space available which you may not have though of. They don't cost an arm and a leg and really do work.

General

- Really deep drawers (I have some over 30cm/1ft deep) need subdividing internally so that tall containers don't fall over and leak as you slide the drawer in and out. These are obtainable in a wide range of sizes (from Ikea, Holding Company and Muji – see My Directory). Shallow drawers are also better subdivided internally, and you can find nifty compartmented plastic trays which are perfect for visually sorting small things like lipsticks, cosmetics, hair accessories and trinkets. Another tray might take care of First Aid stuff, baby bits and pieces or home office essentials – stamps, paper clips and pen refills.

● Another system booster, and timesaver, is to replicate items in frequent use in different parts of the house (see page 39).

Hallways

● An associative gambit might include provision for outdoor stuff – muddy boots, coats, umbrellas and school bags – in the porch or hall. Provide a boot scraper outside and a large doormat inside and resign yourself to a hallway that looks more like a transit camp than anything out of the glossies. At least that way, you might save muddy footprints and puddles elsewhere.

● Bikes are a nightmare indoors; if your space won't run to the tiniest lean-to outside, and chaining them to the railings is too risky, forget pretty and accept transit camp. However, do fix pegs on the wall so the bikes can be hung up where you won't fall over them rushing to the doorbell.

● If books are your weakness and space is running out, see if you can't contrive shelves that climb the staircase walls. Paperbacks don't need deep shelves and as well as adding considerable character, are a useful reminder when you need a book to read on the way up to bed.

● Shelving can handsomely frame a door at the end of a narrow passage, if wall space allows. They can display just about anything: antique bottles, fossils, seashells or simply hold more books.

● To save running up and down stairs unnecessarily, make sure there is a table right by the foot of the stairs to take clothes, books and shoes, etc. For small items, a stair basket, with a built-in step, keeps the stuff safe until the owners take the next step of putting them away.

Bedrooms

● The backs of cupboard doors are underused for storage. As well as wire racks (see page 33), add rails for belts, ties and scarves. Screw-in door knobs or hooks can take strappy handbags or necklaces.

● Hanging rails (on castors) are the business for clothes storage if their functional appearance fits in with your style or you have a dressing/box room. Having your clothes on view is good –

moth infestation is less likely than in a dark, warm cupboard – and seeing items together can be inspirational.

● Some wardrobes are roomy enough to take a shelf, above the hanging rail or below the garments. Use these for stashing shoes in wire trays, thick woollies in zipped bags, hat boxes, etc. If short clothes (jackets and suits, etc) are hung together, a space can perhaps be cleared to take a small chest of drawers.

● Multi-hanger. This is a great space saver rather than a mind-clear. Jeeves, the dry-cleaning chain, stock an ingenious hanger for trousers, made by Russel and called a Slack Rack (see My Directory). It has four chrome bars which each take a pair of trousers, which (this is the cute bit) can be individually detached by lifting them out of their socket, which are, in turn, hinged to swing out for easy removal – ie, without impatiently dragging all four pairs out at one go. It is rather nicely made (I think Eileen Gray would have approved) in chrome with non-slip rubber sleeves to the detachable bars. Do we talk about 'slacks' these days? Eileen Gray did, and went to the lengths of designing a purpose made, waist high, cabinet to take care of them neatly. The Slack Rack costs £7. Carousels in the same range provide a tidy

way to store ties, belts, scarves and even beaded necklaces. They hang up on your rail, but the spiky bits swivel round!

● Plastic wheelie bins, with lids, are a big help for stashing out-of-season clothes and sports gear, etc.

● Keep spare blankets, pillows or duvets under the beds in plastic bins, but do check the clearance space first! Make sure any woollen items are clean: ie, clear of moth larvae. A few mothballs or anti-moth sachets are an extra safeguard. Use a magic marker to identify contents clearly. This can be wiped off with meths when no longer needed.

● Colour sorting does work for bedding (see Bathrooms, page 39); double bed stuff in one colour, single beds another.

Kitchens

● A narrow shelf 7.5–10cm (3–4in) wide, running right round kitchen or dining room at picture rail height makes a fine decorative feature for attractive plates, jugs, figurines or sports trophies. It needs a lip, or groove, to hold plates securely. It can be supported on wooden brackets, plain or decorative as you wish, and should be painted to contrast or tone in with the décor.

- If your under-sink space is crammed full, another plasticised wire invention comes apropos: a tier of baskets on runners for cleaning things, soap pads, etc.

- Ceiling as storage is no new thing. The glossies have explored baskets festooned on old beams and kitchen paraphernalia slung off a suspended steel grid or rack.

Living rooms

- Most people find plastic storage bins invaluable for a rapid tidy-up of kids' toys.

- Happy snaps are great, heart-warming reminders, but they lose relevance and status dumped in shoe boxes and unvisited drawers. Be ruthless in whittling down your collection and selecting the best, and mount them in photo albums. My favourites are those with thick black pages – and the photos labelled using a white pen.

Bathrooms

Bathrooms have changed out of all recognition in the past decade or two; most are centrally heated, lavishly tiled, have a shower as well as bath, His and Hers basins, large mirrors and decent lighting. However, they tend to be small, so storage of the traditional bathroom clutter still needs to be addressed – soaps, bath oils, towels, toilet rolls, cleaning material, cosmetics (don't most women make up in the bathroom?), shaving tackle, shampoos; not to mention dressing gowns and a laundry basket or bag. Keeping some semblance of order in a bathroom is thus an ongoing battle. Bathrooms are where space-saving devices really come into their own.

- Use plastic dividers in shallow drawers to let you see your entire make-up paraphernalia at a glance. This not only keeps them in better shape, and easy to locate, but guards against the sticky squalor that results from throwing stuff pell-mell into drawers.

- It is always a good rule to try to keep like with like: all hair things in one compartment, all bath stuff in another and all cleaning aids housed together in another.

- Medicines of any kind (prescription or over the counter) should be kept in a cabinet out of reach of small, enquiring children. I use those brightly coloured jute sacks from Africa to keep lotions and potions in, out of sight and to distinguish between the His and Hers elements; these are attractive enough to leave out by the basin or on the bath surround.

- Use stick-on plastic hooks on the back of cupboard doors to suspend sponge bags or hot-water bottles.

Towels take up a lot of room. I keep mine in the airing cupboard on slatted shelves so that they are always dry. I also have a heated towel rail; a must in any bathroom. I did attempt to introduce a colour code for towels; a different colour for each family member. It didn't catch on; I think it was too fussy on the admin side and families make short work of such impediments. What makes more sense – and less mess – is to colour towels by size (different colours for different sizes) or, simplest of all, buy all white!

All bathrooms need their own laundry baskets/bins or bags. The advantage of bags (lots of choice, mostly canvas slung on frames) is that you gather up all the bags on the way to the washing machine instead of an armful of dirty clothes.

Keep some cleaning aids close to hand; lavatory brush in a steel or ceramic holder, sponges for wiping down surfaces close to the bath and shower basin. However, unless you can run to a purpose-made cupboard/shelf or drawer for the nitty gritty stuff, keep all these ungainly containers in a separate place on the same floor as your bathroom, in a large plastic tray with a handle, along with all your other cleaning stuff. If you have small children, keep the cupboard locked.

Office/paperwork
See page 284.

THINK BIGGER

Have you ever thought, resentfully, how much time you waste running about the place looking for things? I don't mean treasured things like your amethyst ring, but utterly mundane yet needful things such as scissors, stapler, a pozzy screwdriver or a book of stamps?

In an interview with Minn Hogg, redoubtable former editor of *World of Interiors*, she let drop that she keeps a pair of scissors in every room of her flat. The brilliance of this simple expedient struck me all of a heap. All these needful objects are quite cheap, so why not stack the odds in one's favour by keeping one to each room?

I now have at least one pair of scissors in every room. This doesn't prevent them from going walkies now and then, but it does tend to give me faster retrieval time. I am contemplating chaining them to the relevant wall or shelf. Isn't it the age old moan that no one, but no one, ever puts the scissors, sellotape or stamp book back where they found it? No wonder Victorian housekeepers went about their chores girded with a chatelaine, a belt from which all their vital equipment – mostly keys – was suspended.

It must be admitted that shopping for basic items – five staplers, five pairs of scissors, five Stanley knives – is not exhilarating. It is boring and one resents the cost, however modest. But, believe me, it considerably eases the mind when a courier is pawing the ground at your door to know that, yes, there is a pen to sign off the package just a few steps away and a Stanley knife to rip it open afterwards.

Think big about small things. It could prolong your life or erase those fretful worry lines from your brow. Cheaper than Botox. Consider multiples of any of the following:

● Pens: keep a clutch in each room, kept in a jar, tumbler, flowerpot or whatever you please. What is silly about keeping pens in your bathroom? Often one's thoughts surface there. This leads me to the logical corollary:

● A scribble pad, preferably in its own plastic holder, kept in most rooms for jotting down inspirations, memos and lists.

● Scissors should be hung visibly from a hook or secreted in a drawer or box depending on family traits.

● More than one Stanley knife, equipped with blade, for splitting open infuriating packaging and parcels more quickly and conveniently. (But do be sure to keep them safe from small children.)

● Books of stamps, or better still stamped envelopes, ready to go. I deeply admire Superwoman's – Shirley Conran's – artful notion of keeping a stack of stamped envelopes, with cards, next to her bed so she could scribble a thank you letter to her dinner/weekend hosts while the mood was upon her and the emollient phrases flowing. This could be a proper use for some of those dinky boxes women find irresistible and collect?

● Staplers: maybe place one in the study/office and one in the kitchen. Try to make them identical so one supply of staples works for all the machines. The new-fangled stapler, which works by chomping a little hook through the paper could be an advantage here. One less item to remember.

● Tiny repair/needlework kit. Sewing back a missing button is no big deal; having to hunt about for needles, thread and scissors can mean the job gets put off in perpetuity.

● Elastic bands, paper clips, and sellotape (preferably with weighty tape dispensers).

● Keys. We are moving a bit laterally here. Every time I find myself locked out of my place for one reason or another, I berate myself for not leaving a spare set with my trusted neighbour, Polly. You would do this with forethought, and your eyes open, of course. But in extremis – cold, wet and locked out – what a comfort!

● Thinking not so much laterally as bigger, why not replicate cleaning items on each floor of your house? Get a plastic tub which can contain cleaning materials plus a broom, feather duster, rags, etc.

Space savers

When every square centimetre counts – in a studio flat say – you should major on space-saving items. For instance:

● Flap-up/hinged tabletops are useful for tiny kitchens. Gate-leg tables are ideal for more serious meals.

● Floor cushions provide extra seating, which you can neatly pile up when not in use, and take up less space than beanbags.

● Anything that stacks up is useful in a small space: mugs and bowls. cooking pans, stools, café-type chairs or storage bins.

● Fix pegs to the wall to hook spare chairs on to, Shaker style.

● Multi-hangers (see page 37) are able to suspend four pairs of trousers/shirts from one hook.

● Ceiling-suspended rings or racks are ideal for hanging pots and pans from butchers' hooks. Tip: a photographer friend used an old clothes-airing rack on pulleys for this. You never know, such an item could turn up in a boot sale.

● Fix a steel rack across a window or wall to hold kitchen implements.

● Pricey but clever: pull-out full-height but narrow storage units for kitchen stuff, namely bottles, jars and tins.

● Items that eat up floor space (eg, coffee tables) should be tiered. Think club sandwich! Ditto bedside table: get one with a cupboard below.

● Think dual purpose: thus a trolley (booze, plates and food) is more useful and flexible than a side table.

● Ration your quota of books, videos and CDs. Be disciplined: join a library and hire videos. You will save money as well as space.

A vacuum cleaner on each floor may be pushing it, but worth thinking about if you live on many levels. All vacuum cleaners, old or latest model, are hell to lug around.

● Kleenex or paper tissues. Handy for blowing your nose (surprise), mopping up baby sick, dog widdle and food or drink spills promptly.

● Safety pins. Use these to secure a bra strap, close a gaping décolleté or fix a mad fake paeony to your shoulder?

● Stickies – by every phone extension, in a box, with a pen.

● Spring measuring tape – it's surprising how often you might want to measure something.

SOME STORAGE DON'TS

Boxes

The glossies are never more seductive than when showing stacks of pretty boxes or old armoires piled high with crisp, coloured linens or patchwork quilts. These are more about imaginative styling than real life. Pretty boxes, fabric covered and expensive, are a snare and delusion unless they are instantly accessible and ever-so-clearly labelled.

Most women have a weakness for boxes, doubtless for Freudian reasons. My own collection used to include Georgian tea caddies, Victorian tin spice boxes, lacquered pen-work boxes, Moroccan mosaic inlaid with mother-of-pearl and antique leather jewellery boxes. All struck me as bargains and irresistible at the time. I also thought they would come in useful somewhere. Now I can't think why.

A box is dumb, so to speak: the chances are that once you put something in it – rogue keys, single earrings or old buttons – you will almost instantly forget which box belongs with what. One of my best ideas ever was to get the cream of my collection (with a few beloved exceptions) restored and repaired; hinges replaced, keys made, box-wood banding re-instated and inlaid brass ovals or shields initialled, to give away as Christmas presents to all of my family. Admittedly, this cost me, though less than a designer sweater each. A customised antique box made an acceptable gift, my conscience was assuaged and valuable shelf space was cleared in one decisive move.

If you are a box addict, at least try to make them work for their living: put one by every bedside to hold tissues, make-up remover pads or those stamped envelopes with cards that Superwoman, Shirley Conran, so famously kept to write thank you notes before dinner parties and weekends passed into history.

Chests

There is a trend for using outsize boxes – chests, blanket boxes and steamer trunks – as table substitutes either by the side of the sofa or as a coffee table. There is nothing wrong here – they look sturdy and stylish – and can be relatively inexpensive – so long as you don't fall for the sales pitch about how useful they will be. Once they fulfil their table function with lamps, ashtrays and books laid on top, you will really have to force yourself to clear the top and open them up to retrieve what is inside. One exception perhaps: the chest (rattan, kelim covered, stripped pine?) doubling as a coffee table could be used to hoard back copies of magazines 'in case', alhough it will soon be too heavy to move. You could add castors, where appropriate?

LONG-TERM STORAGE

However keenly you subscribe to the concept of de-cluttering, there may well be possessions you want to hang on to, but don't need right now, which need to be stored in a solid, dry, mothproof container: items such as old kilims, fragile patchwork quilts, sets of lined and interlined curtains too good and too pricey to get rid of even if you are currently into minimalist muslin, etc.

Corn bins

These are outsize metal containers, like giant steamer trunks, used by farmers to store animal feed where rats and damp cannot get at them. Stoutly made and tightly closing, just one of these could provide a household with safe storage for a mass of stuff that is liable to deteriorate under normal storage conditions: moths, mice, mildew and carpet beetles are just a few of the infestations arraigned against you.

A corn bin is a bit like a huge safe, too big to play around with decoratively in the average home, although I can just about see one in the corner of a spacious loft. But you

Corn bins

These useful and sturdy containers are manufactured in sheet aluminium and are sold through dealers all over the country: see My Directory.

They come in three sizes: 900 mm high and 640mm wide and various lengths. The smallest, 800 mm long, is £85.15, the 1200 mm is £96.29 and the largest, 1600 mm, costs £109.53 – all plus VAT. The manufacturer says they should be kept under cover as they are not watertight. However, you will be glad to hear, they are rodent and moth-proof.

could locate one in the garage, cellar or box room for extra, secure storage. They cost a lot more than the tiddly plastic storage bins on wheels designed to slide under beds, but they hold massively more, and have a reassuring Fort Knox feeling about them. I see them as a halfway house between conventional home storage solutions and one of the storage units leased out by commercial outfits at a fairly hefty rental.

Whatever you stash in a corn bin needs to be clean, dry and packed with a little care and finesse. A big label of contents needs to be sellotaped to the outside.

The bin should be checked out periodically if the contents include pile or flat weave woollen rugs. If they have been professionally cleaned or home cleaned (see page 101) these should be OK, but we have all heard scare stories about imported rugs arriving in this country with the odd moth larva on board.

DE-CLUTTERING OR RE-SHUFFLING?

My friend, Anne Maurice (see page 32) is convinced that the British are insatiable clutterers. When working on a house, Anne picks over the stuff looking for some 'nice bits' to make a feature of in the newly de-cluttered home. Everything else is consigned to boxes in the garage or the garden shed, a job she delegates to the home owners. 'What I tell them is this way it is all packed up and ready to move, when the time comes.'

This is the tactful compromise settled upon when she discovered how loath we Brits are to be parted from our hoarded stuff. Her instinctive reaction would be to chuck the lot in the skip. 'The stuff that comes out of those cupboards!' she exclaims, flashing her perfect wicked smile. 'I just gasp. This stuff is so old, most of it is broken and it's all

so durdy.' This being the Maurice pronunciation, uttered with a curl of the lip that sends a guilty shiver through me. Old, broken and 'durdy' is probably a fair summary of what goes on behind the mercifully solid doors of all too many cupboards in the UK. Either that, or it is stuff that doesn't earn house room because we don't wear it, or read it, or use it, or even think about it if this can be avoided because it makes us feel bad.

In de-cluttering circles this shrinking state of mind is defined as 'stuck energy'. De-clutterers affirm that if we took a hold on ourselves, waded into these glory holes – what Le Corbusier, Big Daddy of minimalism, nastily but accurately called our 'dirty corners' – with a load of black bags, we would be doing many helpful things at a stroke. We would release megavolts of 'stuck energy', get our heads round a log-jam of accumulated stuff, create valuable new space in our overcrowded homes, and get to feel in control of the things in our lives, instead of the other way round. This bold exercise, once completed, will make us feel positive and carefree, radiating joyous calm, revelling in our uncluttered spaces instead of ducking and diving round the dirty corners.

As a born accumulator myself (my youngest daughter is the same, so I blame transmitted genes for some of this) I am forced to acknowledge that the de-cluttering concept wraps up a hard nugget of common sense. Don't dirty corners and cluttered cupboards mirror some unresolved dirty corners in the mind? Clear your desk, tidy your drawers and hey, your puckered brow relaxes, and you feel ready for anything.

ORIGINS

De-cluttering hails, as you might suspect, from the USA. Over there it is a proper little industry, with its head in the clouds maybe – emphasis on the spiritual aspect, protest against materialism, a liberal dash of *feng shui* – but its feet on the ground as regards the profit motive. De-cluttering has its spokespersons, busy on the media front, its literature, and its proselytisers: de-clutter

The dining room was a jumble of old books, antique bottles, three shoe boxes full of perforated discs for an old painted music box Dad had found at an auction. A seamstress's dummy stood by the hutch; a cradle, a wooden sled, duck decoys. Books were piled next to it on the floor, on them a sign; DO NOT MOVE – ASK PLEASE. The dining room table had disappeared under piles of magazines that, according to Mum, Dad was trying to sort out … But Dad could not throw stuff out; if it was old, if he could imagine a use for it, if he could think of someone he might give it to someday, he would hang onto it.

Wobegon Boy, Garrison Keillor (Penguin USA, 1997; Faber & Faber, 1998)

consultants who are more than willing to step in, case the joint, analyse your situation and come up with an action programme, for a fee. To have them stand over you, encouraging or dismissive, costs more of course, but what do you expect? It needs training to become so ruthless that you can see at a cool, dispassionate glance, what the client is well able to live without, overriding their pathetic protests 'but this was a wedding present!' with a firm command: 'You don't use it, you don't need it, OUT.' A tough love situation you could say, and it is an undoubted fact that the outsider (who hasn't all these absurd sentimental niggles) sees the game clearly, and sees it whole.

I have no problem sorting and dealing with other people's clutter. It is my own I get 'stuck' and wobbly about. Steaming in, solo, I get sidetracked sorting a million screws into separate glass jars, or piling up adorable antique scraps of lace or embroidery into 'a to be dealt with later' sub-project, which only shifts the clutter from A to B. In the decorating area, which I do feel on top of, I always recommend persuading a friend to act as a sounding board on tricky colour decisions to argue the point, clarify your ideas as well as lending muscle and sharing gossip. The same goes for de-cluttering. Get your best mate round, on the understanding you will reciprocate in kind at a later date.

SO WHAT IS CLUTTER?

Clutter is everything and anything taking up space you cannot justify; an analogy might be the unsold stuff that shows up during a retail stock-taking. If stock is unsold, it is because no one wants it, so it gets marked down to clear the decks for the new product. This can be hurtful as some cherished innovation gets the thumbs down, but looked at from another angle, it is about optimism, moving with the times and wising up to reality. De-cluttering isn't only about sloughing off the old skin of the family past, but opening your home up to the future, new ideas, options, colours and lifestyle, etc. Try that argument on sneering teenagers, and sneer right back!

I think we all secretly know what is meant by clutter. If opening a cupboard door sets off an avalanche this is Big Clutter. Wardrobes with dirty corners, where moths rule and unloved shoes and bags gather, are another example. Ditto drawers stuffed with jumpers, knickers and tights in a sorry and sordid tangle – one of those rainy day jobs. Kitchen unit shelves harbouring a plethora of plastic 'attachments' going so far back you forget what they were originally attached to!

I won't go on, because we all – well, most of us – know very well what we are talking about, and the list of unfinished business is as long as a piece of string. If you have kids, small to teenage, the clutter gets magnified exponentially, but you know that too.

THE DE-CLUTTERING START-UP

Take it room by room; blitzing the entire home at one go is just too much, even if (as happens) the adrenalin starts coursing through you as you achieve breakthrough. One cupboard at a time might be enough. You will need roll after roll of extra-tough plastic bags, and a fleet of empty cardboard cartons from your friendly supermarket or corner shop. Remember, you are also helping them to de-clutter! A supply of stick-on, or luggage-type labels for ID, marker pens and a notebook are also useful.

Strategy

De-cluttering goes much further than sorting and tidying. That follows after, when the inventory of possessions is fresh in your mind and, more importantly, you have created space for them. The plan goes something like this:

● Rubbish gets ruthlessly bagged up and chucked out.

● Stuff too good to treat as mere rubbish (surplus clothes, paperbacks and old magazines) is passed on. (See below for recycling ideas).

● Items with possible re-sale value (furniture, bric-a-brac, specialist books, retro or antique clothing, table linen, coverlets, etc) is sorted for disposal via auction room, consignment shops, internet auction sites, charity shops, boot sales or market stalls. (See pages 49–54 for how to set about this.)

Equipment

Large cardboard boxes

*Sturdy plastic bags
    (bin liners are too flimsy)*

String, rubber bands and scissors

Tie-on and stick-on labels

Marker pen

Notebook

*Cleaning materials to do a number on
    cleared shelves: bucket with water
    and a squeeze of detergent, soap
    pads, soft brush, pan and sponge
    cloths*

*A large basket is useful for family
    possessions that have gone astray
    (toys, games, sports stuff, clothes,
    etc). Explain than anything not
    retrieved and put away will fetch
    up, in bags, on the pavement*

Rubbish

Start here, because getting shot of this flotsam and jetsam is already a mind-clearer, making the rest easier to rationalise.

This rubbish gets bagged up for collection, or driven to the local dump. It would include:

- Hoarded empty jars, bottles, boxes, containers and wrapping paper from last Christmas.

- Falling-apart paperbacks, sans covers.

- Hopelessly stained/shrunken clothing, single socks, suitcases/bags minus handle or splitting at the seams.

- Chipped crockery.

- Junk mail, old catalogues and calendars.

- Old medicines, cosmetics or cleaning materials that you no longer use.

- Dried-up paint, gummed-up paint brushes (some of these can be rescued, but will you do this? Be ruthless!).

- Unidentifiable keys (but do test them first).

- Plastic attachments that belong to the vacuum-cleaner-before-last which you just haven't had time to check out.

- Kitchen gadgets that you will never use.

- Garden tools minus handles, plastic flower pots, seed trays, canvas chairs with rents and crusty barbecue equipment sans handles.

This is by no means an exhaustive list, but you get the drift ... these are things you are better off giving the heave-ho; don't waste a second thought on them. Bag it all up securely and put it out for collection immediately, or take it to the nearest dump.

Recycling

I use the word loosely here, to designate stuff surplus to your requirements, but which might warm a refugee somewhere or give a hospital patient a good read. Mark boxes here in big letters. This list might include old radios, videos, CDs, or pots and pans too battered for a boot sale.

- Paperback books you won't want to re-read and back numbers of glossy mags can go to your local hospital, retirement home, Oxfam, library, etc. Ditto videos, CDs, etc. You will have to deliver your box yourself, but the glow of doing a good deed overrides the inconvenience.

- Clothing that is serviceable, rather than stylish, should be bagged or boxed up for delivery to a charity shop. They will be grateful too for warm bedding, sleeping bags, tents, backpacks, and they might like swatch watches, alarm clocks, etc. Ask. In the West, we tend to upgrade such things almost without noticing. Passing them on to someone who might be thrilled by them (with a new battery, or a little repair) feels less sinful and wasteful than chucking them out.

● Toys, board games, cards, baby buggies (outgrown) – the whole paraphernalia of baby and childhood – can be passed on to someone who will be glad of them, if your family is teenage or grown up.

● Ditto skateboards and sports equipment (but do check with owners first)!

CONSIGNMENT SHOPS

This is US-speak, now gaining ground over here, for shops that sell on superior, preferably designer, clothing and some accessories, in perfect nick, and fitting into either the 'good classic' or 'still trendy' categories. They used to have names like 'Nearly New' or 'Beautiful Bargains'. Now they look pretty much like boutiques at first glance, with spiffing window displays in upmarket locations, where they are stocked up by the sort of wealthy women who wouldn't dream of wearing a designer frock more than twice, but hope to recoup some of the cost via the consignment shop. The usual deal is that the shop puts your stuff on display for an agreed time, and any cash raised if it sells is divided 50/50 between shop and seller, which goes some way towards pacifying those annoying conscience pangs over a buy which you fell out of love with as soon as you got it home.

But don't push your luck. The style of these shops may be fluffy and genteel, but their proprietors have pretty exacting standards. Clothes must be immaculate; designer label; and either last season's, or the season before at the most. Good classics – cashmere frocks, silk shirts, leather gear – keep their resale value longer, as do swanky accessories such as Italian boots and bags. If the items haven't sold by a certain date, usually six months, you will be asked to take them back.

After this you move a notch down to Dress Agencies, swap-shops, market stalls

> Sorting the basement was easy, because that was mostly stuff to be thrown out. Paint tins that no longer sloshed; mildewed rolls of leftover wallpaper; galvanised buckets so old they'd been patched with metal disks by some long-dead tinker. We crammed them all into garbage cans and hoped the city would collect them …
>
> *A Patchwork Planet*, Anne Tyler
> (Chatto & Windus, 1998)

and boot sales. If this seems too much like hard graft – and it is! – you might do better to simply give the stuff away – to family, friends, the new au pair or your cleaner. No cash back, but you might make someone's day? And you have at least tried.

GOING, GOING, GONE ...
Selling furniture

Most people wanting to get shot of furniture will send it to a local sale room, hoping to make a bit of cash as well as clear the decks. This is fine if the items are bog standard, and you don't set your sights too high as to their value. (By bog standard stuff, I mean such items as three piece suites of fairly recent vintage, undistinguished dining tables and chairs or sideboards.)

The very fact that sale rooms are a good place to buy stuff at a keen price means they may not be such good venues for selling. It is as well to make sure that they are likely to make enough to cover the cost of transport and the saleroom's charges, which are normally around 15 per cent of the selling price plus VAT. Take snaps of the items you want to sell, show them to the person in charge of valuations, and do your sums.

If you are on friendly terms with a local dealer or secondhand-shop owner, you might be better off negotiating with him/her to take it off your hands, since this way you can both cut out the middleman.

Antiques and period items

Where you might score is with quirky or interesting period items. Serious antiques you will know about if you watch 'Antiques Road Show', but it is as well to bone up on current values in the *Miller's Price Guides*. You might not realise that old English oak is currently more sought after than Georgian mahogany, or that '30s club chairs covered in brown hide are more popular than buttoned, spoon-back Victorian chairs and fetch relatively high prices, even in poor condition. Current taste is definitely reflected in saleroom prices.

Where you need to be a bit smart and streetwise is with silver, old books, glass and ceramics, paintings and prints. Georgian silver, for instance, sells like hot cakes, so don't make the mistake of sending a bundle of tarnished spoons to a local sale room when they might fetch a lot more at a specialist sale to which interested dealers flock and bid against each other for the good stuff.

Specialist sales are held at regular intervals by the 'name' auction houses – Christie's, Sotheby's and Bonham's – not just in their London salerooms, but up and down the country (see My Directory). Anything of interest, and possible value, should be entrusted to sales like these rather than a smaller local – and perhaps less expert – auction house.

The first step is to call the head office, describe what you want to sell (silver, oriental pieces, ceramics, etc) and you will be referred to an 'expert'. Any information you can give – hallmarks, signatures, provenance – will be helpful here; the local library may be useful for research. However, you will probably be asked to send photos, or bring the item in for a quick look and valuation. If the item falls outside their scope, you will be directed towards another auction house. At least you will almost certainly have learnt more about the item in question, even if your wilder hopes are dashed.

The snag with specialist sales is that they may happen at long intervals, especially the really oddball ones such as antique toys, Chinese embroideries, or Art Deco figurines, but it will almost certainly be worth waiting for/holding your fire.

The good news is that the grander auction houses charge more or less the same as the lesser ones, with the interesting difference that the charge comes down if the end price goes up – thus 10 per cent instead of 15 per cent for goods which fetch over £1,000; and 10 per cent VAT (instead of 17.5 per cent) on items selling for over £30,000. (Well, you never know in this game!) This is what makes salerooms, at all levels, a bit buzzy and exciting – finally, it is all a bit of a gamble. The remarkable thing is that discoveries do still happen!

The expert opinion

Usually through inheritance, many families own a possible 'treasure' whose importance and value has been handed down orally through generations. Young children are thrilled when a grandparent warns them off handling a particular item, with the solemn explanation, 'This is unique, it was a wedding present to your great-great-grandmother from a Chinese war lord!' Such romantic and exotic possibilities operate powerfully on a child's imagination. The grandparents die, and eventually the now grown-up child inherits the family treasure. However, is it really a treasure (worth a fortune requiring proper care and insurance) or is its importance just a figment of the family mystique? The BBC's Antiques Road Show is thronged with such folk exhibiting their own 'treasures', uncertain whether they have been sitting on a goldmine or a fancy but rubbishy item of sentimental value only.

I inherited two items of exactly this sort. A jade ring, of a peculiarly brilliant green, seemingly carved to represent a cricket or grasshopper, and a rather lovely scroll with what looks like Chinese characters on one half and quite different calligraphy on the other, all set out against a background of silk brocade in blocks of subtle shades. The ring, my mother proudly said, was special because of its colour – not cloudy and subdued (soapstone) but viridian – and thus rare. The scroll, she claimed, was the written record of a treaty between Manchurian and Korean warlords of some long past date. She must have picked these items up in China during the '30s, and was probably repeating to me the spiel she heard from the owners of the curio shops at the time. She gave me the scroll, on impulse, long before she died. During her last scatty years, I found the famously vivid jade creature in her sewing drawer come adrift from its setting. I persuaded her to let me get the gold claw setting repaired, and then returned it to her third finger, left hand, with due solemnity. She wore it until her death; I have worn it ever since; for its odd beauty and out of piety – a link with her that I cherish.

Then, in a Sunday supplement, I read an excitable article about 'jade stone', unknown in the West but startlingly valuable in the East, 'more precious than diamonds'. I suddenly felt anxious about this scrap of family history on my finger, which goes swimming and washes up with me (under a marigold!). It was scary to think that something I was wearing offhandedly, as a memento, might be unique and highly valuable. And the scroll, now pinned to my bedroom wall, a strange and lovely artefact, could this be some vital historical document? I felt a new weight of responsibility and thought it best to get them both checked out. But where and how? I enquired at the Victoria and Albert information desk, and found out about the Opinions and Enquiry Service that takes place once a month (see My Directory).

This is how it works. Phone first, then take the objects in question (in some cases photographs may be sufficient) to the museum, and you will be sent on to an appropriate curator. However, you can't expect an evaluation; after all this isn't the Antiques Road Show. However, you will get a knowledgeable opinion as to the object's rarity, interest and authenticity.

On the appointed day, I presented myself at the Museum's information desk, with my ring and my scroll, and was referred to the Oriental Department, which took some finding in that labyrinthine building. Here I joined a queue; all of us clutching a putative treasure. After a brief wait, I was summoned behind a screen and met by a chic Chinese woman, expert in this area. We sat, along with a small crowd of other aspirants, round a large table. Against a background of discreet murmurs from other experts, my expert, after a brief glance at my ring and scroll, gave her opinion.

My ring, she said crushingly, was not 'jadeite', this newly desired and fabulously rare and expensive stone said to be worth more than diamonds. She darted a sharp glance at me as she said this, as if checking my reaction, to this sad news. So what is it?

I asked, blank-faced. It is ordinary jade, good colour, but jadeite is quite different, much more vivid, unmistakable. I ventured that my mother always claimed it represented a carved grasshopper. No, it is a dragon, very small, see the head here. Sorry Ma, I thought to myself, but you can't get much more Chinese than a dragon. The ring put in its proper place, not without a stir of resentment on my part I have to admit, we moved on to the scroll. She showed more interest in this. My mother's notion that this inscribed some historic treaty between China and Korea, she dismissed briskly but not unkindly. No, it is the record of an honour paid to a provincial official by the Emperor, in return for good services, maybe in the late nineteenth century. Maybe a bit like a CBE? This scroll praises him in a nice way, of course. The two scripts are because one is official, Mandarin, the other local, demotic.

Should I, I asked, take special care of my Chinese 'CBE' scroll? She shrugged. Maybe hang it out of direct sunlight? All around me, murmured comments greeted far more extraordinary artefacts than mine: carved lacquer, lengths of Tribute Silk, elaborately painted scrolls. I thanked my expert, replaced the bright but common jade dragon ring on my finger, rolled up my Chinese CBE scroll and left. A touch disgruntled, as you will have divined. But this is often the fate of 'treasures' exposed to the expert's eye.

Your fantasies are punctured with a few knowledgeable words. What you gain is valuable information, provenance, date, a smidgin of local colour. Not a clue as to the value of the item concerned, which is fair enough as this is not the brief of the museum curators, as explained beforehand.

I dropped in at the Chinese Gallery on my way out to remind myself of what museum quality artefacts are about. Illusions are sweet, but the truth – matchless jade, porcelain, embroidered imperial gowns – is better, I decided.

Anyone determined to sell, at auction or privately, will have gained vital information through this museum service, which is free, incidentally. Quoting the V & A expert opinion shows you have done your homework, and lends useful clout to your story.

MARKET STALLS AND BOOT FAIRS

A chancier way to offload or sell on your clutter because these have their good days and bad days, for no ascertainable reason. It takes quite a bit of organising too: the venue, the time, the transport, the 'display' (old hands recommend decorators' pasting tables, which are cheap, fold easily, and are reasonably sturdy once set up on site; plus a 'cover': old curtains, fabric lengths, quilts. However, the upside is that if you hit on a good day, you might clear a complete jumble of accumulated stuff and be quids in at the end. It seems people about to move house often use boot sales as an outlet for the stuff they suddenly see as surplus.

For information about London markets consult *Time Out*. Established markets such as Portobello, Camden Lock, Camden Passage, Spitalfields, White City, etc, charge more for a pitch (£25–45) and competition for a site is keener, so you need to be in the queue horribly early – 7 am is about right – with your goods and display ready to go. The regulars tend to get priority and the favoured locations: ie, at the posher end, or under cover. Given our uncertain weather, an open-air pitch will need some sort of protection from showers.

Mei Hui, a sparky young Taiwanese designer who has been a Portobello regular for years – 'On a good day I clear £400, on a bad day maybe £50' – advises anyone looking for a market stall to do a recce first; to get a fix on prices, display ideas (you need a hanging rail for clothes), shelter ideas, and the buzz. The stuff that walks off your stall in one market could die in another. What gives the established markets their edge is that most young, struggling designers use them for their first step on the ladder towards recognition, fame and orders from foreign buyers. This is irrelevant to someone trying to sell on a load of household clutter, except that it guarantees a wider, more free-spending sector of the public, including loads of spend-happy tourists.

Boot sales are altogether less formal, more of a pot-luck for both sellers and buyers. Check out venues in local papers. A pitch will cost less – £5–15 or thereabouts – and the whole thing may launch off at a more reasonable hour (9.30 am onwards). Parking too is not such a problem as they tend to be held in giant parking lots next to a station or a market, deserted at weekends. Dealers may skim through briefly, but on the whole, boot sales are local affairs, attracting local people, so prices are that much more realistic.

Anna, a jewellery designer friend, who has done loads of boot sales to raise spot cash over the years, never puts a price tag on her offerings. She has an idea of her bottom line, but she likes an open-ended situation where she negotiates a price with a potential buyer. The danger of sticking price tags on your stuff, she says, is that you can so easily get it wrong – especially if you are new to the scene – and either pitch it so low that you sell it but feel cheated, or so high you are left with a load of unsold goods, which have to be packed up and driven away. Best to do a quick recce of the other stalls on the day and arrive at your prices accordingly. Only use price tags, she advises, if you have an idea of your bottom line much like an auctioneer's reserve price, below which you are just giving it away.

DOWNSIZING

To plummet from careless extravagance to anxious penny pinching is a traumatic experience for anyone, at any age. If the economic downturn forecast everywhere in the media really gets to bite, a lot of people are going to be struggling – fat cats, young Turks and especially young women – 20-somethings – flagged up in a *Company* magazine survey as habitually in debt. In this survey, they owed an average of £5,000 each, but 25 per cent were down by as much as £15,000 which could represent a year's income before tax. Of course they should have known better, but these are the people who have been most ardently courted by banks, and shops dishing out those seductive bits of plastic with a 'buy now, pay later' message. When you can't pay your debts, then the situation becomes a very different, and scary story: the cards are rejected, cut in two by a stone-faced shop assistant, the landlord gets threatening, the post is full of those buff envelopes with red printed warnings, cash is needed to get stuff back from the cleaners, to pay the milk bill and so on. Being cut down to size is frightening and humiliating.

The 'yoof' culture has been predicated on spend, spend, spend, or shop till you drop, its iconic image some rock chick snapped on her way out of a ritzy boutique bowed down under the weight of her expensive loot. Spending money is just so much easier, and more fun than earning it. As for saving it … puhleeze!

The likelihood is that all that is changing as corporations downsize, companies trim their fat, and the last to come are the first to go. A cab drive through the City of London takes half the time because, as my cabby pointed out, the workforce is dwindling; its roaring boys being laid off.

Having gone from prosperity to penury twice in my life, I think I am placed to give a front-line report on how to handle the shock of your ladder suddenly turning into a slippery snake. You will feel depressed, sleep badly, drink too much, wake in a sweaty panic around 4 am, convinced your life has imploded. It can sometimes help to treat this as a wake-up call; cook and eat a lonely (but appetising) breakfast. Getting a head start on the waking day feels good once in a while, and between slurps of tea and comforting bites of toast, you should plan your retaliatory campaign, scribbling down your ideas or brainwaves in a notebook. The critical thing is to view your predicament – being skint – as a challenge, not a punishment.

I wrote my first published book, *The Pauper's Cookbook*, in 1970 out of a real-life situation; four of us living close to the breadline in a small rented flat in a seaside town in Dorset. I had become quite adept at feeding us cheaply: foraging for free food such as mussels on rocks at low tide, blackberries, blewits (mushrooms); learning how to make bread and pasta; and cooking the cheapest cuts of meat, or a poacher's gift of rabbit or pigeons.

When someone suggested I put this all down in book form, as recipes costing no more than half a crown per head (as this was then) I leapt at it. We lived on the advance meanwhile, but it was the challenge of researching cheap but rewardingly tasty food and recipes that saw me through months of bashing away on my kitchen table, with my two-year-old daughter clutching at my knees for attention a lot of the time, that drove me on. It saw me through the testing and tasting, and at length to publication, interviews on World at One, and sales that briefly made me Penguin's blue-eyed girl.

Looking back, I marvel that I pulled it off, fitted the endeavour into a pauperish lifestyle – small, underheated flat, demanding child, no regular income – without cracking up. But I recall these as some of the happiest, most fulfilled days of my life.

CUTTING BACK

I assume that you will already have come to some agreement with your bank, which may or may not involve surrendering your crucial credit card, and cancelling any other plastic, such as store cards. The bottom line is going to be retrenching on all fronts to save enough from your earnings to start regular repayments. Believe me, playing ostrich will only prolong the agony. If you have never had to economise, you may well be wondering where to start. If you value your independence, and bolting home to Mum and Dad is out of the question, some small sacrifices will be needed.

Here are some suggestions that may help. If you have never scrimped before, they will strike you as horribly petty, but they will gradually reduce your outgoings and allow you to manage your debt. As this happens, you will regain confidence and the economic restrictions will feel less niggling.

MONEY

● Cancel all store credit/charge cards – these often charge as much as 25 per cent interest.

● Take out a fixed sum of cash each week and make it last.

● File all your bills, invoices, bank statements, receipts, etc, and try to get a handle on preparing your own tax returns. If this is beyond you, having all the paperwork to hand will save an accountant's time and thus reduce his fees.

FOOD

● Eating in saves money and learning to cook can be great fun once you get into the swing of it. Get one basic how-to book, cut out recipes from the Sunday papers and shop cleverly. These are, after all, life skills which will stand you in good stead for a long time to come.

● Don't buy pre-prepared foods such as washed salad greens or peeled sliced carrots. Prepare your own vegetables (using a sharp knife or swivel-blade peeler) and save at least 30 per cent. Plus, they last longer.

● Take a home-made packed lunch to work.

● Make your own mayonnaise, salad dressing, pasta sauce and mashed potatoes – cheaper, nicer and healthier.

● Mineral water is expensive – get a filter jug

Vicarage Mutton,
or the story of the Sunday joint

Hot on Sunday
Cold on Monday
Hashed on Wednesday
Curried on Thursday
Broth on Friday
Cottage Pie on Saturday

Food in England, Dorothy Hartley
(Macdonalds, 1954;
Little, Brown & Co, 1996)

Some joint; a whole sheep's leg. But it should really be Shepherd's Pie on Saturday, because this is made from mutton. Cottage pie is traditionally made from beef.

and store filter water in the fridge in small recycled plastic bottles.

● Major on traditional staple foods: potatoes, rice, pasta, pulses and polenta. They are all tasty and nutritious if you read up on sauces and trimmings. Don't buy these pre-cooked, tinned or ready-to-go in the microwave. Read up on some basic cooking methods.

● Try making your own bread? Irish soda bread is easy (no yeast involved) and delicious. Defrosted bread tastes fine and one large loaf can be allocated to suit your requirements

● Waste not, want not: get clever with leftovers. Make chicken carcases into stock, keep any gravy to add to soups or sauces, use cooked vegetables for warm salads and purées or add to a catch-all omelette – call it an *eggah*, and add a little chopped chilli. Make surplus milk into white sauce, cool, bag up, label and freeze. This is a great time saver.

OVERHEADS

- Get into the habit of turning lights off, thus saving energy as well as cash.

- Turn the central heating down a few degrees and wear more layers of clothes to keep warm. If your house has fireplaces and flues, try real fires (see page 81) using scrap timber.

- Cut down on cooking/fuel bills by using a pressure cooker or by cooking several dishes at once in the oven.

- Get a bike with panniers. Bicycles are the cheapest form of transport and brilliant exercise for everything below the arms. Panniers will hold a change of clothes, office doodahs and a last-minute shop. Remember to buy a protective helmet and fluorescent armbands to wear for visibility and safety.

- In some city areas, a resident's parking space can be rented out – I found out that mine is worth over £3,000 per year!

- Get ahead on the DIY front: clean your own windows, do your own decorating, stitch your own covers, curtains, etc. Teach yourself how to change a fuse, unblock a sink, replace a low-voltage bulb or unblock a vacuum cleaner.

PERSONAL MAINTENANCE

This covers both clothes and, erm, beauty.

- Launder your own clothes instead of stacking up dry-cleaning bills. (See page 172 for safe options.) Hand-washed clothes feel nicer, smell sweeter and stay cleaner for longer.

- If you are into hair colouring, keep the professional hairdresser visits to a minimum – maybe once a month max – and ask your colourist to prepare your 'colour stuff' and tell you how to use it. A veggie colour, such as henna, is easy to apply oneself.

- Forget laundries (especially you men!) and learn how to wash/iron and starch (see page 179) your shirts yourself.

- Buy classics (cashmere cardigans and jumpers, etc) via mail order (see page 75) as their prices are often lower than similar items in designer/boutique shops.

- Use your public transport journeys to knit a lavishly long stripy scarf in your own wild colour combination.

- Check out thrift shops while retro (cunningly mixed with designer stuff) is street smart.

● Clear your unworn extravagances via consignment shops, boot sales and market stalls (see page 49).

● Look out for kids' clothes in thrift shops and jumble sales.

● Try home-made beauty treatments (see page 277). Do your own nails, hands and feet.

● Get nifty on a sewing machine for alterations, repairs and even creative stuff of your own. Convert thrift shop finds (such as knits) into cushion covers or hot-water bottle covers (see page 216), adding your own flourish. This is an excellent idea for Christmas presents or even the start of your own cottage industry! No kidding. Loads of young designers started out from one home-spun, cute idea and moved into the big time when the orders started rolling in.

MAKING DO

This is the scrimping bottom line, but I make no apologies for adding it.

● When a tube of toothpaste, etc, seems empty, it rarely is. Cut off the end with scissors and squeeze the other way. There is often more left than you thought.

● When plastic bottles release (almost) nothing more, stand them on their heads for a last innings.

● Cook up a debris of pasta shapes (too little for a meal) until *al dente*, and use as a base for a mixed salad.

● Half empty tins of emulsion paint? Wearing gloves, peel off the thick skin on top, add a little water and stir well. Decant what you might need for touch-ups into lidded jars (label these) and then consider whether you might intermix what is left? Space forbids a lengthy treatise on colour mixing here, but it is worth a try – at worst you end up with an interesting sludge shade for the garage; at best you have enough of a new 'individual' shade for your spare room.

● Old shirts galore? Rip or snip the best: large pieces (usually the back) can be added to a future patchwork. Shirting is ideal for this: it is dye-fast, good-quality fabric (forget acrilan/polyester mixes) and usually comes in harmoniously traditional shades.

● Light bulbs get dingier even before they go phut. To gain maximum lux, wipe them over with a just-damp rag.

DOING IT THEIR WAY

NICK CURTIS

Nick Curtis is Features Editor of London's *Evening Standard*, a position which often involves rushing out what we used to call a 'think piece' for the next day's editions, pegged to some topical theme that has floated up through the zeitgeist. It may be serious, controversial or frivolous. The piece that caught my eye was perhaps a bit of all three, and grew out of Ruby Wax's admission, to camera, that she is hopeless around the home. (I happen to know this is no word of a lie: when I came across Ruby on a country weekend, she was lying out by the swimming pool while her husband, described as 'rather gorgeous', rustled up an evening meal for the family.) Anyway, this unblushing statement of Ruby's struck a chord with Nick, who went on to disclose that his 'lovely, intelligent, kind and witty wife is a slut'. 'I'm the neat one,' he went on, 'the one who applies vacuum cleaner to carpet, who unites knicker with knicker drawer.' I thought that a man brave enough to label his wife a slut, albeit in the nicest possible way, to maintain that 'the male of the species is tidier than the female' and know that there is such a thing as a knicker drawer, was someone who could throw a search-light on domestic matters seen from a male perspective.

I asked him to tell me more, which he obligingly did in my kitchen over a frugal lunch, en route to Top of the Pops with Victoria Beckham. While admitting that he might have ratcheted up the Curtis home situation fractionally to give edge to his views, Nick was not about to back down about the male being tidier, etc. 'It's not just me speaking. I went round the office and asked all the men there what was the most annoying thing women do in the home and they all said – this was from 22-year-olds to 60-year-olds – it was the way women cover every available surface with stuff!' This male solidarity seems to make Nick feel better about some of Ann's sluttier habits, such as scattering the bathroom floor with lipstick-blotted tissues as she prepares to step out of the Curtis home, glossily immaculate, the very pattern of a rising advertising executive. This did make me gasp inwardly, I have to admit. A picture of Ann was forming in my mind: one of those sophisticated sirens played by Hedy Lamarr, Joan Crawford or Bette Davis in old movies, sweeping out of the home in a whirl of mink and perfume, throwing husky double entendres over her shoulder as she pauses to adjust the spotted veil on her absurd hat in the hall mirror.

Nick meanwhile came up with an intriguing theory, that all men have a touch of something in their make-up which makes them obsessive, anally retentive, control freaks. For instance, he has taken over half of a majorly useful cupboard to store his collection of *2000 AD* comics, going back to 1974, sorted by year into plastic packs and labelled. He seems to feel a tad uneasy about this fusspot side of his character.

During a twelve-year stint as theatre critic, prior to the day job as Features Editor, – and before he met Ann – Nick became a nocturnal animal. A working schedule would be a play in the evening, followed by eating out somewhere, followed by sitting up over his review till 4 am. Rising around midday, he had hours to kill before the next play and this was when he became house dproud and evolved a routine. He sees it as part of a larger movement – the return of *l'homme sensuel*.

It began with washing up, which he did by the book: cleanest things first (glasses and cups), then cutlery and plates, pots and pans. All thoroughly rinsed and upended to drain. He didn't learn this from his mother, but from girls at school with him. 'There were a couple of black girls I remember, who told me about rinsing as you go along. They said only black people bothered to do this.'

Then he might vacuum the des. res., which is sizeable: two reception rooms, four bedrooms plus the usual offices. Dusting didn't figure on this checklist, though he spent time tidying videos and CDs into their orderly compartments. Once a week or so he would tackle his ironing, with video or music as company. 'I got to feel a sense of achievement – 14 shirts ironed!' He tackled home improvements, such as converting a metal medicine cabinet, inherited from his father, into a cocktail cabinet lined with mirror and packed with retro cocktail shakers, glasses and different bottles of booze.

Any writer will recognise that a lot of this was displacement activity; the blank page, blank screen angst which makes lowlier chores irresistibly attractive.

So there was Nick, bachelor lifestyle nicely under control, home in apple-pie order (how much mess does a tidy bloke with time on his hands get to create?), shirts crisp, cocktail cabinet stocked and gleaming, a modest but reassuring ongoing routine and what happens next is this. He meets Ann, the stylish, amusing 'slut' whose fridge in Kensington is so choked with food past its sell-by date that Nick's investigating arm comes out covered with brown sludge! Captivated, disarmed and amused by this insouciance, our man woos and wins his Sally Bowles. They marry and she moves into his South London des. res., scattering knickers and tissues about, designating one of the four bedrooms as her dressing room. She gets the decorators in (actually her brother) to paint the connubial bedroom red (it was all white before), imports a dishwasher, engages a cleaner to die for (through a colleague at the agency) who not only keeps an eye on things while the Curtises are on holiday, but actually purchases a sheet or towel out of her own funds when she feels their linen is on its last legs. The Curtises now give more dinner parties, on Saturday nights as a rule, shopping for them in the morning. Nick, who is a bit of a foodie, does most of the cooking still but Ann is learning fast.

One control-freakish trait from his old singleton life Nick has hung on to is that he always washes up and clears up after a dinner party, even if it means staying up, hungover, till the early hours. He also de-frosts the fridge every two weeks. However, a trade-off is taking place between anal-retentive Mr Tidy and insouciant Mrs Slut: Nick, to his surprise, likes his red bedroom. He has amiably relaxed his fussy standards: 'As long as the living room looks tidy, I'm fine.'

Ann, meanwhile, is showing signs of mending her ways. She sometimes helps with the washing up. She is learning to cook and, clever lady that she undoubtedly is, she has clocked on to the fact that while husbands can be cajoled by a charm offensive, a first-class cleaner demands considerable respect. Once a week Ann flies around the house 'in a frenzy of tidying and straightening. No matter how slovenly a woman will be in front of her partner she always, always, cleans up before the cleaner arrives.'

SORTING

SHOPPING

THE BIG SHOP

A weekly fixture in all our lives, supplemented by dribs and drabs in between. The big shop is best dealt with at the end of the week – Thursday or Friday – as parking is easier, supermarkets are not chock-a-block and the bread counters have not been stripped bare. However, working people inevitably gravitate towards the weekend, possibly picking up fresh organic produce at a Saturday market alongside a trip to the supermarket for the staples.

Who shops?

One person armed with a list makes shorter work than two unless you have two lists and two trolleys. I think women are usually cannier shoppers than men for the following reasons:

● they enjoy it more.

● they are more knowledgeable in this area.

● they can think laterally, keeping an eye out for what is seasonal, which means fresher and cheaper produce. They also keep an eye on what is on offer or a Best Buy.

My partner, Richard, has done most of our big shops recently because I have been laid up with a fractured ankle. I make a list, of course, but he departs from it freely, adding things that take his fancy – usually bundles of out-of-season asparagus – overlooking boring essentials such as Cif, soap pads and loo paper. He certainly doesn't regard my list as canonical – ie, I have checked out stocks thoroughly – so we end up with six bottles of soy sauce, balsamic vinegar in spades and enough lentils to fill a neck pillow. Now I make a list which starts with No/No items and carries on with the Yes/Yes. Not that I am ungrateful, but we soon run out of space.

The list

Shopping has to start here and the list has to start with checking out the contents of the fridge, larder (if you have one), shelves and freezer. Do this the day before.

This is also when you bin mouldy bread, mushy vegetables, yoghurt growing fur, sour milk and invent an interesting meal using leftovers. In addition, take the opportunity to clean out the fridge so it is neat and sweet for next day's provisions (see page 149).

As a general tactic, try to keep stocks of dry goods – rice, flour, lentils, chickpeas, burghul (bulgar wheat) and spices – to a sensible minimum. While they will keep for months and look attractive lined up in glass jars, they do deteriorate over time, getting harder and drier and thus requiring longer soaking and cooking time. Spices, especially, lose their pungency. Dried chillies seem to be the one ingredient that lasts for years on end.

Women at home are best placed to know what their family's consumption is likely to be over a week. They will also have evolved a shopping (blueprint) list and have a plan of sorts, and the time to implement it so that waste is kept to a minimum. The cost of wasted food, through overbuying, lack of planning and impulse buys, runs into millions annually in the UK. All of us slip up occasionally, myself included, for lifestyle reasons: sausages get pushed to the back of the fridge and then look and smell dubious by Thursday, or the tomatoes (left in their pack because you were in a hurry or distracted) are deliquescent. There is a real comfort factor in a full fridge and generously stocked shelves, especially with hungry children or teenagers around.

The real wastrels are young, well-paid single people with expensive tastes and impromptu eating habits. Too 'tired and emotional' to cook after a long day's work, they often grab a bagel or phone for a takeaway; the perishable contents of the fridge and cupboards going to waste for yet another evening.

Wasting food is not a crime; only your purse suffers. However, it does seem unnecessary if you have a freezer. My freezing compartment is always much more crowded than the fridge. This is good: unlike fridges, freezers apparently work better when packed.

POST-SHOP

Keep perishables, to be eaten in the next two to three days, in the fridge. These might include fish/shellfish (always best eaten on the day of purchase), a joint of lamb or a bird. These products should be stored in the cold zone – just above the salad bins (see page 149). If I have time, I prefer to unwrap them (removing all those soggy and bloody paper mats), transfer them to pyrex, china dishes or plastic containers and squeeze lemon juice over with a sprinkle of dried thyme, or splash on a little white wine with a few crushed mixed peppercorns. This is not a serious marinade, but it looks and smells more appealing and contributes something to the final dish.

Other perishables (organic sausages, whole crabs, pork loin and duck breasts) can go into the freezer, as found. This means they remain safely edible even if your eating-in plans change, or you opt for comfort dishes such as pasta. However, to de-frost safely, transfer to the fridge the night before. Or failing that (you simply forgot), leave out at room temperature on the day you plan to eat, in its packaging or in a dish. Even if I had a microwave, I would rather the food thawed out naturally than rapidly in a microwave, both on hygiene and foodie grounds.

Cooking meat, poultry and shellfish that might not be completely thawed out is a food hygienist's no-no (see page 152). I feel it is one intervention too many, robbing it of succulence and flavour. I would rather rustle up a quick store-cupboard dish such as *penne all'arrabiata*.

Two items I never freeze are mince (I buy minced lamb-going-on-mutton from local halal butchers for freshness) and steak, which I prefer to marinade. We rarely eat steak anyway, because it is so pricey. By the same token, whenever I do splurge on steak, of the right purplish colour with yellow fat (never buy scarlet wet-looking steak from supermarket shelves unless you plan to casserole it), I feel it deserves thoughtful treatment: a rub with cut garlic or balsamic vinegar, a dribble of wine, sprinkling of crushed peppercorns or dried chillies. Any of these will both keep the steak in good condition for several days (in the fridge) and enrich the flavour on the plate. Fresh mince is juiciest eaten the same day, but surplus mince, zapped up with your preferred flavourings – chopped garlic, shallots, herbs and turmeric, etc – can be refrigerated and eaten the next day. My family adores meatballs, so this is a frequent dish *chez moi*.

Greenstuff

This will probably include both organic and non-organic vegetables, salad stuff and herbs. Organic produce deteriorates so much more rapidly than produce helped along by pesticides, irradiation and waxing that it needs either to be eaten a.s.a.p. (two to three days max) or further processed by yourself – blanched, frozen, puréed, lightly cooked and dressed to be eaten as a salad – to keep it sound and tasty for a bit longer. Whereas a standard cauliflower, for instance, will still be white and crisp after four or five days, an organic cauliflower begins to develop black patches, a slimy stem and mushy bits much sooner: 48 hours? Salads and herbs go off even faster. Root vegetables – carrots, parsnips and celeriac – are a tad more tolerant if kept in cool and dark conditions. Potatoes tend to sprout in less than a week. The bottom line is – don't buy organic unless you care enough to deal with it promptly, otherwise you will just be adding to the mountains of waste foodstuff we chuck out nationally.

● Plan to eat as much of it as you can, fresh and unmediated, as soon as possible to enjoy the undeniable pungency of flavour as well as its ecological purity.

● Put salad stuff to crisp in cold water for an hour or two. Remove any discoloured leaves, spin in a salad dryer, and store in freezer bags in the fridge salad compartments. This gives lettuce, radicchio and oak leaf lettuce an extra lease of life but watercress and rocket should be eaten as soon as possible.

● I find that carrots and turnips, etc, fare better taken out of their wraps and stored in the fridge, if there is room (chop off the leaves), or in a cool larder. After day two, it would be wise to cook, cool off, then freeze in bags, whole or puréed.

● Cauliflowers make an excellent warm salad, broken into florets, steamed till *al dente*, then dressed and refrigerated. Broccoli ditto.

● Tomatoes: eat raw within 48 hours or cook up into a sauce with garlic and onions, freeze or refrigerate.

● Less urgency is required with potatoes, small new, waxy ones especially, but at the first sign of sprouting, or greening, cook them up, purée and freeze. Mix the mash with other root purées, garlic or mustard/brie.

● Herbs: eat fresh as much as you can, to add a waft of scent and flavour to soups, salads, roasts, gravies or what foodies annoyingly call 'jus'. Soft, leafy herbs such as parsley and coriander turn slimy quickest. Dunked in cold water (glass or jug) they last a bit longer if you change the water daily. It's safer to dry them, or more laboriously, blanch briefly, chop or process and freeze.

Old gadgets

How is this for a weird coincidence? Rooting about for a contrivance to reduce a pan full of cooked quinces to a purée without pips, stalks, etc, I came across two elderly gadgets which arrived in a box of stuff from my mother's, and had been sitting at the bottom of a cupboard, gathering dust, ever since. On inspection, they turned out to be a Mouli Legumes and a Mouli Julienne, a bit rusty here and there, but complete with their sets of cutting attachments and handles. Compared with the chore of setting up my massively weighty food processor, the Mouli Legumes was a cinch to assemble, and did the job efficiently, without pushing through pips, stalks, etc. I looked upon it with new respect and decided to flag it up to you, dear readers, on the grounds of simplicity and effectiveness.

So why had these items languished unused all this time? I decided – a frivolous reason I know – that it was because they looked a bit dated and decrepit compared with the lustrous mandoline in stainless steel I have had my eye on, and which costs all of £120. I phoned David Mellor, my favourite kitchen shop, to enquire whether they stocked updated versions and what they cost. 'Yes,' the sales assistant said, 'we do still have some Mouli Legumes in stock and they cost £36.' Then she paused. 'It may just be a rumour' she added, 'but I think you may find Moulinex, the company that makes them, has just gone out of business.' And so it proved.

So the Mouli Legumes and the Mouli Julienne have become overnight rarities. I advise you to look out for them in boot sales or market stalls. Glamorous they are not, but functional, light and blessedly straightforward (you can see at a glance how the bits fit together and how to operate the gadget) they undoubtedly are; chomping their way through bumpy soups, dried out chunks of Parmesan, or bunches of parsley with dogged efficiency. And of course we are not talking here about paying £36. More like a fiver – but make sure they haven't lost their sets of cutters. To bring them up to scratch, a blast of WD 40, followed after ten minutes by a soap pad, will brighten them up and remove loose spots of rust. A light coating of oil – vegetable oil, applied with a pastry brush – will keep them protected and operational.

● Fruit: eat soft berry fruit that very day, or purée with sugar and freeze. Refrigerate ripe fruit, but leave hard peaches, pears and melons at room temperature to ripen, to eat at once or refrigerate. Some exotics – papaya and mangoes – seem to keep well and ripen in the fridge for up to a week. Apples should keep well on the whole, but pick them over and discard ones with brown patches or speedily peel and cut off the brown bits. Then cook and purée – apple sauce for a pork roast? Once cooked, this will keep several days.

Standard fruit and veg

Much the same advice holds good for these with the difference that the heat is off, and you can expect up to a week's keeping – or longer – from most of it. Salads and soft fruit are the least satisfactory, as you might expect. Unless your family's consumption of potatoes is mega, it can be a mistake to buy these in large bags because by the time you get down to the last spuds you will – unless the weather is really cold – find them green and sprouting. With all fresh produce, whether standard or organic, the best insurance against having to bin the lot is a daily once over, picking out any dodgy items. If you have a compost system up and running, this becomes a positive way to re-cycle them, though expensive compared with potato peel and grass cuttings.

Storing eggs

Do not wash eggs because they might have picked up nasties such as salmonella, and washing could pass this on to the egg by removing its natural protective coating. Opinions vary as to the best ways to store eggs. Hygienists advise you to keep them in the fridge, whereas foodies urge storage at room temperature to retain maximum flavour.

Other foods

● Bread: I regularly freeze a couple of loaves, bringing them out as the week goes by. Thawed, they are indis-tinguishable from fresh loaves, although they do go stale quicker. Freshly brought bread goes mouldy in a few days if stored in a metal or earthenware bread bin with a glazed lining; the moisture is trapped and mould results.

Stale (not mouldy) bread, dried out in the oven, makes bread-crumbs, or it can be used undried in peasant salads, soups or bread-and-butter pudding. I sometimes buy an immense round, crusty peasant loaf in our local farmers' market. This is expensive but it goes on being delicious, from fresh, to toasted, to crostini and so on, the remains being turned into de luxe breadcrumbs.

● Dairy Produce: I tend to buy organic here for the rich magnificence of its flavour. Everyone, at least once in a while, should treat themselves to organic – even unpasteurised – Jersey milk, cream and butter, as a reminder of what phrases like 'the fat of the land' are all about; a greedy, celestial experience. Organic yoghurt may be higher in calories, but tastes divine, as does my recent discovery, goat butter. We eat these so sparingly – a scrape on the breakfast toast or a tiny knob with the veg – I feel justified in making this a priority. When I eat low-fat, processed and otherwise denatured dairy products, I feel poor cow, all that patient munching, all those stomachs churning and refining away, to produce this!

Goose fat

I have recently discovered goose fat as an ideal means of frying. It comes in tins from France and the brand is *La Truffe Cendrée*. I use it for browning birds or meat, cooking sausages, and roasting or frying potatoes. Leftover Anya potatoes, peeled or unpeeled, slowly browned in goose fat, sprinkled with rosemary and sea salt to finish, are delectable. The great virtue of goose fat is its high burning temperature: you can take it to a higher frying temperature than oils or ghee (clarified butter) without the food catching and burning. It is transparently pure, a viscous liquid straight from the tin. It sets to a snowy solid in the fridge but is still soft enough to spoon out. It keeps in the fridge indefinitely. Unlike ghee, which I find over-rich and cloying, goose fat has no discernible flavour. I haven't yet used goose fat for frying chips, but I suspect it would make an excellent job of these if the chips are small and fairly uniform in size,

Does goose fat pose a high cholesterol risk? I think this is debatable, and many chefs and food writers would agree. Used at a suitably high temperature, goose fat instantly seals food surfaces so the meat or potatoes absorb minimum fat. However, if you are on a cholesterol-controlled/free diet you shouldn't be eating fried foods at all!

MAIL-ORDER AND INTERNET SHOPPING

Mail-order and online shopping are now well established as an alternative way to shop for anything from leather upholstered sofas to light bulbs. Mail-order catalogues get bigger and better looking all the time, with some – notably Toast (see My Directory) – setting new standards in styling and presentation with their 'real' looking, fresh-faced models and scrummy but helpful photography (you can actually *see* the clothes)

PRICING AND PAYING

On the whole, pricing is competitive (which you would expect since mail order cuts out the middleman) though postage and packing can bump this up. One example: I was looking for a towelling robe as a birthday present. In a local shop, a black version was marked down at sale time to £80 from over £100. However, the one I ordered, from Lands End (see page 75), was a mere £46 and it came in denim blue, the guy's favourite colour. A while back, White Company (see page 75) offered a plain white terry robe for a mere £15 if your order exceeded a certain sum – I think it was £200. So it can pay to shop around between catalogues.

Some problems are endemic to this form of shopping. Security is one concern: some card holders are becoming wary of giving out details over the phone or online to a complete stranger. If ordering online, check whether the site is secure, although any mail-order service that has been up and running successfully for a few years should have this sussed.

DELIVERY

Delivery is the big bugbear. The charm of ordering via phone, fax or email (some companies give a small discount of approximately 5 per cent for email orders) evaporates if the delivery service misses you and you have to schlep out to a depot address or the nearest post office to collect the goods.

While some outfits, notably Lyco (see page 74) pride themselves on delivery within 24 hours, smaller companies may well be out of stock on the very item you set your heart on because an unanticipated response has cleaned them out, for weeks or even months. Alternatively, your order may come in dribs and drabs, which is annoying as you need to keep tabs on the order until 'closure' is reached.

MAIL-ORDER/ONLINE SHOPPING WITHOUT TEARS

Mail-order is such a self-indulgent, spoiling operation I find, and thus the smallest setback can be seriously off-putting. Silly, perhaps, but true. Here are some tips for mail-order shopping without tears.

● Always make a photocopy of your order/order form. The advantage of emailing your order is that it is automatically stored. Note the date of your order in your diary too.

● Arrange for a second address for delivery (a neighbour, friendly shop or local pub for example) in order to avoid the hassle if the van arrives in your absence. Warn your proxy, obviously, and give the company a contact name, since the delivery man may need it to be signed for.

● Most well-organised mail-order companies accept returns these days for a number of reasons: wrong size, colour, disappointment over quality of fabric, finishing, etc. In the USA the policy is clear: keep the customer happy, and everything is returnable with no questions asked. In the UK, we are nearly there, but you may run into dopey staff, interminable delays of the 'bear with me while I speak to my supervisor' sort. Obviously, don't mess about with the product in the meantime, such as wear the clothes; let your pet scratch the hide upholstery; or enlarge the screw holes in the new bathroom cabinet.

● Keep a measuring tape handy in the run-up to an order, I know it is an old joke that things that look big in the catalogue shrink in reality. However, it remains true that what looks like a useful, bargain buy in the catalogue may prove doll sized – like a sea grass stool I noticed, pumped up in the blurb as handy extra seating or an 'occasional table', which turned out to be only just over 30cm (12in) high: in fact, child sized.

● Study the small print before picking up the phone. The information should make it clear what credit cards are acceptable. Nothing is more exasperating, after carefully noting down the product number, page numbers, item names, sizes, etc, than to find at the end of a long chat with your mail-order operator that they won't accept Switch, so you have to laboriously copy it all out again on the order form. I had to do this with Lands End and nearly gave up on the deal. Mind you, in this situation, you do have the reassurance that a cheque, properly filled in (stub too) is more of a safeguard than giving out all your plastic details.

Incidentally, most order forms are vertically and horizontally challenged. Use a fine-tipped drawing pen to fill in the details, not a felt pen that writes thick and fat.

● Some catalogues, notably Lyco, are chiefly aimed at commercial customers – hence the impressive savings over normal retail – and demand attentive reading in order to decode the relevant information. Supposing you want to order 60-watt golf-ball light bulbs, pearl finish, bayonet fitting, you will have to spend some time scanning the many pages of information and photographs, not to mention somewhat confusing tables of product types, wattages, diminishing costs per order, etc, to locate the item you want. Lyco is a business-like production for business supply managers used to ordering in bulk. However, the savings (up to five to six times cheaper) are impressive and do make the research beforehand worthwhile.

● A return of any item, large items especially, is always going to be a pain. A trip to the post office or organising a collection is often involved. It is worth checking out whether the mail-order company will do this at no additional cost.

CONVENIENCE VS. MISTAKES

I have tried mail order in many areas, from clothing to perishable food and I love it with some reservations. So easy to pick up the phone and lo and behold the goods arrive at your door (usually within 28 days). In addition, you are saved sore feet, too much mind-blowing choice and the whole tedious quest for boring yet essential items.

However, I am sceptical about ordering clothes online or via mail order. There really is nothing like trying a garment on in order to arrive at a decision. Basic stuff like T-shirts, pyjamas, cashmere jumpers in classic shapes and a good colour range are pretty safe to go for.

It is easy to get seduced by the sexy copy – silky soft pima cotton, hand-picked – and fetch up with an expensive item which looks just like the pic in the catalogue, is a triumph of workmanship but weighs a ton – and this they don't tell you of course. Had you tried the garment on you would have discovered this immediately.

Paid for, in eager anticipation, delivered in layers of tissue, the thought of arguing the point is just a nightmare; so you end with a knitted masterpiece which you rarely wear. Sad, because it cost a fair bit too. In the meantime, the moths get at it. Alas we all make these mistakes. Move on.

Where I feel mail order stars is opening up a world of foodie delights (such as Suffolk cured ham, Loch Fyne kippers, oak-smoked venison sausages and wild boar rashers) which you might not happen upon in your shopping round. Or classic garments (T-shirts, pyjamas) with a keen price, or where shopping around for household staples – towels, sheets, etc – seems a serious waste of your time and energy. Life really is too short to spend slogging from store to store to get a feel of their bed linen or towels. Mrs Wonderful would do all this, maybe hit on a fab bargain, note the sale date in her diary, but she leaves most of us fuming guiltily behind. Mail-order offerings in the basic white goods areas are well priced, and good – if not top whack – quality.

Furniture, especially classy, expensive furniture such as leather-covered sofas, chairs and cushions, is another potentially dodgy area. A mirror-fronted bathroom cabinet is one thing, but a sofa is a big item which I would always want to see, feel and sit on before committing myself to a purchase: a return for something this big is clearly going to be a big hassle.

Until the coming of electricity in this village a few years ago, the lighting of cottages in the long winter evenings was always a problem … Until about the beginning of the last century most country cottages used rushlights … First the rind or the skin of a green rush was peeled away from the pith … then grease, specially kept for the purpose, was heated in a long pan … the rush was dipped into it, and held in it sufficiently long to soak. Then it was taken out and laid on a bit of bark until ready for use

Ask The Fellows Who Cut The Hay,
George Ewart Evans
(Faber & Faber 1956; 2e 1977, 1999)

Where mail order by phone or email wins hands down, if you can negotiate the somewhat confusing catalogue presentation, is with deeply dull but absolutely essential items such as light bulbs. I used to make a tube journey to Peter Jones in Sloane Square as the nearest place where I could see the whole dizzying range of available bulbs clearly displayed; small bayonet fittings, screw fittings, halogen, pearl, clear; all the different wattages or voltages flagged up. Having failed to streamline my lighting design requirements from square one, this was a safeguard against sudden blackouts (usually bedside lights) and infuriating gaps in my supply system. Having run across Lyco, I have turned over a new, smart leaf. I order the damn things in bulk, because it works out cheaper, the order arrives within

24 hours and I have a warm and comforting sense that at least one aspect of running a home is under control and saving money.

It is worth checking out any item you consume in quantity (loo paper, cleaning products and disposable nappies, for example) to see if you can't find a cheaper, quicker, save-on-foot-slog alternative to the weekly big shop. Mail order can help if used in an intelligent and imaginative fashion.

MAIL-ORDER/ONLINE COMPANIES

NOTE: See My Directory for phone numbers and website addresses.

Lyco Direct

Lyco has been going eight years and is exceptionally clued up. Their fat, 200-page catalogue covers a huge range of products – tools, cleaning materials, security systems, first-aid kits, etc, aimed at commercial customers, although householders will find great buys, especially in the lighting section, which covers all sorts of light bulbs.

Savings on shop prices are considerable. The more you buy the more you save: for example. a 60W pearl bulb RRP at 87p costs 27p if you buy 10, 22p for 50 and 19p for 100. There is a next-day delivery service. A no-quibble guarantee allows you to return unsatisfactory goods within 30 days. They collect; you get a refund.

Viking Direct

Huge catalogue of every imaginable type of stationery and office equipment: from paper and pens to furniture and vacuum cleaners. Can be very useful for hard-to-obtain supplies for aged computers, but keep an eye on prices and shop around. Next-day delivery is free for orders over £35.25.

The only drawback to this company is that once you buy with them you will be bombarded with catalogues on an all-too-regular basis.

Green Business Co / Consumablemad

Supplies at keen prices for computers: paper, inkjet and laser cartridges, CDs and storage racks, etc. Delivery is £2.50/£4.75 depending on weight with free delivery on orders over £85.

Ocean

A glossy 131-page catalogue of various home products with a clean and contemporary feel. Their range includes lots of steel, glass, leather and blonde wood. Some good buys include anglepoise halogen desk lamps at £65; a galvanised letterbox at £34.95; leather cushions in black or brown at £34.95; some stylish leather-seated dining chairs with steel legs at £89; and a stainless steel kitchen wall cupboard at £375. Ocean will accept Switch as well as Mastercard in payment.

Nicole Farhi Home

Small, elegant selection of upmarket goods: fur throws, knitted leather cushions, crêpe de Chine bed stuff. Fairly pricey but distinguished. The cushions retail at £150. If you like Farhi's style in clothes, this collection should please.

The White Company

A good range of classic bed linen, mostly white, with emphasis on crisp fabrics, waffle picque and nice touches such as cording and drawn thread work. Specials include cotton rib blankets in white and natural (£80 for double-bed size), mohair and cashmere throws, flannel sheets and cable knit cushion covers. Towels and robes are also available.

Goods should arrive within two to four working days, stock permitting. Perhaps I was unlucky, but I have waited up to a month for parts of an order to arrive.

Volga Linen Co

Very classy linen (looks handwoven, made in Russia) sheets, robes, tablecloths, etc. Jasper Conran has some. Me too: bedding in natural/white checks, which actually improves with washing and wear. Pricey, as you might expect, but worth it.

Cucina Direct

Classy kitchenware for 'people who love to cook': cast-iron griddles, Sabatier, Henckel and Global (Japanese) knives, granite pestle and mortar, professional quality mandolin. The latter is £120 and I mean to save up for it. Unexpected items: telescopic ostrich feather duster (£30) and stainless steel dustpan with bristle brush (£14). Not a bargain counter, but good gear.

Lands End Direct Merchant UK Ltd

Sporty clothes for both sexes: jeans and T-shirts keenly priced in good, strong colours. Also canvas field jackets: goose-down gilets at £24.50. They accept Mastercard but not Switch payment.

Delivery is usually within a couple of days from despatch with a £3.50 delivery fee.

Peruvian Connection

Elaborate hand knits and lavish fibres – alpaca, silk, pima cotton – are their speciality, made up into coats, cardigans, slinky frocks and tunics. Their wools, especially baby alpaca, feel luxurious. The hand knits are gorgeously colourful, and the designs constantly updated, but the plain styles are easier to wear. I find the pima cotton separates droopy. Prices range from less than £200 for jumpers and cardis to £815 for an alpaca/lambswool reefer.

Tightsplease

Retailers, from supermarkets to Sock Shop, have clicked in to the way women buy tights.

We like everyday tights (black, opaque) in packs of three or more, and cheap. Fancier jobs, sheer, patterned, coloured, tasselled or spattered with glitter, are a fashion item, and more expensive so these we buy on impulse. Likewise, all variations on the hosiery theme – stockings, knee-highs, hold-ups and socks.

A website dedicated to the whole range of hosiery seems a cute idea; it gives you a vast amount of choice (Pretty Polly, Aristoc, Jonathan Aston, Couture, Charnos to name but a few), which you can scroll through at leisure rather than losing your mind in a crowded department store. From great value multi-packs (work tights) to the funkiest fashions: fishnets, polka dots and Burberry plaids.

Organic meat by mail

Eastbrook Farms sell a wide range of organic beef, lamb, pork and poultry, etc. A catalogue is available on request.

THE BIG E-SHOP

There has been talk of computerised shopping for years. When I worked on *Cosmopolitan* as Food Editor in the mid 80s, I agreed to test out what must have been a fairly primitive system linked to a chain of Greek-owned stores. A large monitor was installed in my kitchen. It flashed up a lengthy list of items, from which we chose and clicked our order through, which duly arrived, delivered by van, the following day. I say 'we' because my young daughters joined in eagerly, and the three of us played with this enchanting new toy rather like the monkeys which, let loose on typewriters, eventually come up with Shakespeare sonnets. What we came up with on one never-to-be-forgotten occasion – one paw must have slipped – was 120 bottles of household bleach. Perhaps this contributed to the demise of the idea for the time being? We were not devastated to be dropped from the project but agreed that it had been fun while it lasted.

When flyers from Sainsbury's appeared offering a free delivery, I decided to give it a whirl, despite my stated reservations about supermarkets and the fact that I prefer to shop on foot and in person.

Accessing the website is straightforward for anyone used to surfing and emailing procedures. You tap in the website address, fill your details into the questionnaire – ie, email address, home address and telephone number and card details. You will need to decide on a password too, to quote should there be any queries or problems with an order. Formalities concluded, you are free to step into a virtual supermarket, and click off your order against their list of products. The next thing is to agree on a time slot for delivery. This is where a cloud appears in the blue sky notion of the e-shop: no same-day delivery. Deliveries can usually be arranged for some time the following day and the delivery runs operate long hours – from 8 am till 10 pm – designed to help people working late and getting delayed on the homeward journey. Many people arrange for deliveries to their workplace, to be on the safe side. Another solution is to designate a fail-safe address close by if you can't take the delivery in person, warning your proxy too, of course.

Like most systems e-shopping needs forethought and intelligent handling to work well for you. My instinct would be to make use of it for bulky household staples – all the stuff it is tedious to shop for, pack into the boot, transfer to the kitchen. This should be registered as a regular, rolling order once a week, or a fortnight, or month, but well ahead, so you get to pick the most convenient time slot for delivery. A £5 delivery charge may seem piffling if it relieves you of the heavy duty side of shopping. It must be a real concern to many pensioners, however, and here the solution must surely be to club together with a friend or two?

As emailing becomes a standard mode of communication, and the other supermarket chains jump on the bandwagon, I guess e-shopping will become increasingly popular. Dealing with email orders must represent a saving on overheads for the companies involved, as against phone orders, which tie down staff for minutes at a time. So synergy

is at work here. My main concern is that the delivery charge will creep up: £5 feels like a loss leader, designed to tempt us into the virtual supermarket. And if people increasingly use the delivery service for their bulk buys, as I would, the vans will be packed out with loo rolls, disposable nappies, cans of pet food, and the profit margins per delivery will drop, delivery charge notwithstanding. But this is still in the future, and meantime the notion of browsing through a virtual supermarket is gaining new adherents and few complaints.

What I would seriously consider is an email cash-and-carry option, where I could bulk-buy at near wholesale prices, with delivery part of the deal. That may be a pipe-dream, even assuming I can blag my way into a cash-and-carry operation with a business card and the right plastic. Supermarkets are good at driving prices down for their customers, but to do this they cut their suppliers' margins ruthlessly, to the point where they go pear-shaped or, in the worst cases, commit suicide, as sombre surveys indicate. There are no easy options in the world we live in.

ORDERING
The Protocol
Having run on at some length about the joys of ordering up stuff by phone (or email), I have to say that the first rush of gratitude can

turn sour when you find this blessedly simple act has entangled you in a Laocoön of unforeseen complications.

From four placed orders I made, not one delivered the goods exactly as promised. One company sent me the same order twice over. Another, after two weeks, sent me half an outfit; the other half arrived half a month later (despite having promised delivery within 28 days)!

One company delivered to the wrong address and another (Argos) delivered my new cordless phone the very next day. This was most impressive, except the phone proved to be faulty and mysteriously infected my existing cordless phone, so that too is now on the scrap heap. Furthermore, I can't remember where I bought the first one and certainly haven't kept the receipt. I mean, this was over two years ago! So big slap on the wrist for me.

It would be nice if someone benefits from my foolishness. It may only take minutes to place your order but checking up on it (as was the case with the faulty cordless) can take hours as you punch button after button in search of a 'real person' to pour your heart out to. I name Argos, not to shame them (because on balance they performed rather well; see later) but to fill you in on the protocol that drives these situations. The devil, as they say, is in the details.

- Keep track of *everything* when placing an order: date, price, catalogue number, your order number, name of item. I mean everything. Yes, I know, dragsville, but this can save precious minutes hanging on the phone while your order details are tracked on the computer, your ID details are scrupulously checked, and your ear is assaulted by blasts of 'bear with me' muzak.

- In a perfect world you would photocopy everything to be on the safe side (easier if you work in an office). It may be worth a walk to your nearest print shop.

- Staple all this stuff together, and spike or file it until 'closure' happens, ie, the items are safely delivered, in working order and paid for. If you are not satisfied on any of these counts, hang on grimly to the paperwork.

- Avoid this situation. The bell rings, the box is in your hands, you tear open the packaging and in the excitement of the moment the invoice and order number gets thrown out with the packaging. At this moment you aren't thinking coolly; it doesn't occur to you that the phone may not work, or the jacket may be two sizes too big. It's all singing and dancing celebration time!

● The moral of this tale is:

a) open the package with care, and b) spike or file any paperwork enclosed. You cannot have too much evidence in the case of mistakes, wrong sizes, etc. Keep the packaging in case you have to return the goods. Lamentable as it may sound, some of us would rather write a mistake off to experience than actually make it up into a parcel and take it to a post office. No wonder the Royal Mail is millions in the red.

● What is excellent and admirable about the really Big Boys in the mail-order scene is that they are cool about returns. Argos and Lyco, for instance: faulty cordless? No probs. They aren't about to interrogate you beadily about what went wrong or come and test it out under your nose. Customer satisfaction rules. It did involve a trip to my nearest Argos in order for a swap to take place, and there was a snag. Because I chose a cheaper cordless phone (my first choice was out of stock) and had lost my receipt, I had to accept a £20 voucher instead of a refund. However, I liked the style. No doubt, poring through my up-to-date Argos catalogue, I will find something to blow a £20 voucher on.

● In search of a 'real person'? Usually, this magic moment arrives at the very end of the menu of options, after you have been issued with countless blind alleys. Perseverance and patience is the key.

HELPING CONSUMERS: WHICH?

WHICH? is the Consumer Association's monthly publication. Of all the consumer information services, it is the longest established, founded in 1957, the most prestigious, and the source regularly trawled for news stories by the rest of the media. Where WHICH? scores over consumerist columns in the broadsheets and magazines is in the range and depth of its research into current consumer concerns. To take one recent issue, the magazine reports on the following: British beaches, flexible mortgages, travel cots and South African white wine.

WHICH? surveys are impressively impartial, and the reports published in the magazine or online after much testing by knowledgeable, anonymous experts, simply give you their findings, both for and against, invariably presented along with their Best Buys, flagged up with the red star which must cause ripples of alarm in manufacturing circles. WHICH? for instance, was first to give the much hyped Dyson bagless vacuum cleaner a low rating in its survey of vacuum cleaners on the market (a verdict confirmed by retailers I spoke to, and indeed by my own experience).

WHICH? is only obtainable via subscription at a cost of £59 a year, which seems high till you recall that this is a publication without advertising revenues, for obvious reasons. The sub buys you many services: a Helpline, previous reports stored in their archives, free of charge, back-up in disputes with retailers, tour operators or Building Societies – you name it. Non-subscribers will have to access WHICH? via local libraries.

WHICH? strikes me as a wholly admirable organisation that deserves the support of all of us driven to make (often) expensive choices, our ears still ringing with sales patter, and more than a little dazed and confused. WHICH? has markedly altered since its inception in 1957. It is now colourful, with lots of photography, its remit has widened considerably, and it has sharp teeth, pursuing readers' complaints and often using its undoubted clout to rectify them and reach a fair settlement. Such cases are reported under the heading 'briefcases', and invariably have you punching the air delightedly, caught up in the David vs. Goliath drama of it all.

WHICH? has now grown sideways, with sister publications: WHICH? Health, WHICH? Gardening, Which? Holiday, WHICH? Computing. Now that these publications are online, the information can be accessed via the website by any WHICH? subscriber, the usual route taken by people who don't want, or can't afford, several subscriptions concurrently.

All packed with relevant information, surveys, reports on topical matters close to your heart, head and purse. To my mind, the WHICH? set-up stands out, an oasis of integrity and impartiality, a watchdog for us consumers barking and biting when needful, regardless of commercial pressures, hype, disingenuous marketing departments and pass-the-buck manoeuvres that consumers so often get landed with.

WHICH? runs a members' (ie, subscribers) helpline: see My Directory for phone number and website address.

Factsheets are free to members, and are also available online. One rare plus of calling up WHICH? in my experience is that you get to talk to a real person, often straight away.

THE LAST CHEAP LUXURY:
A COMFORTING BLAZE

Is there anything more welcoming, more centrifugal to any social gathering than a real open fire; crackling logs or briskly flaming coals? A good fire draws people to it, not just for warmth but for the sheer spectacle of flames leaping round its incandescent heart. Even boxed into a domestic hearth, fire feels like a wild, almost demonic, creature. We sense this even though we take constant hot water and food cooked at the click of a switch for granted. Fire is both friend and enemy all at once. Perhaps it is this friendly warmth edged with danger that makes us gather round and raises the convivial spirit to a higher power?

I like to make a fire any evening the temperature drops, even in summer, especially when I have people around. I can get a fire burning well with no trouble, but I notice the younger generation seem baffled by real live fires – how to lay, light and maintain them.

A century ago almost everyone, except the hopelessly genteel, knew how to lay a fire and get a good blaze going. During the cold months, it was the housemaid's first chore of the day. Building a camp fire to cook sausages used to be every boy scout's epiphany. I now observe that young people seem to have lost touch with this ancient skill. Ask them to light a fire and they cast around for packets of firelighters, which give a good and gratifying blaze, they then smother this with outsize logs or a shower of coal and then wonder why it goes out! They don't seem to recognise that a good fire needs a draught to kindle it and hot nucleus to further it, not to mention patient coaxing and attention to reach the point where the fiery element takes over and devours whatever you feed it with.

If this is regarded as a somewhat arcane skill with the prevalence of central heating, how come the recent craze for fireplaces in the home? Do people hunt them down in shops with punning names – Amazing Grates – just to make a 'feature' on which to stick cards and dried flower arrangements? Sad if this is the case. A fireplace that is just for show is a dismal, black hole and a pointless architectural feature. I concede that bedroom fireplaces in old houses have probably passed their sell-by date. However, it would be lovely to reinstate them for a special occasion – a lovers' tryst, a favoured guest or a sick child. It is a bit of a performance, but nothing confers such a glow of wicked luxury as one's own personal fire sparking and crackling in the grate as you recline in bed with a favourite book. As luxuries go, compared with a day in a health spa or dinner in a swanky restaurant, it is absurdly cheap and deliciously novel.

MANAGING OPEN FIRES

Fire is as dangerous as it is bewitching so make sure you are always in control.

Sooty? Then sweep

Have your chimney (flues) checked and cleared by one of the intriguing characters Victorian fiction called 'sweeps'. They do still exist and can be found in the Yellow Pages under Chimney Sweeps. You have no need to fear that they will send tiny boys ahead with ferocious oaths and imprecations! Nor will they make any mess to speak of. Although your modern sweep will use a traditional brush the debris will fetch up in a tidy plastic sack and you will not detect a speck of soot.

Chimneys in regular use should be cleaned out every five years or so; more often if you burn a lot of softwood scrap timber. This causes a gradual furring up of the flue which can give rise to a fire in the chimney.

Grates and baskets

The key to a healthy blaze is to raise the fire off the hearth level so air can reach it from beneath and create a strong draught. If you don't have a built-in grate, you will need a freestanding basket grate or fire dogs for burning logs.

Some chimneys are fitted with a metal plate with a hinged flap in the throat operated by a lever. If in doubt, ask a sweep to show you how this works.

Laying a fire

Make a small heap of scrumpled newspaper sheets. Stand a wigwam of kindling around this. Set light to the newspaper here and there. Once it is all ablaze balance some slightly larger logs and a few lumps of coal on top. All firewood should be dry – damp logs covered in green lichen are slow, if not impossible, to set alight and give off clouds of smoke.

When you are confident that the fire has really got going you can lay on larger logs and more coal. From time to time, riddle the fire with a poker from the bottom to brisk it up. The old trick of stretching a double page of newspaper across the fire surround works wonders should the fire look in risk of fizzling out. However, do this carefully because the paper can easily catch fire.

Fireguards

If you are in and out the room or have young children around, a fireguard of some nature is essential, both to prevent sparks burning holes in your carpets, or to protect lively youngsters from burning themselves.

Perhaps the most elegant type I have observed (for spark protection only) is a sort of curtain of fine steel chain fixed above the grate. Although this can be moved out of the way while cleaning the grate and laying the fire it does not obscure the latter once lit. Moreover, being metal it probably increases the radiant heat quite considerably.

An old-fashioned nursery fireguard, of fine wire mesh in a metal frame, will act as a barrier to slipping logs, coals and flying sparks – as well a children. A fender that fits round the hearth stone – made from steel, brass or wood – is a useful second line of defence.

Fire tools

A sturdy poker and fire tongs are standard equipment for a well-kept hearth. They can often be found hooked to a metal stand in junk shops and should include a hearth brush, poker and small shovel for clearing out the fireplace.

If you burn a lot of large logs, a set of bellows is a useful accessory: by acting as a sort of squeeze box which puffs a jet of air through its nozzle while you pump away on the handles. Handled in an adroit manner, a bellows can wake up a fire that has sunk to what looks like a mound of ashes and get it licking at new logs in minutes.

Firelighters

Firelighters come in very handy if you are in a hurry or the wood is a little green. If your first attempt dies, poke a firelighter into the middle of your kindling and relight it with a spill of paper.

Fuel

If you live in the country, finding logs should not be a problem though do make sure they are sufficiently dry. If you have space, store them in a shed or outhouse to dry out before winter. Failing a shed, logs can be stacked into a woodpile along a wall with a plastic sheet stretched over them weighted down with stones to keep off the rain.

A small sharp axe is invaluable for splitting logs or reducing a pile of carpentry offcuts to kindling. To split a log, bed the axe head with a powerful blow into the cut end, then smack the log up and down on a hard surface using the tool as a lever – it will usually split along the grain. If you are a town dweller (and do not live in a smokeless zone), consult the Yellow Pages for log suppliers or check out your local farmers' markets. Try to avoid those string bags of logs and kindling sold on garage forecourts as they are both shockingly pricey and often unseasoned – ie, green or sappy.

Most small Victorian basket grates were designed to burn coal, which gives off more heat than wood. Sadly, it hasn't got that great woody tang and lingering smell of scented smoke. Coal merchants do exist but they are becoming fewer and far between. Again, I suggest the Yellow Pages. If you live in a smokeless zone, the coal merchant will probably be able to suggest suitable smokeless fuels.

SOLID-FUEL STOVES

Cast-iron stoves with their own chimney pipes are the best option where you need maximum radiant heat rather than just a cheering glow in a grate. These come in many shapes and sizes from tall cylinders of polished iron to retro versions in enamelled iron with little mica windows. You can even find antique versions imported from Scandinavia with charming little 'crowns' as embellishment on top.

One of the most efficient and altogether sociable models I have come across is an update of the nineteenth-century Franklin stove (named after President Benjamin Franklin, its inventor). This has a wide base, or 'lap', with doors which can be opened up for people to cluster round and an outsize stovepipe to carry away fumes and smoke. Stovepipes also pump out extra heat all the way up their length which does a good job of space heating in a chilly weekend cottage.

GAS FIRES

Gas-fired 'log' or 'coal' fires have been sneered at by purists since their arrival on the scene. In some situations however they have admirable qualities. Not only do they provide a safe and instant mimicry of a real fire but they give off a decent aura of radiant heat as well.

I reckon that fake 'coals' look more convincing than fake 'logs' and have often debated installing a fake coal fire in my study. The latter only tends to be in daily use when I am writing a book. I would be – indeed I am – tempted by the prospect of a warm and friendly glow in the fireplace at the flick of a switch.

My Victorian cast-iron grates would easily convert to a gas coal fire. The bonus here would be that the gas pipe to fire it could be run up the chimney to keep a second 'instant' coal fire going when needed in the bedroom above.

There are other forms of fake fires than the 'log' and 'coal' variety. In my view one of the most interesting of these is my neighbour's tiny enamelled stove which stands snugly in a corner close to her chairs and sofas. Because the fake coals are hidden behind mica-paned doors it looks remarkably similar to the real thing.

WEEKENDING – THE WELCOME

People get fussier as they get older! During your student days, friends would be glad of a sofa and blankets. Ten years on and, dammit, they expect a proper bed, clean sheets, central heating, reading lights and a tasty selection of book or mags. In a word, they want comfort. Of course, good food and copious amounts of booze go without saying.

It is not that they don't want to see you, reminisce until the small hours and bond with you all over again, it is simply what I call 'the inertia factor' setting in. I mean, travelling is such hell today, the working week is so full and one's own place is both comfortable and familiar. What this means is that as host/hostess, you have to up the ante by offering a cocoon of comfort and menu of treats so that they are left dying for a repeat.

In my experience, the people who have got this hospitality thing sussed are upper-class types who entertain weekend parties as a matter of course and are deeply aware of the thoughtful touches that keep guests happy and relaxed. These tend also to be wealthy people, so you may need to scale down the lavishness of the treats while upping the USPs (unique selling points): a bunch of wild flowers by the bed, lavender-scented sheets, a trip to a local boot sale, pottery or mushroom grower. In the reverse situation, country types venturing to the big city, you lay on urban experiences: shopping (sales often go down well), a booking on the London Eye or a boat trip down the river followed by a reviving cocktail in one of the metropolis's chillingly trendy new hotel bars. This they may enjoy hating for all the right reasons and telling their mates about back in the sticks.

Hospitality may come at a high cost today, but of course it is fuelled still by sensitivity, imagination and a generous wish to make your friends feel comfortable and content. The following suggestions should help:

● Try to get your guests to arrive on a Friday, even if it means eating any time up to midnight and waking up with a cracking hangover. Having all Saturday to play with gives more of a holiday feeling.

● Welcome them with a chilled bottle of champagne. This strikes the right celebratory note.

● A crackling fire spells welcome in any language and to a city dweller is sheer luxury.

● Warm the bed beforehand; hot-water bottles and electric blankets are both options here.

- At least one bunch of flowers to a room. Wildflowers win hands down (if you are a country host) backed up with some spikes of lavender and rosemary for fragrance.

- A bottle of mineral water and glass on the bedside table is a sine qua non, set out on a tiny tray or one of the Chatsworth tin versions of old porcelain plates. This saves hungover friend slopping water over your nicetable and looks neat.

- A juicy selection of books and mags piled on table or chair should be to hand. They have probably read the current best sellers so try something more arcane such as old copies of *The Countryman*, Dorothy Hartley or one of those vintage green Penguin 'mystery' stories.

- You know friends' tastes in food/drink. However, don't overlook the delights of what is fresh and local. A full-on Sunday roast with all the trimmings is invariably a winner, but do check they haven't gone veggie since you last saw them.

- Treats should be a cinch if you know your locality. Boot sales, Saturday markets, WI markets, fêtes and fairs are all rich with possibilities for urban visitors itching to take back a souvenir of rural life. Drop in on local craftspersons: weavers, potters and artists. Your guests many not buy anything but it shows willing and earns you brownie points.

- A visit to your local hostelry is good for real ale and a smack of local atmosphere; a quick fix on local concerns from planned bypasses to foot and mouth. Cits (as they were called in the eighteenth century) love to brag about rural matters hot from the village pump, as it were.

- Surprise them as they leave with a bunch of flowers, blossoming twigs, newly cut rhubarb or some herbs, etc. For safe transportation, wrap in newspaper and then in a plastic bag.

- Cits love the idea of a country walk, beautiful scenery, fresh air and healthy exercise. However, don't push it too hard (maybe a few miles before the Sunday roast) and don't make it punishingly far. Forcing unfit townies to toil up precipitous hills without a treat at the end is to appear a puritanical bully.

I realise that I have put all the emphasis here on country hosts laying on a weekend for their townie friends. Should the situation be reversed, there should be no problems that the local paper, or *Time Out/Evening Standard* (for London) cannot solve. Any town deserving of its title is usually abundant with treats and surprises on to which you need only put a personal spin.

Nor have I mentioned kids. With luck, your mutual offspring are close enough in age to be interesting to each other. With luck again the home team will enjoy showing the invitees around and a lot of surplus energy can get burnt up exploring the locality. Make sure everyone has wellies and lots of warm clothing. Videos and computer games are a useful means of buying a few hours of peace so the parents can do their thing.

One solution might be to conscript a charismatic local teenager to act as pack leader for the duration of the stay. Perhaps for an agreed sum of £10–15 a day? Try to hit on the right candidate: knowledgeable, enthusiastic and above all sensible. Meanwhile, the adults in the party can relax and get on with the purpose of their weekend: sharing anecdotes, swapping confidences and generally being freed up to do as they wish.

DIY BEDLINEN

On reflection, I decided Polly Hope's notion of running up sheets, pillowcases and duvet covers (see page 102) was not so impractical after all. Anyone who can sew a straight seam on a sewing machine could run off bottom sheets, with a hem either end, in next to no time.

Pillowcases and duvet covers are essentially bags, with a fastening system along one side (ties, snaps or buttons).

There is a considerable saving in cash terms over ready-made versions. Fabrics in sheeting widths are obtainable in a range of yarns and prices per metre.

Top quality Irish linen (1400 thread count) would set you back – gulp – £60 for a single-bed (2m/6ft) width, or £150 for a double-bed/king size (250cm/10ft) width. It still works out approximately one-third cheaper than buying the finished articles. But working with such aristocratic fabric could be excessively challenging. Nevertheless, Givans do sell it to skilled needlewomen (see My Directory). More my mark would be Ian Mankin's Belgian linen (see My Directory). This is a tad coarser, but only £34 per metre in a 240cm (9ft 6in) width (double or king size). It only comes in white, but linen dyes beautifully.

A top sheet, with two matching pillowcases, would make a great wedding present for a daughter or close friend, especially if you worked a monogram of their initials in satin-stitch. In the USA, with their craze for 'personalising' everything, adding initials and monograms has generated a small luxe service in posh places such as the Hamptons. Pricey too. Hand stitching takes longer, of course, but it is not that difficult and the brownie points must be quite dizzying.

Down to earth with a bump, John Lewis in its 18 UK branches sells pure cotton sheeting in 228cm (9ft) or 278cm (11ft) widths, at under £8 per metre. The 278cm is available only in white and ivory but the more popular 228cm fabric comes in a wide colour range, including red, lime, cobalt and dark blue. Here you can let your creativity run wild: blue sheets with lime borders, white sheets with red borders and so on.

That is just for starters. If a sheet needs 2.5m, a duvet cover (being shorter) needs 4m and pillowcases approx 0.5m each, you are looking at a total cost of about £68 for a whole bed set, which is not bad for pure cotton.

Of course, this estimate does not include your work and time. Still, if you enjoy straightforward sewing and have time to spare, it is worth considering. No household ever has too much bed linen.

If you need to make some serious savings, Asian wholesalers such as Z Butt in Brick Lane, London (see My Directory), will send you 10m (11yds) of a 50/50 cotton polyester for a mere £22.90 including VAT. How would you like a sheet, duvet cover and four pillowcases at a snip price of £22.90?

'Within living memory sheets of unbleached calico were given out in the church porch. Priscilla Savage said: "The churchwardens used to have a table in the porch and they cut sheets of calico from a big roll – one sheet for each family; two if the family was a big one. The sheets lasted a wholly long time. I got one now as good as new and washed nearly white."

Ask The Fellows Who Cut The Hay, George Ewart Evans
(Faber & Faber 1956; 2e 1977, 1999)

First aid kit

This is an essential in any household and is best kept in a carefully designated case so you can lay your hands on wipes, plasters, etc, in a second. The traditional red plastic case seems appropriate. I assembled the following with the help of a WHICH? booklet (see page 79) and a Lyco catalogue (see page 74). Lyco do a neat motorist's kit for £9.99, but I would add a few items for a family situation. If you include painkillers, you will need to keep the kit locked away from nosy kids and their prying hands.

- Antiseptic wipes
- Antiseptic cream
- 1 triangular bandage (for sprained wrists)
- 1 crepe bandage
- Assorted perforated plasters
- Assorted waterproof plasters (Lyco also do 'fun' plasters with a dinosaur design for kids)
- Gel-impregnated burn dressings
- Eye wash/pads
- 1 roll of gauze
- 1 roll of micro porous tape
- Painkillers – aspirin or paracetomol (for those allergic to aspirin), Junior Disprin or Nurofen
- Clove oil (this quietens toothache)
- Friars Balsam: inhalant for sore bronchials, chests or sinuses
- 1 or 2 moist dressings to promote healing of wounds or ulcers.

You probably have sharp scissors and safety pins around your house, but these can be added if your want the kit to be self-contained.

GET A PET

Family life feels incomplete to me without a pet. Dogs and cats are my favourites and I have kept both. In my experience, children often find smaller pets – gerbils, hamsters and rabbits – poor company after the initial thrill of possessing a small furry creature has worn off. Whereas cats and dogs positively enjoy human company, I see no possibility of bonding with a hamster. A dog's life seems infinitely preferable to that of any rodent, frantically racing around its cage.

Likewise, all a pet rabbit can do is stuff its belly and mope because it isn't enjoying the social life of its wild counterparts. An artist I know keeps a large pet rabbit, to which she is devoted, in a London loft. Maybe the rabbit loves her back. It is house-trained, which suggests it wants to please. On the other hand, it sometimes bites, which gives an ambivalent message.

CATS

I find the recent statistics – that the UK is now more of a cat- than dog-owning society – a bit sad. I can see where this current trend is coming from. Cats are people's first choice as pets if they live in a city as they are easier to house-train, don't need walkies, eat less and keep their own counsel. Kittens are playful and adorable and adult cats are independent and handsome creatures. By the same token, they are hostages to fortune in city areas. During the time I have been writing this book, my neighbour has lost two handsome cats, *desaparecidos*, both males and neutered, but young, agile and venturesome, off and away over the rooftops, or slinking along the street outside, hiding under parked cars. They were not precious pedigree cats, so theft seems an unlikely explanation. Cats have come and gone in her household, but the sole survivor, who lived out her proper span, was female, spayed and Siamese, which are famously intelligent and home-loving.

It is possible to become as attached to a cat as a dog and its disappearance is heartbreaking. You can circulate descriptions and rewards, but they rarely return, and you are left wondering if they found another home, got run over, or just went walkabout and lost their way back. Having owned and lost three cats myself, and monitored my neighbour's cat situation across the fence, I have views about cat ownership and how to make it work.

Going walkabout

Tom cats, the hunters, neutered or not, will roam much more widely than their female counterparts. This is perhaps OK in suburbia, but dodgy in inner cities because of traffic, crowded streets and lack of garden space. Even the smartest of cats can wander outside a known territory and get confused and lost.

Cats are famous for trying their luck and using their wiles on other households in an area, establishing a second home you don't even know about. Cats are cool – for reasons you cannot fathom, the other home may suit them better – and they can decamp without so much as a backward glance.

However, and I think this is a key factor, I doubt they do this unless their domestic routine is altered. My neighbour takes two- to three-week breaks twice a year in Greece where she has a second home. Although there is continuity, an au pair to do the feeding and looking after, I can't help noticing that her cats usually take off while she is away. It appears that cats resent their owners going away, seeing it as a betrayal or scary change to their status quo.

If you put your cat into a 'holiday home' while you are away, at least you can be sure it will still be there when you get back. However, it might decide to punish you by doing a runner shortly after? Age and sex seem to have a bearing on this. During a holiday, I left a young male cat, Spider, in charge of another young male, friend of a daughter. On my return, Spider greeted me rapturously, slept on my bed that night, and vanished the very next day, never to be seen again. I often caught glimpses of shiny black cats with white markings, but they never responded when I called 'Spider'. My guess is that he charmed his way into another household while we were away, and returned there after his courtesy visit the day I got back.

My advice would be to get a female moggy, less venturesome and less likely to be cat-napped than a fancy breed. Fix her up with an ID disc with your phone number on one side and reward on the other. Time it so you don't go on holiday until her routine is well established.

However, in the last analysis cats are opportunists, and choose to lead secret lives. I once sat a small distance away from a lioness in a South African game park, in a large vehicle along with about 20 other people including our guide and ranger. Having just devoured half a baby antelope, the lioness was languid, stretched out in the wispy grass, her great yellow eyes flicking indifferently over our clumsy vehicle with its silent human freight. At one point, she seemed to be staring directly at me. I went cold all over, like a small creature caught at night in a car's headlights. We were pretty safe, of course, the big cat sated and our ranger and guide both armed. But when a lioness gazes at you, to freeze seems like an instinctive reaction, the sudden awareness of the gulf between our species.

When a small domestic cat turns that look on me, I feel a twinge of the same unease under its scrutiny. People love their cats, grow besotted with them, but I always feel cats remain coolly outside the range of human sentiment and emotion; they accept our care and homage, but we can never penetrate that feral core and become the best of friends.

Living with a cat

Even so, you may have decided that it is about time to have a cat in your life. There are good reasons for having a cat around the place. Perhaps you have moved into a new apartment and can finally have the cat you've always wanted. Maybe you and your partner have agreed that your children need a pet and that a dog would be too much bother. Cats can provide a happy compromise.

Whatever your reasoning, there are a number of factors to consider before rushing out to a pet store or cat home. The fact is, too often pets acquired by impulse often don't work out – and this is especially true of cats.

Although cats are low maintenance compared to dogs, they require plenty of human companionship and can become quite desolate if this is lacking. Cats like to vocalise as if to confirm their presence within the household. A friend of mine has a cat who mews as if to say: 'I am here, I am here!'

You need to ensure that your lifestyle is suitable for the ownership of a cat.

Have you got young toddlers or expensive furniture? If so, it is perhaps not the ideal time to acquire a cat. Kittens are naughty by nature and could very easily scratch a young child and destroy your Queen Anne chair. Face it, cats need to sharpen their claws and a good scratching post is a must. Cats need feeding and caring for – cat litter trays need to be cleaned out on a regular basis. Although these tasks can provide a useful means of teaching children responsibility, an adult should always be around to supervise.

As with dogs, cats need to be taught the rules of the house from day one. You cannot expect your pet to be perfectly trained from birth: it is a two-way thing. I know of someone who allows her six cats to sit on her kitchen table throughout supper when *en famille*, but they are ceremoniously thrown out of the room when guests are in attendance. Of course, the cats are confused and thus badly behaved.

Finally, are you willing to spend the money necessary for spaying/neutering, vaccinations and veterinary care when necessary? You wouldn't neglect your children's health and neither must you overlook your cat's medical requirements. Hopefully, you have considered the above points (which are by no means exhaustive) and have come to a carefully deliberated decision to proceed with your cat acquisition.

Feeding your cat

Cats are what they call obligate carnivores, meaning they have to eat meat or fish – ie, animal protein – to survive. In the wild, cats arrive at a balanced feline diet by eating every scrap of bird, mouse or vole, etc, except the gall bladder. This provides them with all the protein, vitamins, fat and roughage they need. Any carbohydrate comes from devouring the contents of their victim's stomach.

Most cat owners feed their pets on proprietary cat food, partly for convenience and partly because these include ingredients like taurine which cats need. A taurine deficiency can lead to premature feline blindness. There is a concern that proprietary foods are tending to bulk up carbohydrates because this keeps the price down. You should compare the listed contents of different brands.

Where possible, cats are best fed on the little-and-often principle. Cats are snackers by nature. They are also very crafty. A cat may get addicted to one brand of cat food and act hungry to get another helping. This clearly results in a fat cat! An overweight cat loses its abdominal tuck and becomes lethargic. So steel yourself; you must be cruel to be kind to a greedy cat.

DOGS

The great thing in favour of keeping dogs in a city is that they can be confined pretty much, as long as you give them adequate exercise, which of course is very good for both parties.

On balance, I think dogs star as family pets. Children love all that eager jumping up, licking, wagging and sheer boisterous enthusiasm towards us bipeds. That doggy overreacting which brings weary grimaces to tired adult faces suits children just fine because they have a lot in common temperamentally. The rapture with which the family dog greets a travelling teenager after six months skimming the world really touches their hardened young hearts. It is the dream welcome-back scene.

Where dogs score as members of the tribe is not only do they love madly and extravagantly, but they never forget their past loves, even when old and creaky on their pins. I think all children, especially teenagers, take enormous comfort from unconditional doggy love, and thoughtful parents might set about providing it. And, of course, the other big plus is that dogs are funny – comedians on a slapstick level.

I am convinced that dogs have a conscience, that they know when they have done a bad thing. It is harder to join in the laughter when the bad thing is crapping on the doorstep or chewing the guts out of a

Pets and health

- Your vet will give pets immunisations at prescribed intervals, at nine weeks and twelve weeks for cats, and at eight and twelve weeks for dogs. This protects cats against cat flu, leukaemia, enteritis; dogs against distemper, leptospirosis, parvo virus and para influenza. Rabies shots (for pet passports when going abroad) are given separately. Vets advise annual repeats in young animals, the second being the most critical, in case any part of shot one didn't take.

- De-worming should be done three or four times a year in both cases, using tablets prescribed by the vet. More outlay (ouch), but they point out that their medication is cutting edge compared to branded products from chemists or pet shops – about ten years ahead.

- Fleas: Frontline, another prescription, involves squirting a flea-killer on to the skin at the back of the animal`s neck, much easier than old-fashioned powders or sprays and, in my experience, effective. Twice a year should do it, but meantime watch out for heavy scratching – a sign of fleas at work – or for bites on family members. For a full-on flea infestation, you could call in your local council pest-control department, but vets prefer you to use Vet Cem Acclaim 2000, which is non-toxic and zaps both existing fleas and their future offspring.

- Feeding: the consensus is that commercial pet foods are the safe choice since they contain all the supplements an animal requires for growth and health, with some reservations. All-in dry foods are cheap and convenient, and acceptable to pets if nothing else is offered. A dog`s insatiable appetite is thought to be a genetic throwback to their wolf ancestry, wolves stuffing themselves after a successful kill, but then sleeping it off for days. So if your dog is greedy, he/she just thinks he/she is a wolf?

- Grooming: Regular brushing/combing is good, getting rid of loose hairs, dried mud and burrs, and pets enjoy it as a rule. With dogs, too much shampooing removes natural oils from the pelt, though extra fluffy creatures do need more help from you in this area. Fluffy dogs benefit from a clip towards summer, to make them comfortable in the heat: dogs can only sweat via their tongues, in case you didn't know.

buttoned antique chair and of course they ham up their response, cowering under a chair and making big doleful eyes at you, even shuddering dramatically like the cornered villain of a Victorian melodrama. Later, once the dust has settled, you may just be able to manage a wry smile. Perhaps it is just a small lesson in forgiveness, an underused muscle.

Have I persuaded you that a dog is a serious option? Good. the next problem is how to get one.

Acquiring a dog

All my dogs were happenstance. A neighbour foisted one on me, and my daughter started working on me to claim one of a litter born to ineptly named Rosie, a brindled Staffy, big as a barrel, who often spent the night whilst her owner was out clubbing in Hoxton. So Bella, lithe and black as ink with sexy touches of white, has moved in, ostensibly to jolly up the declining years of ancient Padge (so named after a character in *Diary of a Nobody*, a bit of literary pretension which worked out OK because, when I call him, everyone assumes I am shouting 'Patch'). Talk about April meets December. They are hacking it quite well at present. Padge barks sharply and angrily when Bella goes too far, which is only right and proper. I mean, if you were 120, would you enjoy having your ears nipped? Sometimes I find them curled up together like two spoons, asleep.

Having had dogs sort of visited upon me, I was staggered to find how difficult it can be to locate a suitable puppy these days unless you are privileged, as with Bella, to be on good terms with its mum and her owner. OK, if you are into a pedigree pup, changing hands at many hundreds of pounds, there is no problem. A local kennel will put you on to a breeder, you sign up and troll along, and make your choice. Where I ran into difficulties was looking for a mongrel pup for my granddaughter, Ottilie. I knew just what she had in mind, a small cute doglet on the lines of Padge but much younger. Mongrels, as you know, are tougher, live longer and are often brighter than pedigrees. It wasn't the money thing, we were just into mongrels then and Ottilie found Padge adorable.

Battersea Dogs' Home is a Londoner's first thought, doubling the joy of finding the perfect mutt with the noble thought that you may have saved it – gulp – from a lethal injection after its sell-by date. No longer. I was so wrong. Adopting a Battersea canine today is almost as problematic as offering a good home and wider life to one of the street orphans of Rio de Janeiro. You have to join a queue, fill in a questionnaire, agree to a visit from the Dogs' Home 'just checking' to see that their inmate is going to a decent home and finally, if you are lucky, that raggedy little terrier that declared its passion by scrabbling halfway up the cage is yours, for a fee.

As a dog lover, I approve of these restrictions and safeguards. However, my problem was that I wanted a young puppy, in dog terms a three-month infant, rather than an older dog that might have been mishandled, to say the least, and emerged neurotic, apt to snarl or snap and needing lots of patient TLC. Of course these dog casualties can be turned around through lots of care and patience, but as a thrilling gift to a young child could be worrying.

Strangely, Battersea had no pups on the books, or in the offing, so I called up every dog rescue home I could think of up and down the country; Blue Cross, PDSA, RSPCA. Having spent hours on the phone, I finally lost my cool. 'Where are all the puppies?' I demanded. 'All I want is a cute mongrel pup around eight weeks old. They used to drown them in a bucket in the old days!'

'Maybe you don't realise. The reason we don't get puppies these days,' snapped my vis-à-vis, 'is that most dogs have been neutered so they don't breed any more, like they used to.'

Maybe I am soft and/or eccentric, but I jib at the idea that pets should be instantly trimmed of their parts, let alone their tails and ears (for stylistic reasons), and would you believe, their bark? To de-bark a dog strikes me as abominable. You would be better off with a robot, hamster or a fluffy toy.

In the end, coincidence provided the puppy. Richard, my partner, rushed back from a Sunday-morning trip up Brick Lane to tell me that he had found a whole box of young pups outside a shop with a notice stating 'Good Homes Wanted'. Daughter and husband set off to reconnoitre and, of course returned with a large squirming tough-guy pup with size three paws who promptly barked defiantly and peed wherever he could reach, including our feet. I figured him for a future giant, perhaps a German Shepherd with a touch of Doberman, even a pinch of Labrador? Miles away from a fluffy mongrel pup. Ottilie promptly christened him Otto.

A few years on, Otto now looks like the Hound of the Baskervilles; a big lad with a blood-curdling bark and stunning fluidity when running or jumping. My son-in-law, who has spent hours on training, really loves him and Ottilie, now into larger animals such as horses, treats Otto with impatient familiarity, cuffing this big sweet thing out of the way; 'DOWN OTTO, DOWN!', and like all well-trained dogs, he obeys. Otto was a gypsy dog, I guess, a genetic salad, but proof that if you catch them young enough and work at it, the canine species are biddable, domesticated rather than feral. But training takes time, patience and dedication.

House-training your puppy

Start as you mean to go on. A new puppy will whimper piteously to begin with when you leave it alone in its basket. Try to resist the temptation to take it to bed for a cuddle and don't let your children do this either. The best place to keep its basket is in a room with a hard floor so you can clean up the messes more easily and install a dog flap on the door so that the puppy can do its jobs outside. Failing a dog flap, a tray thickly lined with old newspaper is probably your best bet, for the time being.

The difficulty is to make the connection in the little creature's mind: need a pee? Go to my tray, or go outside. The old aversion therapy of rubbing the pup's nose in its mess is now frowned upon as both unkind and ineffectual. The trick is to catch the pup the second it hunkers down and then hastily put it outside or in its tray so it begins to realise the most important house rule of all. According to the experts, the times a puppy needs to relieve itself tend to be on waking, after feeding, on a walk or during a big play session. This may be true but it suggests you need to be on case pretty much all day, which is impossible. Regular short walks on waking, after feeding and before dossing down for the night, combined with heaping lavish praise on the pup when it does perform (pooper scoop at hand, naturally) reinforces the message. However, it may take months rather than weeks. In the meanwhile, I find the only solution is to keep room doors closed unless you are on hand

and be extra patient and tolerant. Think how long it took to pot-train your babies.

Pups do pick up eventually, especially as they settle into a routine, gain better control over their functions and learn what wins your approval. On the whole, a family dog wants to please and this is the fundamental trait to work on. In my experience, there are bound to be slip-ups, even with older ostensibly house-trained animals: locked into a room by mistake, a sudden bout of diarrhoea. You just have to exercise the forgiveness muscle.

Chewing

As everyone knows, young pups chew madly, partly because they are teething and partly because genes tell them to, against the day when – in the wild state – they might need strong jaws and sharp teeth. Squidgy rubber toys with a 'chew' threaded through will keep them busy for a while and smelly, discarded shoes are often acceptable. Brushes can be exciting too, maybe because the bristles have something of an animal-like appearance.

But what do you do if you surround your pup with chewy toys, old slippers and chunks of wood, and it still does a really bad thing and chomps a big piece out of an upholstered chair? Pups, and even older dogs, do these awful deeds when they are (a) bored, (b) locked in inadvertently or

(c) unsupervised. (The forgiveness muscle is in overtime here.) All I can suggest is that if the pup or dog is to be left alone for any length of time without human company, make sure they are confined to where they can do least damage should ennui get too much. Buttoned chairs are a special attraction – first they worry at the button, then it gives and hey it is soon into the gut of the thing and your treasured library chair has been eviscerated!

It is easy for pups and dogs to get locked in as they have sneaky ways of hiding themselves for a nap. Loud policing is the only defence and do not leave the house until your pup (or dog) is present and correct, fed, watered and safely out of harm's reach. Tough Yankees (the heroine of a Patricia Cornwell chiller I am reading) lock their dogs into a cage filled with toys when they go out, but I haven't got the heart to do this.

Puppy-training classes

I am in two minds about these. You will find your local vet either runs them or can put you on to someone else who does. For me, the 'socialising' aspect was the draw. Theory has it that your puppy needs to make contact, in a controlled environment, with loads of other canine contemporaries so they accept that it takes all sorts, shapes, sizes and colours to make up a doggy world. The socialising bit, where all the pups are unleashed to frolic, growl and attempt to stomp the other guy into submission, is both hilarious and a mite alarming. Having watched my Staffy, Bella, having fun with her mum, Rosie, where jaw-lock seems to be the aim, I already knew that pups like rough play.

Frequent meetings with a puppy peer group is good training in 'socialisation'. A pup should learn to get on with both sexes – bitch and dog. Scrapping occurs most in

Pet toys

The best are designed to work off bothersome instincts and energies, and/or help in training. Better your puppy chews a rubber toy than your furniture, and your cat scratches a piece of rough timber than the upholstery, though cats are resistant to 'training'.

The King Kong, a German-made rubber toy obtainable from vets, is the only 'chew' to withstand powerful canine jaws. A scratch post for cats you could make yourself from wood, rope or scraps of carpet.

same sex encounters, or with staid, elderly canines who resent boisterous puppy overtures. Shout, stamp but *don't interfere* as you may get bitten by mistake.

Walks

All vets are unanimous that what urban dogs need more of is exercise. An hour a day is not too much for a young, strong animal. Dog-walkers abound today in big cities (from about £5 an hour). It is not so bonding as being walked by a family member, but an option if you are short of time.

Your vet will refer you to dog-walking candidates. Or stop the next person you see in the park with a pack of dogs and check them out.

THE BOTTOM LINE

Running costs of keeping pets are high, what with visits to the vet, medicines, etc. Urban pets will set you back more than their country cousins, who can hunt and forage and run relatively free. But family pets occupy a special role in an urban lifestyle: dependent, friend, love object, long-term responsibility. Children learn a lot from this relationship, I think, if it is handled well.

But if you are in doubt – don't get a pet. Simple.

DOING IT THEIR WAY

POLLY HOPE

Polly Hope is a long-time neighbour and friend. She is also a talented, multi-valent artist: painting, ceramics, textiles, soft sculpture and writing. An opera, for which she wrote the libretto, is being staged in Düsselfdorf in 2002. Work projects may whisk her across the world at short notice, but because she keeps a menagerie of pets, she has to have reliable live-in staff to walk the dogs, hunt for straying cats, feed and muck out the chickens and parrot. A widow herself, Polly gets part-time help from Mary, another widow, and at least one au pair. This is currently Joss from Turkey, a smiling young man sans attitude.

In my view, what gives Polly's household its defining note is the fact that she is an English general's daughter. There is a clear schedule, a firm weekly, monthly and annual routine. Polly herself keeps an eye on the bottom line. She is forthright about the way to run what she calls a 'decent home, not luxurious, but civilised' and her views on the subject are crisp and tough minded.

● The fridge is cleaned out thoroughly before the weekly shop, which she does on Thursday to avoid weekend crowds at the supermarket.

● Her kitchen is 'shipshape' every night, crocks washed (she has a dishwasher) and put away, surfaces wiped down and everything made tidy so breakfast at 8.30 am is ready to go. 'I like my kitchen to be left super-clean every night, like an operating theatre.'

● Her rubbish bin is emptied and bagged up on a daily basis.

● Dusting, floor mopping and vacuuming are carried out in a regular manner.

● Bigger jobs such as window cleaning and the turning out of cupboards are spaced out as time offers and need arises.

- Bread is made weekly with the help of a huge old Kenwood mixer. Polly's eggs come seasonally from her chickens and the tomatoes from the tubs on her riotous roof garden. Would you believe, she and Mary forage locally throughout the East End of London with bags and snippers to make 'elderflower cordial'. They now have gallons on the go. Self-sufficiency or plain old hippy? Nonetheless, it is most impressive.

- Twice a year (spring and autumn) Polly's extensive collection of antique and ethnic textiles, plus her own Japanese designer clothes, are taken out, brushed down and moth-proofed with blasts of anti-sachets (see page 161). This is a fixed bi-annual duty as these are both her artistic inspiration and working tools.

- Although special garments are dry cleaned, Polly does believe in soap and water where possible. For instance, her ethnic or flokati rugs are hauled outside in sunny weather, hosed down, sprinkled with soap powder or flakes, scrubbed with a stiff broom, rinsed at length and then hung out to dry. (I have tried this and I can vouch that it works. Not only is it a big cost saving but wonderfully reviving to both colours and wool pile – but of course you need to first check that the dyes are well and truly fast.)

- Polly stocks up on stationery and light bulbs, etc, via mail order or online for both convenience and economy.

- She stressed the need to take intelligent care of all domestic gadgets and machines. All her au pairs are drilled to test the 'suck' of a vacuum cleaner before each use by running a hand carefully under the machine. DIY servicing comes first. Should this fail, she dispatches it to be serviced professionally. Polly reckons that she gets at least ten years working life from all her domestic appliances alike.

- Waste not, want not: old sheets, duvet covers and towels are recycled as rags or dog towels. Typically, if bed linen is running low, Polly would consider buying Egyptian cotton wholesale and making it up in house. (As a textile artist she has a state-of-the-art sewing machine.)

● Polly's guest room, with en suite bathroom, is 'always ready for use, freshly hovered, clean bed linen and *tous conforts*'. Given the hospitable soul she is, there is invariably someone staying.

● In order to deter thieves, Polly paints all her high-tech appliances (computer and printer, etc). This also makes them appear more decorative.

● Generous but thrifty, she prefers to give home-made prezzies. We often get a fruity cake buried in marzipan and icing at Christmas. An architect friend received a snap of himself busying around his country kitchen, tricked out in a cute frame.

A tall Saxon-looking woman with bags of energy, despite being a grandmother, Polly gets up at five every morning and starts the day three times a week by swimming half a mile. She keeps abreast with friends in Moscow and Istanbul and never fails to enjoy a good party. Every year there is a musical event adorned with fairy lights and buffet chez Polly. She is now considering the restoration of a lovely ruin on a 'new' Greek island. Superwoman or what? OK, she is not strapped for cash but neither is she extravagant. Her home is *sui generis* and Bohemian yet clean, orderly, civilised and welcoming.

To me, an artist and general's daughter seems to be a good mix.

CLEANING

PRODUCTS, TOOLS AND METHODS

Shopping for household cleaning stuff along the supermarket aisles is no treat, although we all do it, ignoring the sickly reek of the room freshener section on the hunt for some lowly items such as Brillo pads, which seem never to be in the same place for two weeks together. If I had ample storage space, like my sister with her walls of walk-in cupboards, I would buy the basic materials – scouring powder, bleach and cream cleaner – by the van load from a Cash and Carry, saving both shopping time and money. As it is, I buy in triplicate, having found that a work station on each floor of a house saves endless running up and down stairs for dusters, rags, scrubbing brushes, pails and so forth. I even keep a vacuum cleaner on

each floor, because nothing except a baby buggy is so unwieldy to lug around. (No, I did not go out to buy three vacuum cleaners in one go: I bought two spaced over several years and inherited one from my mother.)

I am sure I am not the only person who mourns the gradual disappearance of the old-fashioned hardware store, signalled on the High Street by bouquets of mops and bunches of brooms guarding the entrance. They are still to be found in small country towns and I make a beeline for them, because there is something inspiring about their characteristic pong: birdseed, beeswax and linseed oil. Ruminating among their seemingly chaotic shelves invariably triggers helpful suggestions to round out my shopping list. Where else can one find decent brooms with luxuriant heads of resilient bristles, feather dusters that do not moult in the hand, those endearingly modest and un-trendy packs of hot-water starch and soda crystals, not to mention household ammonia and spirits of salt?

My fondness for these stores is not pure nostalgia. Well-crafted, sturdy domestic implements – brooms, scrubbing brushes and string mops – are increasingly hard to find as plastic substitutes take over. Brooms with heads of synthetic fibres are virtually useless at sweeping: they merely stir the dust around. Whoever dreamed up the mop with a head made from shredded J-cloths should be set to clean a restaurant kitchen nightly as a penance. The same goes for that humblest tool of all, the washing-up brush. Every season a new plastic model arrives on the market, oddly shaped about the head, with a handle that is hard to get a grip on, and which turns to a soggy mess in weeks.

Granted, most of these cleaning tools are cheap; on the other hand, a gutless implement that fails to deliver is a waste of money and something of an insult to anyone who finds satisfaction in completing household tasks fast and effectively. Imagine if chefs were unable to buy any knives other than those wimpish sets with serrated blades and plastic handles which clutter the pages of mail-order catalogues. To paraphrase the

bard, attempting to seriously sluice down a floor with a mop that feels as ineffectual as a bunch of wet Kleenex is an expense of effort and a waste of time.

Elbow grease

My role model in the cleaning line was spry 60-year-old Lily, who had been an ATS driver during the war. She brought a certain military briskness and precision to her cleaning 'routine'.

I once asked her which cleaning aid she valued most out of her 'kit'. With hardly a pause in her dusting activities, she shot me a sharp glance and said 'elbow grease'. There were no short-cuts to cleaning in her book; clean meant clean and no bones about it.

In her twice-weekly three-hour sessions she whirled through a small maisonette on two floors, dusting from the top down, wiping down with a damp rag, washing spotted, sticky surfaces en route, rubbing up the few good pieces to a gleam with a clean duster. Once in a while she might use a little beeswax, but as she said 'it's the rubbing that makes the difference'. Tidying, other than straightening magazines and piles of paper, she left to me, though cushions were thumped and curtains shaken to release any dust. Lastly, she would race round with the vacuum cleaner sucking up the fall-out from her dusting activities.

The glory of Lily, for an inexperienced person like me, was her professionalism. I never had to point out what needed doing around the place; she had already spotted what was due for attention. Watching Lily at work, 'at the double', was engrossing, like watching a skilled tradesman lay bricks, or chisel a rebate in a length of timber; it instilled proper respect for skills honed by long practice. I felt bereft when Lily at last retired, but after the first dismay wore off, I realised that with Lily I had been to graduate school. The hours I had spent watching her in action had grounded me in the value and purpose of 'routine'.

STATE-OF-THE-ART CLEANING MATERIALS

When it comes to cleaning materials for the home, HG, who retail all over the country, is a heavyweight contender. Think of a surface (marble, tile, wood, leather, vinyl, laminate, plastic) or any item in the house from cooker to chandelier and HG is there for you with a a specific product to clean, de-scale, protect, add shine. They have a website (see My Directory) which you can consult about any cleaning or maintenance problems. They even have a product, HG Cleaning Spray, to remove fungi, algae and moss from graveyard headstones.

Thoughtful or overkill? Is it really necessary to acquire a multitude of products – no fewer than eleven, including the headstone spray – for dealing with marble? Or three separate products to remove algae, stains or accumulated grime from your patio when a dilute application of spirits of salt will deal with all three? And isn't it just a little exasperating to find that so many of these restorers, renovators and shiner-uppers then require a separate HG product to clean them off again?

It is not just spending money on all these boring products that is the problem so much as finding space to store them. I am not saying the products don't work. I have used the HG Impregnator on my brick kitchen floor and find it does give a degree of protection so the floor seems to need mopping less often. But we certainly don't buy HG remover to clean it off again – mopping and foot traffic effectively take care of that.

What firms like HG have identified is that the average consumer with a cleaning problem (green slime on the patio, mould on the shower stall, grimy grout or limescale) is a sitting duck for a smart sales pitch. Instead of stopping to think what alternative treatment they may already have in the house (such as common bleach for algae and mould) they go for the job-specific product that presses the button. HG Green Slime Remover? That has to be the business; and how about a can of

HG Patio Cleaner as well, just in case the Slime Remover doesn't clean up everything else in sight?

I don't mind admitting that I have been through this phase of knee-jerk response to clever marketing; mind elsewhere, under pressure and pushed for time. But I am becoming increasingly sceptical. I have not found a stain remover that works 100 per cent, or a product that really obliterates white rings on French-polished furniture. When it comes to keeping my yard paving (York stone flags and granite setts) looking wholesome, neither mouldy nor slimy, a regular hose down with water and brush with a stiff broom has got it looking good without resorting to commercial solutions, which usually contain a cocktail of chemicals.

I am coming round to the idea that the simplest solution is often the best. Most times this will be no more than a regular application of elbow grease. Our mistake is to imagine that technology can provide an alternative and effortless solution. To a greater or lesser degree most cleaning activities involve physical effort. Scrubbing, rubbing and mopping are all physically taxing activities, but by the same token are excellent aerobic activities for tightening the upper arm muscles, firming the bust and limbering the spine – so it's not all bad news.

There is another factor that should weigh with you. By reducing your cleaning aids to essentials you will be cutting down on many of those dodgy emissions and dubious chemicals which linger around in the air and finally settle on the carpet and turn it into what a recent *Guardian* article called 'a toxic sponge'. This is a quote from environmental engineer John Roberts – known to his fans as Mr Dust – and I suspect him of exaggeration to make his point. However, it does seem likely to me that the indiscriminate use of inessential cleaning products, whose chemistry remains a mystery, may be a factor in the reported increase in allergenic disorders, especially amongst very young children. As Mr Dust reminds us, small children spend a lot of time very close to the carpet and thus breathe in a lot more nasties in relation to their body weight than adults; their respiratory systems work more rapidly than ours.

ESSENTIAL CLEANING PRODUCTS

Having got that off my chest, I have to say that there are some modern, commercial cleaning products I would be bereft without.

Cream cleaners

Liquid cleaning agents with a mildly abrasive action, often containing bleach. There are stacks of these to choose from, with supermarket own brands the cheapest. My favourite is Cif (formerly Jif), which I use for scrubbing stains off my kitchen table or the sink, and for any cleaning operations that call for more than a wipe down.

Bleach

Most household bleaches are chlorine based. Chlorine is strong stuff. Don't think if a little is good, more will be better; follow the maker's directions. Like most people, I keep a bottle under the sink but use it less than my other cleaning products. Where it scores is for disinfecting kitchen sponges and cloths. I soak them in cold water with a little bleach every day or so. Now and then I fill my ceramic sink with cold water, add an eggcupfull of bleach and let it stand. This clears all surface stains. You can also use a bleach solution on paving that has developed green algae patches.

There are gentler bleaches such as lemon juice, hydrogen peroxide (in solution) and borax, mostly used to lighten fabrics.

Household bleach comes with childproof caps but should always be kept securely away from small children.

IMPORTANT: Don't mix chlorine bleach with ammonia as this can release a toxic gas.

Scouring powders

More abrasive than cream cleansers, and cheaper – otherwise pretty well inter-changeable. Lots of brands to choose from. I like Barkeeper's Friend, which I use mostly for shining up copper pans. It cleans them up without leaving lots of black gunk. It can also be used to clean stainless steel, chrome and brass.

HG Impregnator

Used on stone, brick or tiled floors (unglazed tiles), this helps to seal the surface and make it stain resistant. It is easy to apply (use a mop) and adds a faint sheen without altering the colour. It wears off gradually underfoot.

Soap pads

I am not fussy which make I buy. I find soap pads invaluable for cleaning stains off mugs and teapots, getting the grease off casseroles (earthenware and cast iron), and the base of saucepans. Occasionally I use them for heavy-duty spot cleaning on stone flags, the Aga or my four-ring gas hob. I use them once and chuck them although my au pairs keep them till rusty, despite my pleas. A pad of soft wire wool rubbed over a bar of soap would do the same job more cheaply, but soap pads are less hassle.

Detergent

This is a generic term for a grease-busting agent that enters into a multitude of cleaning products such as washing-up liquid, washing liquid, various spray cleaners and shampoos. Some detergents are more powerful than others and thus less eco-friendly. On the other hand, I find 'green' washing-up liquids less effective: you use more, so you are back to square one.

Clothes-washing liquids

These liquids (both biological and non-biological) contain detergent plus other ingredients: surfactants, whiteners and brighteners.

Biological washing liquid used in pre-soak mode in your machine is an effective stain remover but should not be used too often as it seems to weaken fabrics. (I once left some sheets soaking in my bathtub overnight, with biological washing liquid. Not only did it lift the stains but also cleared rust and limescale stains off the bath enamel!)

My washing machine guru (see page 173) claims that powders are more effective than liquids because they dissolve more thoroughly; you can alternate powder and liquid.

On the eco front, salve your conscience by using less detergent than the makers suggest – half as much still does the job – and/or get yourself a Washsaver (see page 175). The Great Lakes in the USA, once heavily polluted, have cleaned up their act remarkably in just ten years thanks to both commercial and private initiatives. Every little always helps.

Heavy-duty cleaning powders

These powders are for when you want to get surfaces – floors or paintwork – extra clean. I use Flash powder (cheaper than Flash liquid) in warm water for floors, and any brand of sugar soap, diluted according to maker's instructions, for cleaning up grimy paintwork. Apply with a sponge, squeezed out to prevent drips, then follow with a damp cloth dipped in clean water.

To stop damp getting at these cleaning powders and turning them into a solid mass, transfer them to glass jars with lids, but make sure they are clearly labelled.

Dishwasher tablets

A secondary use for these tablets (outside the machine) is to clean crusty casseroles and burnt pans. Dissolve a tablet in boiling water, and tip the solution into the sink, filling up with hot water.

Leave the dirty pans and dishes to soak in this overnight and you will find the grots have floated clear.

Silver-cleaning cloth

The fastest, least messy way to shine silver cutlery, etc. These are soft cloths that are impregnated with silver polish.

To use, simply rub the cloth over the silver surfaces until the tarnish gives way to a bright gleam. Most effective on what people in the USA call 'flatware'.

Carpet/upholstery shampoo

Another, but job-specific, detergent cleaner, useful for removing surface dirt from upholstered furniture, rugs, carpets, etc. 1001 is a well-known brand. Highly effective used in conjunction with a steam cleaner (see page 116). Otherwise, apply foam with a soft brush, as per instructions, trying not to soak the surface, and follow after with an old towel, rubbing hard to dislodge the surface sleaze. 1001 also comes in a spray version. I use the hands-on method to spot clean stains on carpets. Best to shampoo upholstery before it gets too grimy – little and often is more effective.

A hair dryer can be used to dry off wet surfaces. To restore the pile on velvet or chenille, try running a steam iron an inch or so above the surface.

TRADITIONAL CLEANING MATERIALS

Faced with supermarket gondolas packed with all the cleaning aids the modern housewife is thought to need, it makes you wonder how women managed during the eighteenth century when they even had to make their own soap.

The answer to this is that soap was used sparingly, if at all, and scrubbing and scouring was the usual recourse. Plank softwood floors were scrubbed with silver sand, which scoured stains off as well as smoothing the surface. Wooden table tops were similarly treated, while wooden tubs, chopping boards and other portable items were first scrubbed, then scalded and taken outside to dry in the sun and the wind.

I am not advocating a return to eighteenth-century practices but I find it interesting that 'friction', as in scrubbing and scouring, is now recognised by hygiene experts as the most thorough way to get a surface clean and keep down the micro-organisms.

Wood contains tannin, which inhibits bacteria, mould and other nasties. Sunshine is a natural disinfectant. Working from precept or instinct, our ancestors were wiser than they knew. It seems not beyond the bounds of possibility that an eighteenth-century kitchen, its few surfaces attacked vigorously on a daily basis, was actually more hygienic than a contemporary one where elbow grease has been replaced by a half-hearted wipe down using a manky old sponge cloth. Finishing with an antibacterial spray might seem like a smart compromise, but then we slide into the problem of overkill. (See Hygiene Hypothesis, page 150).

I have always been attracted to traditional solutions, mainly for their simplicity. I mean, why pack your shelves and cupboards with job-specific cleaning materials if one product will deal with several instances?

Take spirits of salt, for example, which I was pleased to find on sale again (after an absence) in one of my local chemists. A squeeze of this, left overnight, cleans your lavatory bowl beyond the bend, removing limescale and stubborn stains. In solution, poured down a plastic funnel, it will effectively flush out sinks and drains. It contains hydrochloric acid, which is powerful stuff; used by mosaic workers to clear cement smears off a new mosaic. Therefore, it must be used with care and kept under lock and key in a house with small children. But then the same applies to bleach, limescale removers and a good many other domestic cleaning products. I also use spirits of salt to clear green mould, algae and mildew from paving stones.

So you have one product with several uses, thus saving storage space as well as cash. This speaks to me. As for the risks, I prefer to be allowed to make up my own mind about these rather than have a useful and effective product withdrawn from circulation. Better the chemical you know and are warned about than a whole melange of unknown substances cluttering up your cleaning cupboard.

The following is a list of old-fashioned and traditional cleaning aids, with their uses, followed by a list of recent products which I use constantly and can honestly endorse, hand on heart.

Caustic soda

Not to be confused with washing soda (see page 112) this is a powerful solvent, obtainable from most chemists and hardware shops in plastic childproof bottles. Use in solution with water (see the manufacturer's instructions for the correct proportions).

Caustic soda poured down sink outlets (plughole and overflow) and drains, on a regular basis – say once a fortnight – dissolves clogging grease and helps pipes to run freely, as well as zapping harmful micro-organisms. Congealed fat, bulked up with tea leaves, rice, etc, is the commonest cause of sink blockages. A caustic treatment should be followed by a kettleful of boiling water. Stand back as you do this because the boiling water/caustic mix releases throat-clutching vapours, and a dramatic, noisy hissing as the stuff gets to work.

Wear rubber gloves when handling caustic soda – while less fierce than spirits of salt (see page 111), caustic soda (which is an ingredient of some paint strippers) will sting on exposed skin. If this happens, the area should be immediately rinsed in cold running water.

Although it is mildly hazardous, caustic soda is so useful it should be a fixture in your *batterie de nettoyage*, to be used with care and always kept out of reach of nosy kids. The same goes for most of the following products.

Spirits of salt

This product, a liquid sold in plastic childproof containers in chemists and some hardware shops, contains hydrochloric acid. It should always be used in solution with water, following manufacturer's printed instructions, wearing rubber gloves, a mask if you are sensitive bronchs and lungwise, standing well back as with caustic soda. A tad risky, therefore, but worth keeping to hand in my view because when caustic soda fails, spirits of salt, being that bit more powerful, can often do the trick on blocked sinks, drains, or toilets. A solution will clean up toilet bowls beyond the bend, if poured in last thing at night and flushed in the morning. Mosaic workers use it to chew through cement mortar smears on their handiwork, just to give an idea of its potency.

But, if the sprits of salt treatment fails to deliver, be sure to warn any plumber that you have used it prior to his intervention.

Methylated spirits

Basically raw alcohol with various additions to prevent it being guzzled with impunity, meths is a purplish liquid, widely obtainable (hardware stores, DIY outlets) with many domestic uses. It is a solvent for emulsion paint stains and smears, also for old French polish (see page 128), and a quick – if smelly – cleaner for mirrors, interior window panes and other glass. Rub on neat with a clean cloth, then polish off. On balance, for glass I prefer the ammonia solution (see page 113) but horses for courses here.

Linseed oil

An oil derived from the seeds of flax plants (used to make linen). It has a kindly affinity to wood, hence its use in many oil-based paints and varnishes, as well as traditional French polish formulae. It comes in both raw and boiled formulations, and is widely available from hardware and trade outlets.

Raw linseed oil is an ingredient of my home-made furniture polish/reviver, its oiliness cut with vinegar and white spirit (see page 127). With repeated applications linseed oil builds up a coating both flattering to the wood (mahogany especially) and protective so that stains are shrugged off, but this demands patience, and much friction, to achieve the rich patina of an antique mahogany dining table.

Vinegar

White (ie, distilled) malt vinegar is popular, I recently found, with cleaners on the west coast of the USA (always called house-keepers over there), as a simple, cheap and environmentally acceptable additive to water for cleaning floors, both vinyl and hardwood. Becky, the highly efficient housekeeper I talked to, says she would use Murphy's Oil Soap (see page 126) for preference, because it not only cleans but feeds and revives the woodiness, but in households where purity was a fetish, she would opt for a white vinegar in water solution – approx. 150ml to 5 litres (5fl oz to a gallon) – which cuts grease, lifts most stains, and has a mildly disinfectant action. On really messed up floors she might start with a tougher cleaning solution – detergent in water – but she will finish with the watered down vinegar.

Vinegar enters too into my home-made wood polish; here the cheapest malt vinegar will do, brown or white. It leaves a faint, pleasant smell. It will also clear limescale off a kettle, electric or otherwise. Empty the kettle, pour in a bottle of malt vinegar (enough to fill it) leave overnight, then flush out with cold water next morning.

Salt

Salt water is a natural disinfectant and promotes healing, which is why salt-water baths – water to which salt is added – are recommended for new mothers with episiotomy stitches. But a saline solution – at a pinch – is safe practice for bathing many minor injuries: grazes, cuts, weepy eyes. Use 500ml (1 pint) tepid boiled water, to which you add 2.5ml (½ teaspoon) salt, dissolve thoroughly, then wipe gently with a fragment of sterile cotton wool. Useful to know when you are caught without your usual antiseptics.

Soap flakes/powders, Woolite

I was raised in the belief that pure soap flakes, or powders (Lux, Dreft), were the most gentle cleaning agents for fine or delicate fabrics – silk, satin, cashmere, baby clothes. Well dissolved in tepid water and throroughly rinsed (three rinses). I have never known this to fail. I use Dreft to clean old rugs (see page 101). I am still inclined to think that pure soap, in flakes or powder form, is kindest to fragile fabrics, and vegetable dyes (as in old rugs) but it does call for thorough rinsing.

Woolite is a mild detergent – a newcomer in the field. It can be used in cold water, and needs less rinsing – like twice. But it is relatively expensive, best kept for cashmeres, pricey lingerie, or fabrics whose colourfastness you are not assured of.

Washing soda

Sold in both crystals and liquid form, in supermarkets and hardware shops. You get more crystals for your money, but they have an annoying trick of going rock solid when damp. The solution here is to dump the compacted lump into a bowl and cover with warm water till it dissolves, then decant into a jar or bottle. Label when done.

Don't confuse washing soda with caustic soda. Washing soda is relatively harmless: it is chiefly used to soften water and dissolve grease and limescale. See page 174 for how to use soda to improve the performance of your washing machine. By the same token, a small cupful of washing soda down your sink followed by boiling water, if done regularly, helps flush out pipes and prevent build-up of grease, though you need a stronger remedy – such as caustic soda or spirits of salt to chew through a blockage. I add 15ml (1 table-spoon) of washing soda to my usual floor-washing liquid when surfaces look particularly grubby. Like dishwasher tablets, washing soda will also help loosen accretions from pots, pans and casseroles (see page 139).

Ammonia

If you can stand the reek of ammonia, this is an efficacious grease solvent and water softener in one. Added to warm water, approximately 15ml to 1 litre (1 tablespoon to 1.5 pints), the solution is excellent for cleaning internal window glass and mirrors. Apply with sponge, dipped then wrung out, follow with a squeegee, then polish with scrim or chamois (see page 118). For best results glass panes need to be cleared first of proprietary spray glass cleaners, because these leave a tenacious film.

Another use is for cleaning hair and clothes brushes. Add to water as above, dabble the bristles until the water discolours, rinse in cold water and dry bristles upwards, away from heat. This works as well for synthetic bristles as for the real thing.

Ammonia is also powerful enough to strip wax off lino, vinyl and wooden floors. For this it needs to be used in a stronger solution. Alwayls read the manufacturer's instructions.

Citric acid

A harmless substance (it was used in home-made lemonade) sold in chemists, in packets and sachets. Ann French, a highly experienced SRN now turned monthly 'new baby nurse' and a fount of all knowledge on cleanliness and hygiene, alerted me to citric acid as a maintenance tip for dishwashers. Tip a sachet (say, 30ml/2 tablespoons) of citric acid into the soap box of your (empty) dishwasher – then switch to the hot cycle. Done regularly – every few weeks – this treatment clears fat and limescale, as well as the element, thus ensuring the drying cycle works most efficiently.

CLEANING TOOLS

It is cheering to find that I am not alone in a keen preference for solid, old-style bristle brooms and brushes, sturdy dustpans and wooden-backed scrubbing brushes. I have had my fill of plastic in this area, so I am delighted to find more shops introducing good-quality household tools, sourced from abroad mostly. A brave move retail-wise, since they all cost more than the mass-produced versions offered by DIY sheds and supermarkets. I paid over £20 recently for a bona fide bristle broom (made in Edinburgh on traditional lines) but compared with its mass-produced equivalent, whose synthetic bristles go uselessly soft in a trice, sliding ineffectually over dust and litter, my broom has resilient, bouncy bristles several inches deep, set stoutly into a wooden stock, which whisk up the grots efficiently, in no time. And since it will last for years if properly cared for (see below), it must work out cheaper in the long run, as well as speeding up the chores meantime.

Plastic is great – cheap, light and streamlined for containers (buckets, laundry baskets, drawer dividers, fridge and freezer bowls, etc) – but when it comes to a tough, business-like domestic tool it fails to deliver. See My Directory for stores stocking traditional brooms, brushes, metal dustpans and string mops.

Don't maltreat your decent tools. See below for how to care for them, and prolong their useful life.

Brooms

Though natural bristle is forgiving, no broom should be left standing on its business end, as this flattens the bristles. Brooms are best stored head up, resting on two pegs, clips or hooks screwed into the wall or cupboard door. Use one of the pegs to suspend your hearth brush too.

Bristle brooms appreciate a little TLC. Rake the gubbins out frequently, and dip the head into tepid water with a dash of ammonia. Rinse in cold water and stand outside to dry. The same goes for bristle hearth brushes.

Mops

Squeegee-type mops are excellent for cleaning up vinyl, lino, tiles and other smooth floorings; on my medley of stone flags, bricks and painted boards, I find an old-fashioned string mop is the only answer, coping with surface unevenness. String mops should be used with a mop bucket containing a strainer-like attachment to squeeze out excess water.

All mop heads wear out in time; better to replace swiftly (as with toothbrushes) than plough on with a knackered piece of equipment. Only replace the head, mind. DIY sheds and supermarkets sell squeegee-type mop heads, while the string type can be found in hardware shops. String heads come in two grades: get the one with the most string. See page 115 for how to fix the new head on to its wooden handle, using screws not nails.

All mops get filthy and should be rinsed in clean water after use, squeezed dry, then stood to dry, head uppermost. String mops can do with a spoonful of bleach in the rinse water. Leaving wet mops scrunched head

Changing a string-mop head

String mop heads are usually sold loose, for you to attach to a wooden handle. Don't be tempted to whack a nail in through the little hole provided on the metal ring: this often splits the handle, and is impossible to remove when you want to replace the mop head. Instead, secure it with a small, preferably brass, screw – brass will not rust. A 1cm ($^3/_8$in) screw is about right.

Use pliers to open up the metal ring enough to slide the handle in, hammering down on the handle, then punch a small hole with a bradawl into the handle through the existing hole on the metal ring. Insert the screw, and drive it home with the appropriate screwdriver. When the mop head gets threadbare, you simply unscrew it, chuck, and replace.

NOTE: Buy at least three replacement heads at a time. They are cheap, and life really is too short to spend looking for a new mop head.

down – especially the string type – leads to rank, mildewy smells.

Much as I deplore mops with heads of shredded J-cloths, and brooms with feeble synthetic bristles, similar care will extend their short life span.

Feather dusters

There is nothing more effective than a feather duster for a rapid flick over all dust-gathering surfaces. This attention should always take place before vacuuming the carpet or floor.

There is something to be said for the delicate caress of ostrich plumes – and these can be found – but ordinary poultry feathers are efficient, and much cheaper.

The feathers need to be securely anchored to the handle. If a surreptitious tug dislodges a feather, move on.

Fluffy lambswool dusters are an alternative, available in most department stores. Clean dusters, feather or fluff, by giving them a good shake in the open air.

I use a soft painter's dust brush on picture frames or carved mouldings because this probes a bit deeper, and more purposefully. I only use those yellow dusters, sold everywhere, as polishing cloths.

Washing-up brushes

I prefer these to sponges or cloths, though I expect to replace them around once a month. Here the plastic type (sold everywhere) scores higher than the recently introduced bristle brush with a wooden stock and handle. I pounced on these to begin with, but I find they disintegrate faster than plastic. Mark you, this applies to the cheaper versions. I recently bought a pricier model, imported from Sweden, with firm bristle stitched into a wood head (see My Directory). It was twice the price but has already lasted more than twice as long. Whatever the type, washing-up brushes should be rinsed in water and a little bleach after use to keep bacteria down and stop them from getting rank and smelly.

Steam cleaners

These are a seriously useful cleaning innovation, hitherto priced out of the domestic market but now becoming affordable, smaller models costing around £59 upwards.

What most appeals to me about steam cleaners is their splendid simplicity: no mystery chemicals, just tap water and heat. Steam cleaners look a bit like cylinder vacuum cleaners, but instead of sucking in dust they puff out steam under sufficient pressure to soften stains and surface grime on soft furnishings, carpets, hobs, grouting and even window panes. The makers claim that steam cleaning destroys dust mites. It also clears fusty smells: cigarette smoke, animal pee, mouse activity. Hotels steam clean their public spaces regularly to keep them pleasantly aired and to prevent the gradual build-up of surface dirt on their soft furnishings.

The pricier models (think £200–300) have a larger capacity, and come with a range of attachments, such as pointy nozzles for cleaning grout, and a steam iron. However, they are cumbersome to use and unfortunately take up as much cupboard

Using a steam cleaner

A hot tip from Frances, who supervises the running of my sister's holiday cottages, and meets a lot of stains on the weekly big clean-up day: she uses a steam cleaner regularly, but starts by spraying the spot with 1001 shampoo (see page 109). She leaves this for a bit and then moves in with the steam cleaner. Also, to save time waiting around for the machine to reach steam heat, she pours boiling water into it straight from the kettle.

space as a cylinder vacuum cleaner.

A smaller, cheaper model would be quite satisfactory for a family home, though I would be cautious about using them with small children around because steam can cause nasty burns. Karcher and Pollti, the two big names in the field, are about to launch domestic-scale models. Argos, and most of the supermarket and DIY sheds stock various other brands.

IS YOUR NITTY GRITTY?

This is where it all gets really down and dirty. Cleaning adjuncts – cloths, sponges, sponge cloths, scourers, etc – are essential to the cleaning process, and the right choice can make a difference.

Not all the following products are to be found in supermarkets; you may have to locate an old-style hardware shop (see My Directory).

J-cloth

First choice of hygiene fanatics, who chuck them after use. I find them flimsy, but Ann French, my candidate for Mrs Clean (see page 113) not only swears by J-cloths for wiping up, but gets maximum value out of them. She buys the extra large size, cuts them in half, puts the used ones through the wash with tea towels, etc, and reckons to re-use them two or three times. Where I see flimsy, she sees absorbent.

Decorator's sponge

There is nothing better than these for wiping down paintwork, clearing gunge off work surfaces and whipping around the sink and draining boards. I like the absorbency of these chunky cellulose sponges. They are stocked in hardware/trade shops and cost a couple of quid. They last a relatively long time, but I recommend that you dunk them in cold water with a drop of bleach on a daily basis to keep them clean and sweet.

Sponge cloths (eg, Spontex)

Supermarkets carry umpteen variants on the theme, usually sold in packs of three. Cheap, multi-tasking and useful – but rapidly disintegrating, especially if you follow the bleach suggestion.

Dishcloths

Stockinette (think of loose cotton knit) squares stitched both ends so as not to unravel. They are absorbent, cheap and widely available. Alternatively, you could buy a roll of stockinette sold by weight in hardware stores. You can then cut off as much as you need, and it is so cheap you can blithely chuck when filthy. This is worth considering since stockinette has umpteen uses: as dusters, polishing cloths and wipes. However, I find them too soft to be useful for washing up dishes, and they get slimy in no time, even with the bleach treatment. Yuk!

Linen scrim

Sold in packs of two, a traditional final polishing cloth for window glass and drinking glasses, etc. They are pure linen, look like hessian, but leave no fluff or lint behind. Wash before first use in order to get rid of dressing. From time to time, I run my scrim through the washing machine along with all the tea towels.

Chamois leather

As with linen scrim, these are prized because they polish surfaces (glass and car bodywork) beautifully and leave no residue. The main snag is upkeep – plenty of TLC is required: warm water, soap not detergent, squeeze-squeeze not rub-a-dub, drying away from heat, and stretch and knead to soften once dry. If properly cared for, chamois leather will last and last.

Scourers

Widely available in many versions, plastic, metal, scratchy pads with or without a sponge attached. All have their uses, but abuse can scratch stainless steel and copper, wear through enamel linings to your precious Le Creuset or erode non-stick surfaces. Horses for courses. The kindest scourer is the plastic knit, round type, the fiercest is the green scratch pad, with the metal knit somewhere between. I use all of them sparingly, preferring the soak and brush treatment. My au pairs love the scratch pads, but never know when enough is enough, and should only be given the knit plastic type! All scourers become disgusting with embedded food. At this stage, chuck and replace.

Dusters

There is nothing wrong with the traditional ubiquitous yellow type, except that household rags (see below) do the job just as well, cost nothing, and get you a re-cycling brownie point.

Rags

I keep drawstring bags on two floors – ragbags – into which go torn-up sheets, knackered towels and anything in cotton jersey. Natural fibres make the best rags: synthetics don't absorb sufficiently. Do take trouble to rip or chop off seams, hems or anything that might catch or scratch. I use rags for polishing furniture, leather, metal and glass. However, I prefer feathers or lamb's wool for dusting. I also keep clean rags for straining fruit for jam and jellies. Sometimes I machine wash rags if my supply is dwindling. Otherwise, I bin the stiffly blackened ones. Other uses for rags are as pressing cloths or for removing stains. I find old towelling invaluable for use with upholstery or carpet shampoo. Once the spill, stain or grime is softened, a towel rub really gets at the dirt. These I do wash, having fewer to start with.

Brushes

Soft, old, second-hand brushes – clothes and hair brushes – are useful aids when polishing up carved decoration, or moulding on wooden furniture because with these you can get right into the cracks and detail. Look for these at boot and jumble sales. Ideally, they should be real bristle. If possible, get two: one for applying polish and another for shining up.

A painter's dust brush is the ideal tool for dusting books and book shelves, more thorough but as gentle as a feather duster. They also work well on lampshades, carvings, or picture frames. But remember to whack dust out as you go along.

SPRING CLEAN, DEEP CLEAN

Time was – up until World War II – any self-respecting household would mobilise all hands, under the watchful direction of the mistress of the house, for a seasonal orgy of cleaning. Enshrined in folk memory as 'spring cleaning' this extended the daily and weekly domestic routines to cover just about every surface and item in the home. As the sharp spring sunshine cruelly showed up the grime, dust, soot and grease deposited by open fires, candles and oil lamps, etc, over the winter months, the season of renewal signalled an intensive and comprehensive attack, armed with all the domestic weaponry of the time; brooms, brushes, mops, feather dusters, soap, sand, bathbrick and holystone. There were also deeper resonances: a spring clean echoed the re-awakening of the natural world outside. To make new – by scrubbing, beating, dusting and polishing – in sympathy with the budding trees and greening fields. A sign of healthy optimism as well as the mark of decent housewifery.

That was then. Thanks to electricity and central heating, winter grunge is not the bogey it once was. Vacuum cleaners and washing machines have eased the slog of domestic chores beyond recognition. Women work full or part time, so standards have relaxed as it is generally understood that with jobs to fulfil and children to care for, something has to give: unmade beds, unironed washing and undusted shelves are comfortably accepted, not a badge of shame.

However, atavistic creatures that we are, the idea of an annual 'deep clean' – not tied to spring necessarily; on return from a holiday often works best – still strikes a chord, gets the adrenalin flowing, mind working, dormant ideas on the move and ancestral voices calling. It is still profoundly linked to the desire for renewal, starting over, rebirth and rejuvenation, a distant throb of those pagan rituals embodied in the May Queen and Corn King.

If that strikes you as a bit heavy and mystical, here is another – and right-on –

fact to assimilate. Throwing your energies into a 'deep clean' once a year (twice if you have very high standards) is really, really good for you. Therapeutic for both mind and body. An hour's vigorous dusting (I read in the *Express*) burns up as many calories as a session in the gym. By the same token, a 'deep clean' must equal weeks of pumping iron or working out on the treadmill. I have no statistics on the mind/mood side of this – you will have to take my word for it that a

Awoke again physically depressed. I got up saying, 'Is this
B R Haydon?…' I resolved to do some violent bodily exercise,
so I moved out all my plasters, cleaned the windows myself
(and don't wonder Servants have good appetites). I dusted,
and got smothered, lifted till my back creaked, and rowed the
Servant for not cleaning my plate (2 forks, 1 table spoon and
6 tea spoons, pepper box and salt spoon). In fact, with my
perspiration and violent effort, I cleaned out the Cobwebs
and felt my dignity revive. Now I'm safe.

The Autobiography and Journals of Benjamin Robert Haydon, B R Haydon
(Longman, 1853; Macdonalds, 1950)

Benjamin Robert Haydon (1786–1846) was a self-taught historical painter, failed RA and a manic personality. Although his paintings never brought him the fame he coveted, his extraordinarily candid and revealing journals, first published in 1853 after his death, rank him among the classic diarists. The plasters mentioned above would have been plaster casts used by academic painters at the time.

thorough deep clean makes you feel happy, positive and at peace with yourself.

Getting started is always the problem. Cross that Rubicon, and the rest follows. You may then have another problem: knowing where to stop. The rewards are sweet enough to compensate for aching joints, mucky hair and sweaty clothes.

I think everyone should have a go at a deep clean at least once, because it provides you with a useful time/cost comparison when it comes to evaluating the work of a professional cleaner or commercial cleaning team, should this be your next move. It will teach you the difference between a 'light clean' and an 'intensive clean', and whether the cost of the exercise represents real value. 'Been there, done that' gives you a helpful grip on the situation.

THE DIY DEEP CLEAN

Planning ahead

You will need to plan ahead, if you want covers and curtains pristine to match. You can send them to be dry-cleaned or wash them yourself. What you can wash safely, do: cushion covers, zip-off loose sofa and chair cushion covers. (For dos and don'ts see page 176.)

Rugs can also be sent to the cleaners and there are plenty of specialist cleaners in the case of antique and/or ethnic rugs (see My Directory). More simply, they can be beaten, vacuumed or shampooed on both sides (see page 123). Even washed if colourfast, the sun is shining and you have enough space to dry it again.

Lampshades

Lampshades can be dusted off with a soft brush. Fabric lampshades can usually be washed by being dunked in a sink full of tepid water with a little non-biological liquid or Woolite added. Dry with a hairdryer, over a radiator or over an Aga hotplate. Don't panic if the fringe or braid comes unstuck as a squeeze of adhesive will deal with that problem.

Repairs

While you are in preparatory mode, check out any small repairs needed around the house – cracked picture glass, wobbly lamp fittings, missing castors, and unstable chair legs. Get these seen to professionally as you already have enough on your plate (see My Directory). Knowing that all these niggling details are in hand while you get down to work is a real boost.

Fireplaces

Should you have an open fireplace you might want to consider booking a chimney sweep. These days this is a streamlined operation and there is no mess to speak of.

Storage and equipment

Get in plenty of cardboard boxes for pictures, books, ornaments and other small items. Check out your cleaning equipment: vacuum cleaner, steam cleaner, portable stepladder, soft brushes, feather dusters, rags, mops and pails plus the usual cleaning aids and materials. A painter's dust brush is a neat size for dusting off picture frames and mouldings. Ensure that you have spare bags for the vacuum cleaner, plenty of black bags for rubbish and a spare fuse or two.

Clearing the room

Rope in some muscle to help with the shifting of furniture. There is no sense in struggling on your own – you need all your energy for the numerous other tasks. Start by moving all the big items into the centre of the room or bodily out of the room if you have enough extra space. Take down all pictures, clear all books into waiting boxes. Begin by vacuuming where the furniture stood as this will be thick with dust. Then spread plastic sheets over the floor to collect dust, flaky plaster and other grot. If you have a painter's dust sheet, throw this over furniture.

Order of work

The rule in cleaning is to start at the top and work down. This way you get to catch up and deal with dust, grots and drips as you work downwards – following gravity.

Ceilings and light fittings

Stepladder work first. Use a soft (clean) broom, or periscopic feather duster to whisk over the ceiling and cornice, clearing away cobwebs along with the dust. Dust or wipe track lighting, wipe over halogen or other spotlights with a barely damp sponge cloth and give any pendent lighting flex a good clean. Flex picks up dirt and a grungy flex will be noticeable in your deeply cleaned room.

Lanterns, chandeliers and other decorative light fittings should be carefully taken down and washed.

Walls

Treatment here depends on the finish. Brush down walls painted in emulsion. Cracks, chips and nail holes show up annoyingly on bare, clean walls. If you are the prudent type with a spare can of emulsion in the right colour (and batch) stored away, you could tackle these now. Fill, sand flush and repaint, remembering that the paint will dry darker. Do not obliterate picture nail holes if the pictures are going straight back!

Wallpaper, especially one with an embossed surface, is better dusted with a feather duster. Vinyl-coated papers can be wiped down with a damp sponge cloth but this could be a protracted task. I would concentrate on the really grubby areas, such as round the light switch, behind the bed or around the bath. Old-fashioned (ie, non-vinyl) wallpaper can often be cleaned up with a chunk of stale bread, but again don't overdo it in one spot so the rest looks dingy.

Tiles and tongue and groove need tougher treatment – wipe down with a mild household detergent such as Flash or sugar soap solution (30–45ml/2–3 tablespoons dissolved in 5 litres/1 gallon warm water) to clear grease and grime and then rinse over. If dirty grouting offends you, there are ways to cope – a steam cleaner (see page 116) with a special nozzle being the best solution.

Shelves and bookcases

Now, at last, you can tackle big items like bookcases, shelves or fitted units of one kind or another. Start by brushing or vacuuming dust off the top surfaces. A car vacuum cleaner is handy here. It is a wipe down and wipe clean situation, whatever the surface, because these will be loaded with dust, fluff and sticky fallout, as one wipe will demonstrate. Go thoroughly here: backs of cupboard doors, undersides of shelves, grubby patches round handles, knobs and pulls, because grease and grime accumulate in these areas. Clearing all this away instantly makes a room look brighter.

Woodwork

This comes next: skirting, door and window architraves, window frames and your actual door. Brush, then vacuum loose dust and follow with the sponge cloth and cleaning solution. Change the latter and the rinse water as they get dark and dirty. If your cleaning cloths are damp – wrung out, rather than soaking wet – there should be no drips and splashes.

Floors

Hard surfaces present no untoward problems – sweep or vacuum and then mop over with the same cleaning solution as above. Rinse with clean water. It may be that the spanking cleanliness elsewhere shows up nasties you hadn't noticed before – ground-in dirt, sticky patches, odd spots of old paint – and even, heaven knows, old chewing gum. This requires tough action. Try one of the following: scraping away with an old kitchen knife, sanding with wet-and-dry paper or rubbing back with steel wool or soap pads. An ice cube can help dislodge encrusted chewing gum. Simple friction, aka elbow grease, is usually the most effective solution.

Carpets

Start by vacuuming thoroughly, changing attachments to get right into corners and cracks. Then take stock. Old wool pile carpet comes up brighter with an overall shampoo (hire a machine?) and some spot cleaning here and there. I use a scrubbing brush dipped in the shampoo, followed by a hard rub with an old towel. A steam cleaner works wonders on wool pile, both to clean and revive the pile. A steam iron will lift badly flattened areas. Wool-mix carpets also respond to this treatment, but try not to get them too wet, especially the backing.

Matting

We all fell in love with this for its calm neutrality and crispbread texture but, sadly, it is a whole different ball game when it comes to deep cleaning. Almost any spill, even plain water or white wine, leaves a mark. Traffic areas near doors leave darker patches.

I have tried a whole gamut of solutions, from spot cleaning with carpet shampoo and an old towel to steam cleaning, and my verdict is that while nothing works 100 per cent, steam cleaning is your best bet. A blast of steam lightens and brightens matting overall and lessens the dark patches round doorways. It can also help with pet pee and territory marking, lightening the stains and, more importantly, getting rid of the smell so pets don't keep returning to the same spot.

But if you are extra fastidious, I would either avoid matting altogether or be prepared to replace it every three to five years. Alternatively, scatter your matting with colourful rugs in key spots. On the other hand, you could rip the whole lot out (especially if your family shows signs of allergies) and switch to bare boards with rugs, laminate, marmoleum or any of the other practical floorings that have become increasingly popular and accessible over recent years.

Mirrors

I prefer a soft cloth with a little methylated spirits or ammonia in water (see page 113) to spray glass cleaner. I suspect spray cleaners leave a film or deposit.

Moving back in

Allow your newly pristine space (and yourself) to settle and dry out overnight, before rushing your stuff back in. Probably you can't wait to get back to normal again, but keep an open mind. Clearing a room for deep cleaning can give you a new fix on the place. Maybe you could try arranging your furniture differently or getting rid of some of it (see De-cluttering, page 44), or you suddenly love the extra light and clean effect of no curtains? Or you might decide to clear out your sickly pot plants and replace them with a glossy new collection. (Alternatively, try moving them outdoors if the weather is warm and feeding them with a liquid fertiliser such as Phostrogen.)

Finally, as a reward for so much hard work, how about a 'room present'? New cushions in suede, fur or coloured silk or a fleecy throw to drape enticingly over a sofa or armchair?

CLEANING WOOD

Most wood in the home – this includes floors, kitchen pieces as well as furniture – needs cleaning from time to time, but the way you go about it must vary with the type of wood in question. Is it hardwood or soft wood? Solid timber or veneered? French polished or factory finished? Not all 'brown' wood is mahogany, nor all blonde wood pine nor inky dark wood antique oak. However, it is astonishing how readily the public accepts these crude distinctions, misled only too often by fast-talking dealers, auctioneers and market stall holders.

How you clean wood also depends on its function within the home, what you use it for and what you expect from it. This is especially true of softwoods, which in the average home may include true pine (kitchen pieces, doors and handrails), common deal (floors and stairs) and a motley collection of woods that have been stripped, bleached, stained and waxed to pass as 'honey-coloured pine'. These are often found in the shape of modest items with a 'country' look such as chests of drawers, blanket boxes and wall shelves.

KITCHEN PINE

An old-fashioned kitchen table top made of stout planks, a drawer at either end and sturdy tapered legs is the 'pine' item I see most often. You may like to paint the legs and frame (red oxide is a cheap and tough paint in a sympathetic colour) but the top should be scrubbed. This not only looks handsome and appropriate, but is still the best way to ensure a deeply clean surface (see The Hygiene Hypothesis, page 150). The snag is that scrubbed surfaces readily mark – grease, red wine and tomato sauce are common culprits – so the scrubbing has to be a daily routine. People invariably ask me how I keep my own much admired kitchen table (a mongrel in fact: 2-inch thick pine planks grafted on to bulbous neo-Jacobean oak legs) 'looking that way' and look fairly scandalised when I tell them it is scrubbed down daily. This doesn't take long (less than 5 minutes) and the time seems well spent in order to sit at a table pristine as a newly swabbed deck. Over the years, the daily scrub has etched longitudinal grooves which underline its long service as the family meeting place. Assembled in situ as it was, I only discovered the other day that there is no way that it can now be moved out of the kitchen without removing the back door. In theory, any scouring product would do the job (in the eighteenth century they used sand or bathbrick), but after trying a number of brands, I remain faithful to Cif (see page 106) which is a thick white liquid containing bleach and does an excellent job of removing grease marks and other stains and leaves a pale velvety surface. Other tools needed are an old-fashioned wooden-backed bristle scrubbing brush and a cheap decorator's sponge. This is the routine:

● Squirt a long squiggle of Cif down its length.

● Scrub the length of the table, following the grain of the wood and pressing hard on the brush with both hands.

● Leave for a few minutes to allow the bleach to get to work.

● Using the sponge, wrung out but damp, mop up the thin slurry the length of the table, rinsing the sponge and wringing it out a few times in hot water. The wood looks clearer if you spend a little time over the rinsing, but it won't come to any harm if a little chalky residue remains.

I give chopping boards the same treatment, impressed by my hygiene expert's contention that nothing gets surfaces more hygienic than friction.

ANTIQUE FURNITURE

I am using the term 'antique' loosely to cover any good pieces you care about to the extent of including them in your regular cleaning routine. Maybe 'old' would be more apt, though even that can be misleading. One of my recent finds is a '60s teak Danish-made office cabinet; finely constructed, long, low and elegant.

I include that in my sporadic – say,

Murphy's Oil Soap

It's not often I stumble across a dream cleaning product, such as this, discovered on a recent trip to the USA. The makers claim that this 'pure vegetable' product, going for over 90 years, 'beautifully cleans wood and laminate surfaces. No dulling residue'. An understatement! I have been using it on my pitch pine kitchen cabinet (originally a school bookcase) and on iroko woodwork, and it is simply brilliant.

Use 75ml in 5 litres water (quarter cup to 1 gallon); I used 1 tablespoon (15ml) in a bowl of water. Not only does it clean but it brings up the wood grain, restores colour, and generally leaves wood looking nurtured, instead of dry and faded.

Home-made furniture polish

2 parts raw linseed oil
1 part white spirit
1 part malt vinegar

Mix together and shake well as you use it because it behaves like a vinaigrette with a tendency to separate. The vinegar is the cleaning agent, while the white spirit cuts out the fattiness of the linseed oil. Use sparingly, applying it with a soft rag.

What I like about this mixture is that it sinks into the wood rather than coating it with a waxy residue like most sprays and cream polishes which in turn attract dust and general dirt.

monthly – efforts with rags, polishing cloths, and my own home-made liquid furniture polish (see above).

Although my current au pair dusts the surfaces regularly with a feather duster, I now attend to the cleaning/polishing myself. I have never been able to convince my helpers that it is the rubbing that makes the difference. I banned spray polishes after I found the girls (with two exceptions) had the hopeful notion that anything with the words Wonder or Miracle on the label would bring up a shine all on its own. A burst of spray polish followed by a quick flick of the polishing cloth and that was it!

When I mixed up a bottle of the home-made stuff I found Jana lavishly applying it to the paintwork as well as the furniture, till the place smelt like a carpenters workshop. They couldn't see the point of rubbing. So now I take care of that myself.

My routine:

● Dust the piece first.

● Sticky patches on wood should be wiped Off with a cloth or sponge wrung out in water with a drop of Flash, other household detergent – or, better still, Murphy's Oil Soap (see left).

● If this doesn't clear them, rub the wood lightly with fine grade wire wool, making sure that you follow the grain of the wood.

● Shake some home-made polish on to a soft rag and wipe this over all the surfaces. Leave for a few minutes to sink in.

● With a clean soft rag or yellow duster rub firmly and forcefully in the direction of the grain until you raise a clean shine. The longer you rub, and the more regularly, the better the piece will look and be imbued with that patina that dealers prattle on about. Although the oil brings out the natural colour and markings of the wood, it is the friction (that word again) that develops a shine. Not straight away, not even in a week, but over time.

NOTE: I find this treatment works for just about any wood with a polished surface, including teak and French-polished woods. But go cautiously on veneered pieces, especially marquetry, in case a loose edge of the pattern is lifted up or ripped out.

Hands-on warmth

To work up a fine patina on a small wooden antique, such as a box or similar, first clean it (see page 125). apply home-made polish (see page 127), then patiently rub with your hands – the warmth generated makes a difference.

REFURBISHING FRENCH-POLISHED WOOD

Most superior furniture was given a French-polished finish from the eighteenth century onwards to even the tone, fill the pores and grain, and bring up a high shine. Where the French polishing was done by a trained craftsman and the piece has been cared for, you will hardly know it is there. You just see the mellow sheen rather than a hard gleam. This is how it should be.

Pieces that have been crudely French polished and maybe neglected or stored in a damp place will look patchily discoloured with the wood grain obscured by a misty bloom. French polish abhors damp, water and other spills and can become dark with grime and guess what: old layers of polish.

Removing the original finish, along with grime and wax, etc, can reveal the wood in a pristine state, clean as a whistle; its grain and characteristic colour restored to view. This works spectacularly well on mahogany, but I have also used it on late nineteenth-century oak and the aforementioned teak cabinet, with excellent results. Be warned: once you have cleared a section and the cleaned surface leaps out in all its glory it will be hard to stop. The equipment is simple:

Methylated spirits
Wire wool, medium and fine grade
Scissors to cut strips of wire wool
Marigolds to protect your hands

Meths is the solvent for shellac, a principal ingredient of French polish, so what you are doing is dissolving the old finish and clearing it off the wood with pads of wire wool.

Expect lots of gunky wire wool to pile up, even if you pull it about looking to make use of every scrap. Dispose of these safely and don't think of smoking anywhere nearby as meths is highly flammable.

The procedure is simplicity itself:

● Apply meths quite freely to a section at a time, using a brush, squeegee, pad or whatever suits you best. Leave for a few minutes.

● Take a pad or cut a strip of wire wool (medium grade first) and go over it following the wood grain, backwards and forwards, till your pad is darkly sticky and the clean wood is showing up.

● Repeat this, section by section, using the medium grade wire wool. ·

● When one whole section, panel, door or side is cleaned it will still look patchy. Apply more meths and use the fine wire wool to clear any remaining gunk and reveal a lovely, smooth, warmly coloured expanse of clean timber. Even an undistinguished piece looks transformed when you can see what it is made of.

● If you find it was made of a mongrelly assortment of woods – lowly beech legs, for instance – do not fret. These can be stained to match (see page 223).

NOTE: The original wood colour will get successively paler with every meths scrub you apply. With mahogany, it is best to stop before you get back to the raw wood shade but with oak you might prefer its pale biscuit colour.

Varnish stripper would no doubt clear the wood more quickly but I find it too drastic and swear by meths and wire wool.

Beware of jugs

Flowers look so winningly informal and painterly crowded into an old pottery jug, until you discover a stubborn dark stain on the polished table beneath – the jug leaked slowly and imperceptibly. Next time, stand the jug on a saucer, or take the line of least resistance – glass never leaks – or choose a high-fired china jug.

Advice from the experts

Standards of care and maintenance, as spelled out in the *National Trust Manual of Housekeeping* are rigorous, as one would expect, and hedged about with so many don'ts (when in doubt call in a conservator) that it makes heavy reading for a householder not entrusted with the care of priceless antiques.

However, some of the advice makes plain sense. For instance, we are warned against spray polishes, because they contain silicone, used too liberally they spread a white bloom on your nice polished surface, which nothing will shift short of stripping down the wood to its raw state, which means losing all that old patina.

We are advised instead to use a good wax polish very sparingly, like once or twice a year. (The National Trust makes its own, on sale in all its shops.) This wax fills or masks scratches and small scars almost invisibly, since wax tones in imperceptibly with a wood surface. In between waxing you dust, and you rub, vigorously, to work up a shine.

But – and this is the critical bit – you must use a clean, soft cloth or rag for the polishing up. Using cloths that you have put away gunged up will almost certainly have picked up dust and grit, and this will finely scratch your polished surface and undo all your good work.

The National Trust sternly advises washing all cleaning/polishing cloths on a weekly basis – but of course they polish weekly! However, it seems wise to wash them (boil them, or put them through the washing machine at a high temperature) after each cleaning session. Alternatively, throw them out and replace them each time: old T-shirts or flannel (sheets or pyjamas) make excellent polishing cloths.

When the whole piece is cleaned up, you can decide how to restore the surface. A dealer would send it to be re-French polished, but you might prefer to work up the wood colour and sheen gradually with my home-made polish. It will not present quite the slick shine of French polish, but I find I prefer my wood (such as my cherished mahogany linen press) warmly coloured but with less of an 'in-your-face' shine.

Once the colour is how you like it, try a wax finish on top for more of an even shine.

CLEANING LEATHER

Really old leather – as in book bindings, club chairs and suitcases – tends to dry out over time to the point where it becomes brittle and discoloured. Feeding oils back into the leather looks like your face feels when you slap on moisturiser after a heavy night. Grateful. However, go carefully until it feels nice and supple.There is not much you can do if the leather has split or gone crumbly except stick a patch inside (to hold a rent together) or outside to mask off a crumbly area. Use an appropriate adhesive. See My Directory for leather suppliers.

SADDLE SOAP

Properts Saddle Soap is an old established proprietary name used by generations of the horsey crowd to keep their leather tackle in good order. It is sold in some hardware shops and department stores. It cleans as it feeds and revives – excellent stuff. Using a damp sponge, pick up a good smear of the Saddle Soap and then rub it gently over the leather. Wring out the sponge when it seems to be picking up dark dirt and start again. Old leather may need several goes before it regains its former suppleness and colour. Leave the item to dry before re-soaping. Repeat till you feel the leather looks healthy before going on to the next stage, polishing.

Saddle soap, as its name suggests, is the best treatment I know for tougher, thicker leather (ie, boots, upholstery and suitcases) and with repeated buffing with soft cloths and brushes will bring up a muted shine. If it is a high shine you are after, try a standard shoe or boot polish in a suitable colour. (Choose the tinned rather than tubed versions.) However, these products are not suitable for upholstery because the colour may come off on clothes. Alternatively, you could use a natural shoe polish.

UPHOLSTERY AND SOFT FURNISHINGS

UPHOLSTERY

My new friend the steam cleaner (see page 116), with a little added detergent (1001 Shampoo) does a pretty good job on upholstery, though you will need to back this up by rubbing the damp surfaces with an old towel. This is particularly fun with a white towel as you witness the dirt coming off. As ever, doing this on a regular basis (perhaps every month or so) is MUCH more effective than waiting until it all gets thoroughly dirty and discoloured.

Lacking a steam cleaner, use a carpet/upholstery shampoo such as 1001: whisk to a foam, work into the surface and rub hard with clean towel. Try not to get it too wet. Repeat if necessary. It is mostly greasiness you are attacking, because grease (from our skin, clothes, etc) attracts dust and dirt and leads to that manky, dingy appearance.

For stain removal see pages 192–200.

Cushion covers

Every now and then, I dunk removable cushion covers in the wash (coolest setting and a little biological liquid) replacing them when just damp in order to counteract shrinkage. The problem is that the cushion covers get lighter while the close covering goes darker – notwithstanding shampoo and steam cleaning. When this gets too noticeable, I resort to 'throws' and alternative cushions. Nothing lasts forever.

CURTAINS AND BLINDS

Filmy, unlined curtains, which have been so popular of late – cotton, linen and muslin – should be as washable as your clothes, but do check the instruction label first and accept that they may shrink slightly. Use the cool setting on your washing machine and hang them out smoothed, stretched and as flat as possible.

A light starching (see page 179) will put some life back into fabrics that go limp and sad. Ironing whilst damp can mitigate shrinkage to a certain extent.

Curtains of cotton, chintz, etc, lined but not interlined, should also be washable (as above), but the lining may shrink differently from the curtain fabric. Chintz will lose its glazed finish over time, however starching will also help out here. Opt for dry cleaning if you have any doubt.

Interlined curtains (in any fabric) must be dry cleaned.

Scotchguard™

My sister swears by Scotchgard for upholstery and carpets in her holiday cottages, where soft furnishings take a beating. She has it done professionally, which costs, but she claims the process offers worthwhile protection and keeps immovable, expensive items like pile carpet and upholstery fabrics in better shape for considerably longer. Scotchgard is also sold for DIY use as a spray and could be a sensible treatment for prized items.

Blinds

Slatted blinds of wood, plastic and metal are traditionally cleaned by wiping with damp household (fabric) gloves; running your gloved fingers between the slats. This sounds fine, but the cords and webbing get filthy. Where possible (not with wooden slats) detach the blinds and soak them in a warm bath for a while, using a sponge or brush to get them really clean. Finally, rinse and hang up to dry. Use the glove treatment (or a sponge) on wooden slats. Otherwise vacuum the blind at the cleaner's lowest (curtain/upholstery) setting.

Roman blinds can be taken down and washed in the same way – though only if both the fabric and the lining have been reliably pre-shrunk.

Roller blinds that are plasticised are best cleaned in situ, wiped over and rinsed using a sponge or cloth. Fabric roller blinds can be detached and soaked in the bath – as long as their roller is wood, not a cardboard tube – then rinsed and dried. However, they may shrink. Pressing them damp should help snap them back into shape. Try to avoid getting any metal parts wet in case they go rusty. Dry these carefully before replacing.

CLEANING FLOORS

CARPET

See Spring Clean, Deep Clean, page 119. For stain removal see page 192.

MATTING

See Spring Clean, Deep Clean, page 119.

WOOD

See Spring Clean, Deep Clean, page 119.

LINO, RUBBER AND VINYL

Regular mopping with warm water and a spot of household detergent such as Flash has to be the quickest way to get these floor surfaces clean. Here, the squeegee-type mop makes sense. Get the posher version with a thicker pad of sponge and a lever-operated self-squeezing action.

All of these flooring types will deteriorate over time. As they get scratched, cleaning gets more difficult and dirt gets trodden in. Rubber industrial-type flooring and lino tend to stand up best. Lino gets a nice shine if you go over it with a liquid floor polish. I think this makes sense in a living room, but not in a heavy-use area like a kitchen, because to clean lino thoroughly means removing the polish – requiring yet another cleaning product and more effort. Rubber flooring really doesn't need polishing.

TILES

Glazed tiles are a cinch to clean: mop over with your usual household detergent/water solution and a squeegee mop. Rinse well.

Unglazed tiles, quarry tiles and slate tiles, being porous, collect more stubborn stains, as do brick floors. Sorry to say this, but a good scrub, on your knees, using a scrubbing brush and a stronger solution is the most effective treatment here. Use soap pads to get at really tough stains. Oil and fat are the chief culprits. Rinse twice with clean water and a squeegee, to clear the slurry completely. Let dry, then apply HG Impregnator with a brush, spray, or lint-free cloth. Let dry two hours. This sealant dries matt and barely affects the tile colour. Another coat may be needed if your flooring is extra porous as in unglazed terracotta (or my low-fired bricks). Let dry – or harden – as before. Lotsa work, I have to say, but it will protect against further staining for some time.

If you prefer a shinier finish, and don't mind deepening the colour, use instead HG Golvpolish, which is self-shining but non-slip. On porous tiles, use Impregnator first. If your preliminary scrub with detergent solution doesn't quite hit the mark, another HG product, HG Remove claims to 'deep clean' grease, etc, off old tiles. With all these products, read instructions carefully first, and follow them to the letter.

NOTE: a thought for those wary of HG's hydrocarbons and polymers. Friends of mine used isinglass (once sold for preserving eggs) to seal their quarry tiles and stone flags, with good results. As skilled potters I felt they had a handle on such matters. Worth a try if you can track down isinglass. Like the HG products, it sealed porous flooring, repelled stains, did not alter the colour and, knowing them, cost next to nothing, as well as being quite free of chemicals.

Many hands, etc

My sister employs a dozen cleaners to give 11 holiday cottages a thorough going over once a week and the system runs with military efficiency. Cleaners arrive; a van drives up loaded with big plastic holdalls (like elongated buckets), one to each cleaner, packed with all the cleaning materials and tools they will need. Granted, this is a different procedure from the clean up for a small family, but the well-stocked receptacle – it must have a handle – is an idea we can all copy.

WINDOW CLEANING

My editor, who lives in Brighton, insists that finding window cleaners is no problem in her neck of the woods: the streets are full of them. the Yellow Pages have plenty of names, and she can get most of her windows cleaned for a fiver. Good news if you live outside London.

My experience, living a step from the City, has been quite different. Maybe it's the Georgian sashes (17 of them), the height of the top floor, or the competition from glass and steel office blocks, but any time I have chatted up a guy on a ladder, he has shown up once, or not shown up at all, or charged £30, or refused to go up more than two floors despite cups of tea and sympathy. Moreover, one or two looked distinctly villainous, even by East End standards, and I say that as one who laid floors alongside an ex-con who spent 14 years inside, mostly for GBH.

It seemed easier, and felt better – if not safer – to learn to clean windows myself. I had done it before, amateurishly and on a small scale (ground-floor sashes) but I can now zip round on an extension ladder, apron pockets stuffed with sponge, squeegee and polishing cloths, and do a pretty competent job.

If you can secure a trustworthy window cleaner at a knock-down rate, go ahead.

Otherwise you could follow my lead, and Do It Yourself. But, obviously, go carefully. I can take second-floor windows, but top-floor windows I clean from inside, standing on the windowsill and trying not to look down.

You will need:

A sturdy but light aluminium extension ladder that locks into place, extended (see below for safety tips)

Washing-up liquid and ammonia, for inside. (Spray window cleaners leave a dirt-attracting film.)

Small plastic pail (paint kettle) for cleaning liquid

S-shaped hook

Apron with pockets

Clean decorator's sponge (see page 117)

Squeegee proportioned to the window panes: a small job for segmented panes, larger for picture windows

Clean, dry polishing cloth, chamois or linen scrim (see page 118)

Rag: dirty cleaning water dribbles on to the windows' glazing bars, so a separate cloth is needed to wipe this off.

The Method

(Well, my method...Experts may sneer, but it works.)

- Position the ladder. Make sure its feet are standing on a level surface with no wobble. Stand it approx. 60cm (2ft) from the wall at base for first-floor windows; this is safer than bringing it up really close. When in doubt, get someone to hold the bottom of the ladder. Psychologically this feels safer.

- Hook the small plastic pail with cleaning liquid to your ladder. Dip the sponge in, squeeze out surplus liquid, then wipe over, say, four panes, or a large square to soften the grots.

- Use the squeegee to clear glass, working from the top down in light, overlapping strokes. If you press too hard the rubber leaves skid marks. Experts use a nifty up-across-down movement, neat and speedy, but this takes much practice. The squeegee is brilliant, but needs wiping off on a cloth between goes.

- Use a rag to wipe off the woodwork. Then use a polishing cloth, chamois, etc, to polish off streaks and smears.

- Carry on over the other panes, or section of picture window. This takes less time than you might suppose, and clean, limpid glass gives a lift to the spirits, I promise.

Getting outside panes clean and sparkling immediately shows up inside smuts and smears. Here you are on home ground, using a low step-ladder. Otherwise, use the same equipment, except a little ammonia in your cleaning water is a help.

I don't attempt to clean all my windows, outside and inside, consecutively – maybe one floor one day, the next a day or so later. Once you appreciate the difference cleaning makes, you won't be tempted to skive off anyway.

Don't skimp on the polishing bit, though; glass needs it. Once your windows are immaculate, the next clean goes faster.

NOTE: wash cloths, rags, chamois, etc, after use. Try to keep them for this job only. Any oil, wax or grease on them means you put as much gunk on as you take off.

Last word: by all means try pads of newspaper if you like the idea of recycling. I ended up with damp paper everywhere; a cloth seemed more efficient.

It takes a fair bit of hand rubbing to get windows crystalline, free of smears and streaks. But each time you clean it again, it comes good more quickly.

KITCHEN CLEANING

WASHING UP

For some reason, washing up has come to typify the unacceptable face of housework; the Sisyphean task no sooner completed than round it comes again. thus chaining the unhappy drudge to the kitchen sink when he/she could be curled up reading *War and Peace*.

Well, that was before the advent of the dishwasher, now so high on the domestic wish list. It seems everyone has one – except me. I know it may sound barmy, but I don't want a dishwasher. I actually enjoy washing up! I relish the simple satisfaction of making dirty things clean again. It helps me get my head together in the morning as this is when I prefer to shift the supper things from the night before. I have also tackled the debris of a riotous dinner party single-handedly during the small hours. The Sisyphus factor doesn't bother me. The way I look at it, lots of necessary actions are repetitive – brushing one's teeth for instance.

The wooden tables were scoured white as bone, scrubbed along the grain with sharp river sand and whitening. The wide range shone like satin; the steel fender and stands were rubbed bright with emery cloth. In the wintry sunshine brass pans and silver dish covers glittered on the cream plaster walls.

Food in England, Dorothy Hartley, (Macdonalds, 1954; Little, Brown & Co, 1996, 1999)

Anyway, there isn't space in my kitchen for a dishwasher.

Apparently, D H Lawrence enjoyed washing up. I suspect he may have found it a refuge from the overwhelming Frieda. The latter, a Prussian aristocrat, probably found this daily ritual demeaning and broke things! Lawrence, a genius, was secure enough to find pleasure in performing pedestrian tasks without feeling a wimp. I am sure he went about the job with methodical care, repeating a sequence he must have watched his mother performing endlessly in that little mining village in Nottinghamshire. There is a charm in doing undemanding tasks with your hands which allows your mind to roam free or float off into a quiet reverie.

But if you thought washing up was a straightforward project, you could be unpleasantly surprised. Over and above my own children, a crowd of foreign au pairs and helpers have passed through my kitchen over the years. Although I have talked through the process of washing up with all these characters it seems to have gone in one ear and out the other.

There was Radka, the dreamy Slovakian flautist, whose take on the process was to pile everything into the sink – plates, pots and pans, with a squeeze of detergent – which she then stirred absent-mindedly with the brush. Austrian Eva washed each item individually under a running hot tap. This not only took hours but emptied the tank of hot water. Spanish Angie (see page 26) dashed at everything with the same green pot scourer, scorning my battery of brushes. When I tried to insist that she used the brush she erupted, 'In my village we always use the pad!' and I was forced to acknowledge that a green scouring pad can be as much of a patriotic icon as the national flag.

I should also mention my partner's odd habit of stacking washed wet plates on top of each other, face up, so they chill out as a cold water sandwich. This is an architect. Moreover, he had the gall to query my authority in the matter. This is something like a rookie cheeking a battle-scarred war veteran. You could say I won that round, but it was a pyrrhic victory since he now confines his washing up to the plastic fruit juicer.

What remains with me is the discovery that attitudes towards washing up differ as sharply as our varying notions of what constitutes a decent breakfast. Are you a toast and marmalade or pickled herrings and slice of cheese fan? Early habits die hard.

> Show me one house-husband, she thought, who rinses out milk bottles or makes tea in a pot or does any of those thousand and one small light tasks that drives you nuts, like cleaning the rubbish bin, boiling the flannels, wiping sticky door handles which no one ever notices unless you stop doing them.
>
> *Mrs Fytton's Country Life*, Mavis Cheek (Faber & Faber, 2000)

The Routine

The logic behind the process of washing up is that one moves from relatively clean items (glasses and cups) through to greasy pots and pans. It makes sense to line up items on the right side (left if you are left-handed) of the sink in order of relative dirt levels. The rationale behind this is that the cleanest items are washed in the fresh water whilst the gungiest finish up being scrubbed down in the more heavily soiled water. If you have washed a big stack of plates and side plates, you can always empty and re-fill the sink before moving on.

This immemorial routine was founded on the basis of a limited supply of hot water. Wasting hot water on washing up meant cold or tepid baths later in the day.

A second sink for rinsing is a bonus if you are extra scrupulous about lingering traces of detergent on glass and crocks. All you need now is lashings of water as hot as you can tolerate through your gloves, a decent new brush and a squidge of washing-up liquid.

Stuck yuk

- Fill really gungy pots, casseroles and roasting tins with water and leave to soak while you deal with the rest of the washing up. A few soda crystals often help by softening the water and loosening stuck-on food.
- Scrape any loose debris off plates, pots and pans into the bin using a wooden spoon, plastic spatula or your gloved hands.

Washing glass

My only regret about not owning a dishwasher is the way it leaves drinking glasses sparkling clean. The challenge was to find a self-regulating method which would give the required results with minimum handling. I sped through my household manuals. They all advocated washing glasses in hot water with a dash of washing-up liquid followed by polishing them with a clean cloth.

But the polishing with a soft cloth is just what I was trying to avoid, I thought irritably. Still, I picked up a few tips, which sounded promising. For extra brilliance try a splash of ammonia, or a sprinkle of soda crystals in the washing water? A splash of vinegar in the rinse water? Then I remembered my father telling me that the way to get glasses bright and non-smeary was to wash them in hot water with a soupçon of detergent using a soft bottle brush to reach inside, then dunk them in cold water and leave to dry. He claimed this was the method favoured by butlers in the days when they had pantries fitted with butler's sinks to care for the family's superior glassware.

Naturally, I dismissed this wisdom as old-fashioned tosh now superseded, like butlers themselves. I lined up a set of matching, narrow tumblers on my right-hand teak draining board, filled my sink with hot water plus the merest squeeze of detergent and proceeded with my research. I forgot to mention that a diminutive ceramic sink sits next to the capacious butler's sink – a recent installation, which I mostly use for crisping salad greens and cleaning vegetables, but also, in this case, for rinsing glasses.

'Housewife's' dermatitis

This is a dermatologist's term for skin problems associated with housework. They usually appear on the hands and wrists – usually consisting of redness, swelling, itchiness. They may be caused by over exposure to cleaning products and/or a sudden reaction, or allergy, to – for instance – rubber household gloves.

My own case began with itchy red patches between my fingers on my right hand. I treated them with zinc and castor oil cream, as for nappy rash, and they subsided, vanished in a few days, only to reappear again a few months later – at which point I consulted a dermatologist. He told me the problem is quite common. It often occurs in the first few months after childbirth, because women begin using sterilising or bleaching products far more than previously.

Zinc and castor oil ointment met with his approval, as a healing measure, but in stubborn cases he prescribes stronger formulations, such as Eumovate, which can be bought over the counter, or a range of ointments that are only obtainable on prescription.

Where an allergic reaction seems to be the cause, he also recommends some protective measures, starting with swapping rubber gloves for plastic ones. At the same time he suggests avoiding contact with some products with a history of causing allergic, or eczematous skin reactions. It is quite a long list, including shampoo, hair dye, various polishes, white spirit, washing-up liquid and other detergents. You should also wear gloves when preparing citrus fruit, garlic and onions. All of which is a big hassle – try peeling garlic cloves in gloves. Trying to identify the culprit in this list is, he explains, a lengthy and tedious and – if you go private – expensive business, involving skin patches, repeated visits. You would probably go for it in severe cases . Otherwise the moral seems to be to wear plastic – PVC – gloves during all cleaning operations, and apply whatever cream or ointment your doctor recommends.

The PVC gloves he recommends are called Nitrile, made by Kimberley Clarke in Belgium. These are issued to hospital staff, by the box. They are a fetching lilac colour, and not expensive. Otherwise – more of a bore – wear cotton gloves inside large-size rubber household gloves.

I began with standard practice, washing a tumbler in hot water plus detergent, rinsing in hot water and upending the glass on my left-hand teak drainer. Next, I added a sprinkle of soda crystals to the washing water, washed a tumbler with bottle brush, rinsed briefly and upended same on the drainer.

Result in both cases? Glasses dried off speedily outside, but pockets of steam appeared inside. When I shifted them to release the trapped steam, water trickled out. The steam evaporated rapidly now, but oh dear!, these streaky, clouded tumblers would never pass the butler test, never mind mine. My fingers itched to snatch up a clean, dry, lint-free glass cloth, but if you recall, 'hand polishing is just what we are trying to avoid'. I reasoned this was due to the lime content of my London water supply (see page 275).

The moment had come to add vinegar to the rinse water, drawing on a confused recollection that vinegar is alkaline, or was it hard water which is alkaline? Anyway, it was a popular tip with my manuals and marched with childhood memories of adding vinegar to the final rinse after hair washing to clear away any lingering traces of shampoo – or was it soap we used then? I tried the vinegar tip and it also failed the butler test. Squinting at my glasses from different angles against the light, I concluded that there was a modest improvement: smears as before but fewer whitish deposits resembling toothpaste.

Finally, I tested my father's tip, washing in the butler's sink, dunking briefly in cold water, and upending on the drainer. Guess what? A 95 per cent success rate: a clean, bright, non-smeary tumbler with the merest hint of clouding near the rim as the water ran off. I repeated the hot/cold treatment, this time leaving the glass the right way up and this was the clincher. It took longer to dry naturally, being cold, but came closest to giving clear, bright glass without manual assistance. Dad, I take it all back, you were right to trust those Jeeves types with their centuries of experience.

USING A DISHWASHER

Not having a dishwasher myself, though I have loaded up a few, I called up the ever helpful John Lewis customer service line and was put on to Robbie Turner, who not only knows his machines backwards but, like all his colleagues, is both friendly and enthusiastic without sliding into a sales spiel.

It used to matter how you loaded up your dishwasher a few years ago because the older models (three to four years back) needed the lighter, cleaner stuff (glasses, cups, side plates) stacked up top, with the dirtier plates and serving dishes stacked below, so the water jets could operate most powerfully where they were most needed. If your dishwasher belongs to this category, this is still the way to go. The newer models are equipped with sensors. These automatically adjust the wash process to the size of your load. Also, the water is recirculated – as in a water feature, Robbie explained, thus using less water, and less energy, which is both more economical and eco-friendlier. This does mean that you need to clear out the filter often, because more food debris will be accumulating in there.

Robbie advises alternating powder and liquid cleaners because the powder performs a mildly scouring action, ridding the tub of any sticky gloop left by the liquid. At longer intervals, try the citric acid tip suggested by Ann French (see page 113) for a thorough clean out of lime-scale deposits.

The quickest solution for what Robbie calls 'heavy soil', is to wash the stuff by hand. Alternatively, soak in warm water with a spoonful of washing soda, scrape and then add to your dishwasher load.

Dishwashers make sense in large families, or for couples who entertain regularly. But they may not be the best option. They take up space, require a panoply of extra products and are not as eco-friendly as your two hands and a sink.

SINKS

Stainless steel sinks are easy to clean with a quick wipe of Cif and a sponge. A polish with stainless steel reviver pretties it up, though only until you next use it.

Fashionable white ceramic sinks, modelled on the old butlers' sinks, are more of a hassle. Over time, the gleaming surface chips and gets discoloured. Any scouring/bleaching agent – Cif, Vim or Barkeeper's Friend – will restore whiteness. Rub on, leave for a minute or two and then rinse. Once in a while, fill the sink up with cold water, add a spoonful of domestic bleach and leave to soak. After this procedure your sink will once again be spotless. For a while.

More important – and this applies to both steel and ceramic sinks – is to zap the outlets and overflow with caustic soda to clear any grease or tea leaves, thus forestalling blockages and destroying any lurking bacteria. I use caustic soda in crystal form and tip a little into the plughole and overflow, then follow up by sluicing with a kettleful of boiling water.

Ensure that you stand well back from the subsequent hissing and bubbling noise as the fierce mixture gets to work. Once this subsides – usually a couple of minutes – it all looks and smells a lot more hygienic. This does it for me as I don't believe in anti-bacterial sprays. Regular caustic treatment can save plumbers' bills.

HOBS

It really is no big deal to wipe down the hob – gas or electric – after every use, and ceramic

Sterilising by scalding

The World Health Organisation hygiene manual – aimed at caterers and other food professionals – contains one nugget of value to all and any of us; namely that 'scalding' is still the most effective and cheapest method of sterilising many – not all – surfaces that come into contact with food preparation or disposal.

This means using boiling water, straight from kettle, to sluice down sinks, overflows, waste masters, draining and chopping boards, etc. This need not be a daily operation in a domestic situation. However, once or twice weekly, get the kettle on the go and pour the contents down the sink, the overflow (these are hot spots for bacterial activity) and your chopping boards.

This simple expedient ties up nicely with the ancient practice of scalding tubs, churns and dairy or kitchen equipment before leaving them outside to air and dry in sunshine or a cold north wind. This process feels so instinctively correct that I don't marvel that our forebears made it good, regular practice long before anyone knew about salmonella or listeria. Furthermore, it helps to keep pipes clear and nasty smells at bay.

hobs positively invite this little attention.

Use your chosen wipe, and a little water with detergent, plus maybe a touch of ammonia or soda crystals to cut the grease. Every week or two, remove any detachable bits, dunk in hot water and use a soap pad to clear grease, etc.

If/when this proves stubborn, use one of the caustic products suggested for ovens, but do this outside, laying them on newspaper, and repeat till clean. Soap pads are helpful, although they tend to scratch a bright chromed or stainless steel surface.

GAS AND ELECTRIC OVENS

The best time to clean your oven is soon after use, when cooking warmth and moisture has helped soften any grease, splashes and other fallout. (Gas burners actually create moisture along with the heat, which makes them marginally easier to clean than their electric counterparts.) At this optimal moment, it only takes a few minutes to whisk around the oven surfaces with a wipe wrung out with hot water with a small squeeze of detergent. Scraping and/or a soap pad can clear tougher deposits. Racks,

Anti-splatter device

Shopping in an Italian supermarket, I lit upon an anti-splatter ring. This looks roughly like a ping-pong bat with fine steel gauze filling a wire ring. My daughter tells me they are available in the UK, so if you see one, buy it! They are cheap, and very useful laid over a frying pan or a pot of cooking jam as they catch any splattering, thus reducing clean-up time as well as the risk of burns. Furthermore, it seems to me that they step up the heat and help to distribute it more evenly, so a fried egg, for instance, cooks both sides at once. My kitchen is full of cute gadgets, which I rarely use – wire whisks and nutmeg graters – but this gizmo has been in constant use since I discovered it.

trays, etc, are more conveniently dealt with in the sink using soap pads. This is a counsel of perfection. If you are dropping with weariness after a long, gruelling day that has ended with a cook-up, you may not be in the mood to tackle the oven there and then. A regular once over is a good move (an accumulation of gunge gets tougher to remove every time you switch on as it bakes hard) but you should be able to catch up before it gets out of hand.

There is another line of attack if you have let your oven become seriously encrusted. Heavy-duty oven cleaners – spray or pads – will help shift the crud; not all at once, but with repeated applications. The snag with these is that they all rely on caustic agents (in varying degrees of intensity) and all of these pack a nasty wallop when inhaled. Therefore,

it is wise to wear a face mask, keep the room well aired and stand back as you work. The spray types (which deposit a fine white foam that fizzes as it gets to work) are easier to use, but they are less powerful and require more repeat performances. The little three-cornered pack (faced with a sponge you perforate with the pin provided) seems to cut in deeper, but the fumes are much more acrid. I suggest that you always begin this operation by scraping away the hardened gunge with a metal spatula or, in desperate cases, a blunt chisel. The more gunk you can detach by scraping clearly removes the need for too many repeat applications. Remove any racks, trays, etc, and deal with these separately outside. Chuck your sponge, dishcloth or other wipe at the end of this foray: the caustic will have made it useless.

Why bother? A gunky, greasy oven is depressing, unaesthetic and the smell of old cooked-on food may not improve your cakes, custards or roasts.

Moral: little and often is better than an annual overhaul.

MICROWAVES

Over to Robbie again here (see page 141), because neither do I own a microwave. These are simplicity itself to clean, he says. Take out the circular plate and wash it in the sink, brushing to remove any food deposits. Wipe round the inside with a damp cloth with a spot of washing-up liquid. This can be done at any time in the standard microwave. In the microwave-cum-oven, it is best done while the machine is still warm, after use.

AGA/RAYBURN/ESSE OR OTHER

Cast-iron cookers, aka 'country ranges', have been an object of desire in well-appointed kitchens since the 1920s when a Swedish physicist, Dr Gustave Dalen, invented the Aga, the first heat-storage cooker: an appliance designed to encompass every cooking method in one compact, well-insulated, massively solid cast-iron box. An Aga costs almost as much as a small runabout car and weighs not much less.

The Aga breakthrough was followed by other marques: Rayburn, Esse, etc. These were smaller and cheaper but less well insulated. So while they were a tad less reliable on the cooking front they kept the kitchen warm as toast.

My own Aga experience (pace Dr Dalen) is that it performs splendidly in all but for cooking methods requiring intense flash heat such as grilling and stir-frying. A two-ring gas hob is thus a useful supplement.

The first cast-iron cookers were run on solid fuel: coke, anthracite and even wood. I once dined in a kitchen whose Aga was consuming the spoil of a huge cedar, and the balsamic glory of the experience remains with me, although I have forgotten what we ate.

My first two cast-iron cookers were Rayburns, old but reconditioned models, run on solid fuel. These required frequent feeds of 'nuts', regular riddling and ash clearance, plus extra stoking if a dinner party was planned. All this created a delicate fallout over all kitchen surfaces. So I joyfully upgraded to a gas-fired Aga in due course. I am devoted to my Aga, along with some half a million other people in the UK, but all things being equal, I sometimes feel nostalgic about the blazing presence of solid fuel, the little fire roaring away in his box lined with firebricks.

Cleaning the Aga

Not much can go wrong with an Aga: no pilot flame to get clogged or gas jets to get bunged up or wiring to go wrong. As Aga's literature proudly points out, the ovens are self-cleaning: that is, the constant heat burns off food residues so you may only need to brush them out occasionally to make sure the vent between the upper and lower ovens is not blocked. Fussy types might feel compelled to go over the slide-in shelves with a soap pad now and then, but this is for looks rather than a necessity. (Note: could Aga not re-design these shelves so that they slide in and out more easily? Even wearing elbow-length oven gloves, the fight to extricate a shelf laden with heavy iron cookware is liable to spot one's arms with little burns that are the honourable scars of Aga ownership.)

While the ovens more or less take care of themselves, the top surface picks up a lot of fallout: grease and hardened deposits from pans that have boiled over. Wiping over the enamelled surfaces daily with a sponge cloth makes them look tidy, but does not really cut through this cooked-on gunk, which finally has to be dealt with much more radically.

The mildly abrasive cleaning paste (containing silica flour) recommended by Aga (trade name Astonish) is fine for cleaning up the front surfaces of the cooker, but useless at cutting through the cooked-on deposits on top. Heavy-duty oven cleaners (a thick gloop containing caustic) which were effective seem to have been phased out in favour of spray cleaners such as Big D, which covers the surface with white foam. When you wipe the foam off some of the gunk comes off, but only what I would describe as loose grease, not the hard deposits. Successive applications of foam might get there in the end but the stuff has a faintly nauseous smell which catches the back of one's throat.

I use an assortment of tools instead, such as old chisels and paint scrapers. Once the blade has got purchase, scraping through the rest of the gunk is quite easy. One needs to avoid cutting into the enamel itself – so go carefully. But Aga surfaces pick up fine scratches: inevitable marks of wear and tear.

Aga servicing

If you live in favoured parts of the UK (such as Norfolk) you may be lucky enough to find a 'service engineer' whose ritual includes cleaning as well as servicing the cooker – doors, hotplates, hotplate covers, rings and basically the lot. A Norfolk owner I discussed Aga with was more than happy with her servicing arrangement, which lasted a morning and left her Aga immaculate, in good running order and cost less than mine. My 'engineer' spent all of 45 minutes on a very basic maintenance, brushing out the ovens and investigating below the enamelled top, where he found and cleared away quantities of dark soot. When he handed me the duplicate forms to sign, I was all astonishment: 'But what about cleaning it?' 'Sorry, Madam, we don't clean the cooker, we just make sure it is working properly. We are engineers not cleaners.' Or words to that effect. It was the sort of put-down you might expect from an orthopaedic consultant if you showed him an incipient bunion.

OK, I got stuck in with the soap pads and my scraper, and got the cooker looking quite shiny and dapper. However, it wasn't just the aesthetic side that bothered me. On my Aga, the steel rings (or maybe cast iron) that surround the hotplates are so heavily encrusted with accumulated deposits of this and that, that any fool can see that the covers no longer fit tightly and hence that the famous insulation which makes the Aga superior to the Rayburn was somewhat defective. My 'engineer', pawing the ground in his impatience to be off, had no solution to this other than to suggest I rang head office. When I rang head office they referred me back to the engineer!

I am fine when it comes to cleaning surfaces I know about, such as vitreous enamel. However, when it comes to great metal rings all bumpy with 'stuff', I am at a loss. Do you take a blowtorch to it, dunk it in a bucket of caustic or what? Or, maybe just order two brand new rings from head office plus another visit from the 'engineer' to fit them? I regret to say at this point I lost the plot, threw in the soap pads and gave up.

The rings look considerably bumpier, the insulation is presumably more defective still, but I have lost faith in the Aga servicing programme for East London, and I don't love my Aga enough to consider moving to Norfolk! I am told that East Sussex is also a good area in which to keep your Aga in perfect condition.

It is ironic that the brainchild of a Nobel Prize-winning Swedish architect should fetch up at the mercy of local 'engineers' and their time sheets. The real irony is that an Aga is such a simple concept and put together in such a straightforward fashion, that engineering skill should hardly come into it. What I am seeking is a trusty mechanic who doesn't mind getting a bit mucky along the way, but who takes pride in regulating and sprucing up our behemoth of a cooker. Considering an Aga, even a two-oven job like mine, costs, as said before, more than a second-hand car, the analogy seems appropriate. Now that Aga is making a sales drive in Central London, maybe they will.

I have also come across the waggish name of Aga Khan, of whom I hear good reports in the servicing/cleaning line, but he is based in Somerset; a longish haul to London.

The DIY clean-up

Forget this if you have an ace 'engineer' in your locality. If not, these simple prescriptions may be of help:

- First, switch off the heat source (gas, electricity, etc) or let a solid fuel model go out. Allow overnight for this (best done during the summer when the famous 'welcoming warmth' might be a bit much).

- Lift off the doors (surprisingly simple) and cart them outside. Ditto the removable collar at the base of your chimney pipe. Ditto also the hotplate covers, held in place by a steel rod which can be gently hammered out with a Pozidrive screwdriver and a hammer. Lay these outside on newspaper.

- Using a strong chisel or screwdriver, lever out the hotplates and rings. Transport these outside also. This allows you to access the dark underbelly of your Aga and the above-mentioned deposits of sooty material. You should just brush the latter carefully into a tiny dustpan or get rid of it with a vacuum cleaner.

- A clever-clogs might see how to do a chimney-sweep number on the pipe, but this is beyond me. Banging it gently will dislodge a fair bit of loose stuff, so have newspapers to hand in order to catch it.

This seems to me as far as DIY intervention should go in dismantling prior to cleaning. Further than, I might add, my laggard 'engineer'.

- The underside of hotplate covers (the 'simmering' one especially, not so hot that the gunk gets burnt off) look better – ie, bright and shiny – for a good clean. A spray oven cleaner is helpful on the simmering plate cover, as this is the one that gets really greasy and darkened. Spray out of doors with oven cleaner where possible. Wipe off, then use a wet soap pad to gently scour clean.

- A stainless-steel cleaner does a nice brightening job on the top side of the hotplate covers, which you can buff to a gleam. OK, this won't last beyond a few cook outs but it is good for the soul, like treating your car to a valeting.

- Oven doors, enamel outside, shiny metal inside, need a gentle go with Astonish, followed by an even gentler go with soap pads to get the enamel exterior bright as new. Pay special attention to the hinges as these attract more old gunk.

- The inside ovens only need brushing out.

- The collar (base of chimney) can be sprayed and soap-padded till it comes clean. Clean round the edges too.

- Hotplates need wire brushing regularly to stop build-up.

KEEPING COOL: YOUR FRIDGE

To do its job properly – keeping a wide range of foodstuffs in optimum condition – a fridge should be kept at a temperature between 0 and 5°C. The only reliable gauge of this is a fridge thermometer: available in any hardware store.

Next, you need to check which bit of your fridge is coldest. In my larder-type fridge (and indeed, in all but an ice-box fridge) this is just above the salad bins. This makes sense if you think about it because – and this may seem odd in connection with refrigerators – warm air rises. Every time you open the fridge door, or pop in a few more items at room temperature, the warmer the air inside gets.

The coldest part is where you should keep the most perishable foods: meat, fish and shellfish. This also removes the likelihood of raw meat or fish dripping on to cooked foods which, as you will remember, is the cardinal sin of food hygiene. The 'cool' zones – top shelves – are where you keep foods best kept cool in order to stay fresh for longer. The warmest zone is the salad bin.

Cleaning the fridge

Obviously the smart time to clean your fridge is the day before the weekly shop, as Polly Hope does (see page 100). As well as making it clean and ready for the new influx, it allows you to check on what is overstocked, past its sell-by date or running low. Polly does her shop on Thursday, to avoid the weekend rush. For most of us it is probably Saturday, so the fridge clean should happen on Friday.

I don't think there is any mystery about cleaning a fridge, but it should go further than a quick wipe over the shelves with a damp sponge cloth. Shelves get sticky, or stuff gets caked on. Quicker to whip out all the movable parts – one by one to avoid taking *everything* out – and stand them in a sink filled with water and a dash of bleach, then sponge or brush them clean on both sides. While a shelf is out give the adjacent fridge lining a thorough wipe too, including the back. Dry the shelf with a clean tea towel and replace, along with its contents.

I used to be selective about sell-by dates, judging by a quick sniff of the contents rather than the printed dates, and I might still cheat in the case of crème fraiche, live yoghurt or soft cheeses. Obviously slimy packed salads or squashy tomatoes get binned. The weekly clean out is a bit of an incentive – and challenge – to think of a way of using up what is left *before* your weekly shop. A big salad niçoise, ratatouille or its Basque cousin, *piperade*, or crostini spread with all those pastes and pâtés. My children tell me – *now* they tell me! – they always had a soft spot for my leftover meals. Call it the Friday-night buffet, let them range freely and mark what they eat and what they don't. This could influence your Saturday shop?

THE HYGIENE HYPOTHESIS

This is the name given (by the media) to one of the more controversial issues to surface around the subject of home hygiene. The hypothesis suggests that an important factor in the steady rise of allergies amongst young children in recent years could be that our homes have become too sterile. This may be due to an overzealous use of anti-bacterial products.

A child develops immunity or resistance to bacteria and microbes through exposure to them in what might be called normal domestic circumstances. This gradual process of acculturation is interfered with where kitchens and bathrooms aspire to operating-theatre sterility. In other words, by constantly spraying kitchen and bathroom surfaces in the name of hygiene you may be doing your children more harm than good.

A hypothesis is just an informed guess – but the correlation between increasing sales of anti-bacterial products and the growing incidence of childhood allergies does seem suggestive. The solution is simple: drop these sprays from your shopping list!

However, this is not to endorse a 'Slut's Charter'. While it reinforces traditional wisdom about not mollycoddling children, the fact remains that there is some new thinking about home hygiene and some of the recommended precautions are both unexpected and convincing.

Bug hunting

For instance, when did you last take a hard long look at your tin opener? If you use it constantly to open cans of peeled tomatoes, pet food, tuna, etc, and it is one of those models that operate via two cutting wheels and a butterfly-shaped handle on the side, you will almost certainly find old hard food deposits gunging up the works. You would probably get a nasty shock if this were placed under a microscope.

The problem is these improved tin openers are much harder to clean than the old manually operated ones where you punch the can lid with the pointy bit and then lever away around the rim. To clean the newer models requires careful scrubbing with an old toothbrush in hot water with a dash of detergent and washing soda. Tough cases may even need previous soaking. You may not need to do this every time you open a can, but it should come high on your agenda of troublespots in the kitchen.

Food processors are another problem area where old food can build up in cracks and crevices. According to Maggie Duke, a hygienist who travels all over the world advising on food hygiene, nasties often lurk in kitchen gadgetry that could become a source of infection. She approves of all-metal spatulas and wooden spoons, but don't use the latter once they have developed cracks or the surface is rough and whiskery. Metal slices and spatulas with wooden handles need careful cleaning around the joint between the metal and wood which is another possible trouble spot.

Food and the fridge

One of Maggie's main concerns is the domestic fridge. The chief culprit in her book is raw meat, which should never be stored where the juices can drip on to either cooked meats or salad vegetables.

Maggie's remit as hygiene advisor is largely in catering, dealing with the problems that arise where food is being produced in large quantities for the public. She mentioned a recent trip to Cyprus where she was advising and monitoring an initiative to put local Cypriot dishes back on the tourist map. A famous speciality of traditional home cooking is the 'green pie' (not unlike the Greek *spanakopitta*), which makes use of wild seasonal leaves and is cooked in a wrapper of filo pastry. Cooked for the family only, the preparation of this dish presented no hygiene problems.

However, once expanded into restaurant-scale production, the picture gets complex and more dodgy. An outworker might not have a fridge large enough to keep the pies chilled; hence the natural bacteria present on the wild greens might have time to multiply. The poor outworker, who has cooked these pies proudly for the family for

years, has never had to think about public health hygiene rules (wash your hands, scrub utensils and surfaces daily, keep animals out of the kitchen etc). As a result, Maggie's basic training requires tact and close observation of every stage along the production line.

You are probably wondering what relevance Cypriot restaurant dishes have to a UK situation. Have you got a summer buffet party coming up? Maggie describes these as a likely trouble zone. For instance, pre-cooked dishes doused in mayonnaise, that don't fit into your fridge, may warm up. Mayonnaise provides an ideal culture for any bacteria carried by flies.

I pointed out that I have eaten countless buffet-type summer meals without ill effects. So isn't this just alarmist talk? Maggie's response, speaking from her professional standpoint, is that her job is to identify potential risks and eliminate them wherever possible by establishing 'good practice' guidelines for food professionals catering for the general public. We all know that one outbreak of food poisoning can make headlines and be a serious setback to tourism and the catering trade in general.

Keep to what you know

I didn't find Maggie a scaremonger. While her scientific training in microbiology might have tilted her towards perfectionism, her hands-on experience advising people working in varied, often far from ideal situations around the world, has given her an insight into the art of the possible. As she points out, it is important to retain a sense of balance.

As I interpret her comments, this suggests a certain conservatism in eating: that is, sticking broadly with the foods you are used to from childhood because your digestive system and intestinal flora are accustomed to dealing with them. A sudden switch to quite different foods (she quoted US tourists stuffing on rich Swiss cheeses or Westerners rushing headlong into tofu and sushi products)· often leads to stomach upsets, indigestion and diarrhoea as your system tries to adjust. Eating active yoghurt is a safe and sensible remedy, plus lots of bottled water.

> Mankind always liked the food he was accustomed to, and his women cooked best, the food that grew around their homes; their babies were reared on it, their stomachs learnt to cope with it
>
> *Food in England*, Dorothy Hartley
> (Macdonalds 1954;
> Little, Brown & Co, 1996, 1999)

Fast food in the kitchen
Her chief short-term concern over food hygiene grows out of the increasing use of frozen foods and microwaves: the domestic fast-food situation. The best and safest way to thaw frozen foods such as meats and fish is gradually in the fridge, from several hours to overnight, depending on the bulk of the item. Thawing via the microwave leaves the chicken joint or fish fillet less flavoursome.

The real danger of cooking short cuts is inadequate de-frosting or thawing time. For instance, if a joint of meat is still frozen in the centre when it goes into the oven it will look brown and juicy from the outside but the oven heat may have only have warmed the core. This creates perfect conditions for any micro-organisms to multiply, with potentially noxious effects. Although there is a fashion for eating certain meats and fish on the rare side, it cannot be emphasised enough that this should only be contemplated when the food in question is either quite fresh or thoroughly de-frosted. If speed is the aim, it is perhaps better to make a pasta dish. Nevertheless, vegetables can be mostly cooked from frozen although with some loss of bite and flavour as a result.

Intensive farming
Maggie's longer term worry has mostly to do with intensive farming methods. These

involve overcrowding to be commercially viable and create unnatural conditions in which any pathogens would have a clear run were the unfortunate creatures not pumped full of antibiotics. Tiger prawns in Malaysia, the media informs us, are raised in ponds that are a virtual antibiotic soup.

Her worry is not that we may fall ill after eating a Thai prawn curry, but that we are unwittingly taking in too many antibiotics over an extended period of time. There is then a risk that they are not effectual when we need them to zap a potential killer such as viral pneumonia. I know a lot of people avoid taking antibiotics on prescription, preferring to tough out the laryngitis or 'flu, yet ironically they are not aware how many antibiotics they are absorbing into their systems via the food they eat.

Other than becoming a veggie, I can see no easy answer to the farmed food situation. Global demand is the nub of the problem coupled with an expectation that what were once luxury or exotic foods should be both accessible and affordable. This situation can only be sustained by intensive farming and mass production in potentially suspect circumstances.

So what's the answer? We can vote with our feet or credit cards and not buy these foods. I haven't bought cheap supermarket chicken – which I take to be battery reared – for years on both ethical, health and taste

grounds. Also, my freezer is no longer stocked up weekly with tiger prawns as it once was. If you are prepared to pay for the privilege, 'wild' versions of these foods can be found at suppliers to the top end of the food market.

However, this will not impact on the mass-production practices which Maggie finds alarming, because the demand for cut-price versions of what were once occasional treats goes on rising. The whole foodie culture – TV chefs, magazine and newspaper columns – has fostered an appetite for the unusual and the exotic. Global travel has overcome many old food prejudices too, hence the number of young guys who can rustle up a Thai green curry as a back-packing legacy.

Unhappily, the bottom line is that we have become greedy and heedless, like a nation of spoilt children. We want what we want, but it must be cheap.

According to a recent survey, Brits spend an average 10 per cent of their annual income on food, whereas the French, Italians and many other Europeans spend as much as 50 per cent. They expect to pay more for eating better, fresher food. So, I suggest, should we. Not only for our family's health, but also to help British farmers, cut to the bone by supermarkets, whose average income is now very often less than £10,000 per year.

METAL AND SILVER

Stainless steel cutlery

Some buffing up is rewarding, now and then, with stainless steel cutlery. The irony is that we all switched to stainless steel cutlery in the first place precisely to eliminate all that palaver, and compared with silver or plate, stainless steel does look presentable with minimum maintenance. All the same, an occasional going over of forks and spoons improves their appearance noticeably.

What dulls cutlery in constant use is surface abrasion; the metal gets minutely scuffed and scratched. Rubbing them over with a stainless steel polish smooths the surfaces again. Followed by a brisk rub with a clean rag and a rinse in hot water, they do look almost as good as new. Steel does not tarnish like silver, but some foods – boiled eggs especially – discolour it slightly and the polishing routine clears this instantly.

I might polish up the cutlery every few months, or before one of those dinner parties where you want your table to look extra special: crisp linen, sparkling glasses and shined-up stainless steel cutlery make a difference here.

I use Barkeeper's Friend, a powder used mixed with water to a thick slurry. It is very fast and effective. Rub it on with a rag, front back and sides, pushing it down between the fork tines, then polish off briskly with a clean rag, rinse and it is done. And yes, you could use it on other stainless steel surfaces in the kitchen for an occasional beauty treatment. There are branded stainless steel cleaners too.

Carbon steel knives

The beauty of old carbon steel knives (ie, pre-stainless steel) is that one can whet them to a razor edge using either a steel or carborundum knife sharpener. An old carving knife, nicely cleaned up and sharpened, gives a new dimension to carving delicate slices of a joint and a set of groomed carbon steel knives makes every steak cut as tenderly as cheese. Cooks' knives, carving knives and sets of old table knives with bone handles often turn up cheaply in boot sales or junk sales because people are put off by their discoloured appearance, freckled with dark spots, and don't know how to keep them bright.

Gentle abrasion is the trick. Butlers used a little gadget into which the blade was inserted and then polished up via fine emery paper by turning a handle. These have probably now all fetched up in National Trust stately home kitchens or county museums. However, one can get the same result, albeit with a little more effort, using a fine abrasive powder such as powdered pumice rubbed on vigorously with a cork. Powdered pumice is available cheaply at most artists' supply shops (see My Directory). Failing powdered pumice, dipping a cork end in Vim will serve though it won't give quite the same finished result.

Tip a spoonful of the powder into a small saucer, mix with water or olive oil to a fine slurry, dip the end of the cork in and away you go. Don't expect the steel blades to come up as shiny as their stainless counterparts; a dull pewtery surface is more the mark but the spots will vanish the more frequently you carry out this procedure. (Incidentally, my turn-of-the-century household manual, called *Enquire Within,* claims that potato peel, dipped on the potato side into powdered pumice, rottenstone or emery powder, makes short work of stains on steel – I haven't tested this myself.)

Another suggestion for cleaning that I have read about is polishing with wet-and-dry carborundum paper and – a new one on me – camellia oil. Wet-and-dry can be found in any car accessory shop. For camelia oil, see My Directory. It is a bit pricey – but intriguing.

Wash the slurry off the knife blades, dry thoroughly, and smear with either vegetable or olive oil to protect the polished surface from contact with air and damp. A dab of Vaseline does this even more effectively and is recommended for use on knives that are not in constant use. The best time to do it is just after honing the blades, but do take care as the knife will now be super sharp.

Bone handles also respond well to oiling but remember not to leave them soaking in hot water because this will discolour the bone as well as loosening the bond between the blade and the handle.

Silver

Silver that is in constant use rarely needs full-on cleaning; rinsed in piping hot water and rubbed dry it comes up bright and shiny. Like most people, we use stainless steel cutlery. However, I inherited a big silver teapot from my mother which used to tarnish quietly at the back of a cupboard. It seemed a bit ostentatious for the early morning cuppa. On the other hand our history of damaged teapots – cracked lids, snapped handles or chipped spouts – was depressing.

I decided the silver teapot should earn its keep, from breakfast onwards. The tea tastes fresher and livelier, I can report, silver being an excellent heat conductor, thus needing less brewing time. It adds a touch of glamour, visually. The downside is it has picked up a few dents, and it is not always shined up as smartly as one might wish. My quick solution is to run the teapot under piping hot tap water, then give it a brisk rub all over with a clean tea towel. When this seems inadequate, I follow this with the blue silver polishing cloth. No longer a tarnishing, untouchable grandee, silver teapot has entered and embellished our lives.

Silver Bath

To judge from the photos on the package, Quickshine, the Quick Acting Silver Bath (see My Directory) is a brilliantly hands-off way to clear tarnish off silver ware. 'Tarnish simply floats away' it claims, and photos show this transformation taking place in three easy steps. Having just run a test on it, I can say that the claim is true, but only up to a point. You will still need to buff up the stuff after its bath, and you should use rags, not tea towels, because some black gunk will rub off, although far less than with conventional silver polish. This American product is non-toxic, and is user-friendly, although wearing gloves is recommended.

The maker tells you to use a plastic receptacle. This is crucial, in fact, because any metal present (ie, a sink plug) will interfere with the catalytic action of the Quickshine. A rectangular plastic tub is suitable for flat items such as silver cutlery, but for bulkier items (sauce boats, teapots, etc) use a plastic bucket.

Silver or not?

Test whether silver is silver by rubbing with your thumb pad. If a bright spot appears, it is the real thing, or at the worst, silver plate.

Follow the Quickshine procedure: put one of the sachets in the plastic receptacle, silver side up, with as many items as possible touching the sachet, or each other. Then pour boiling water over to cover. While the product manufacturers show a kettle being used, my guess is that you need a gallon at a time, so boil up water in your largest pan, and make the trip between hob and plastic tub/bucket as short as possible. Make sure the items are covered with water – top up if necessary – and after 10 to 15 minutes, fish them out of the Quickshine. They will look oddly whitish and non-shiny, but make with the rags and the surface comes up twinkling bright, with some black on the polishing cloth. In my case, there were a few obstinate black spots, like freckles, which old silver seems prone to. If these bother you, try spot cleaning with old-style silver polish. However, on cutlery this is not likely to happen.

I do think that Quickshine saves time, especially for cutlery, but it is not quite such a hands-off process as claimed. And, of course, it costs a bit more, like all labour-saving treatments. In addition, the makers list silver products for which Quickshine is not suitable: lacquered or artificially oxidised silverware, candlesticks with weighted bases, knives with weighted (or bone) handles, or items with porous (wood, leather, horn, bone, enamel, baize) attachments.

Brass and copper

One of the delights of talking to specialists in a really out-of-the-way subject, such as horology, is lighting upon some gem of information such as Horolene Concentrate (see My Directory). This is a very useful product with which anyone on the clock-repair scene is familiar, but which you and I and Joe Bloggs have never heard of – at least till now.

Horolene Concentrate is a solvent designed to clean brass clockworks and mechanisms. It follows that it does a remarkable job of cleaning up any domestic brasses that have accumulated years of tarnish, or what my informant at Horological Solvents Products succinctly calls 'crud'. She mentioned brass coal buckets and fire irons as prone to cruddiness. Maybe you have picked up a set cheap at a boot sale in a shockingly neglected condition? The beauty of Horolene Concentrate is that it does all the work for you; no blackened rags and fingers and no chalky deposits left behind in the cracks. Being an 'impatient type', she uses the product regularly to get her household brass (and copper) looking bright and shiny without lifting a finger.

Well, nearly. What you do first, and she stressed this, is read the instructions. Next, mix the concentrate in a bucket of water – one part to seven parts water – to give enough liquid to completely immerse the item. Then you leave it, checking it from time to time to see where it is at. The more crud to get through, the longer it may take. When it looks nice and bright, fish it out, rinse (to remove lingering solvent) and the job is done. Same routine for copper.

Nonetheless, there is a downside: the smell. The concentrate contains ammonia and the instructions bristle with warnings: wear a mask, wear gloves, and work in a well-ventilated area.

Horolene Concentrate can be found in some trade shops, such as Foxell James . Alternatively, you can order it through Restoration Materials, the mail-order arm of Horological Products, who are fine about individual (non-trade) orders (see My Directory).

PLASTIC AND LAMINATES

Thanks to canny designers such as Starck and Sotsass, once humble man-made materials such as plastic and laminates have been upgraded aesthetically. Juicy colours, frosted translucent surfaces, or subtle patterns have helped make these light, tough and relatively cheap materials irresistible, so it is sad when they lose their pristine freshness and I can understand that one longs to get them looking 'as new'.

Sadly, with man-made materials at this level, you are looking at diminishing returns: they do not improve with age and use.

Wood vs. plastic in the kitchen

Researchers at the University of Wisconsin carried out tests to determine whether plastic or wood is more hygienic. They contaminated both wooden and plastic chopping boards with salmonella, listeria and coliform bacteria. Tests showed that the bacteria multiplied on plastic, whereas on the wood boards 99.9 per cent died within three minutes.

Plastic presents a relatively soft surface, which scratches and scuffs readily and quite quickly. Laminates are much tougher, but they begin to crack up if you treat them roughly: using scouring pads to clean them, chopping on them, or dumping hot plates on them. Laminates are made, after all, from resin-coated paper bonded to something like chipboard. Once the resin wears through you are on a downward slide. However, with TLC you can usually prolong their looks and usefulness.

Plastic

Do not employ any abrasives such as soap pads, Cif or Vim, etc. Instead, use hot water, a squidge of detergent to dissolve grease and sticky film, with a sink brush or sponge cloth. Rinse and wipe. Where hygiene is a concern, fill a sink bowl with cold water, add a spoonful of chlorine bleach, leave for 2 minutes or so until the surface looks lighter and then rinse.

Laminates

These have a tougher surface than plastic. Nevertheless, try to avoid the need for abrasive action by wiping down punctiliously, using a sponge cloth or dishcloth with hot water, on a daily basis, so that gunge cannot pile up.

A drop of chorine bleach will help chase off bacteria if the surface is scarred (see 'The Hygiene Hypothesis', page 150).

Soap pads should be used as sparingly as possible – maybe for an initial clean up if you inherit a shockingly neglected kitchen set-up – but go gently so as not to further damage surfaces. Scour lightly, then mop up with a sponge cloth as above.

If you have worries about using standard household chlorine bleach, use Milton instead, as recommended by Maggie Duke (see page 150).

To remove stains from laminate worktops, try Cif, Barkeeper's Friend (see page 107), or lemon juice.

CLEANING BATHROOMS

Bathrooms come second only to kitchens in their need for regular upkeep, though this comes under the wipe-down heading rather than deep clean. Bathrooms present so many surfaces, all of which pick up so much human fallout of one sort or another: rings round the bath, stubble in the basin, toothpaste spattered on the mirrors, cosmetic spills on the unit tops, plugholes blocked with loose hair, stains round the lavatory bowl, etc.

A disciplined, single person can cope, cleaning up as they go. Sharing with another adult compounds the problem, unless he/she subscribes to your house rules, wipes up after themselves; even – this is rare – scrubbing the lavatory bowl as a matter of principle and hygiene. Sharing with children is already tougher, but sharing with teenagers is the pits.

Luckily many homes today have a second bathroom, and/or cleaner or au pair to lend a hand. Even so you will be well advised to set a benchmark to aim at and keep cleaning products and adjuncts close to hand, and regularly replaced. A cleaner will expect this; au pairs usually need explanations and a demo. But the buck stops with you. If you push yourself to wipe round basin, bath and shower after use, hang up wet towels and swab unit tops, you establish a routine for others to follow and the message does gradually get through.

A well-equipped bathroom needs:
> *a heated towel rail*
> *storage space for cleaning aids*
> *a large laundry basket, bag or bin*
> *a childproof medicine cabinet*
> *cupboards, shelves or drawers for cosmetics, loo rolls, shampoo, conditioner, etc*

Where possible, keep everything accessible and close to the spot where it is needed: lav brush and holder close to the toilet, shower etceteras in the shower stall (you can get plastic containers which grip on to tiles with suction cups), cleaning stuff for bathroom surfaces in the same room, preferably grouped in a plastic 'tidy' and out of sight.

A bathroom cleaning kit should include:

● Cream cleanser for wiping down ceramic basin, bath, tiles, unit tops. (For other surfaces, such as stainless steel, see page 107.)

● Spray all-purpose cleaning liquid for awkward surfaces – taps, soap niches, inside drawers and cupboards.

● Sponge or sponge cloth to apply cleaners and to wipe down (after rinsing out) afterwards.

● Washing-up liquid to dissolve oily residue in baths. It works more effectively here than a cream cleanser. Swab it on first, neat, rinse, *then* follow with cream cleanser.

● Meths or ammonia to clear mirror glass. (See Cleaning windows, page 135.)

● Soap pads are handy for removing obstinate stains but should be used gently, as they can scratch laminates, corian, even marble.

● Limescale remover to squirt into toilet bowl daily, before brushing. I back this up from time to time with spirits of salt (see page 111) which cleans past the notorious bend. (I don't like loo-cleaner tablets that dye the water. Nor do I like air fresheners, which give off a sickly reek. But this is a personal prejudice; you may love them.)

● Household (usually chlorine) bleach. Useful to rinse sponges and cloths (see page 107), and to brighten white ceramic units from time to time.

● Rubber gloves, in your size, preferably several pairs.

All of these should pack away into a plastic container the size of a shoe box. Larger stuff – mops, brooms, vaccum and steam cleaners (see page 116), sink plungers – are used less regularly, and can be stored elsewhere.

Shower curtains

● Shower curtains are best dunked in a warm bath with a squeeze of bio-washing liquid, or, if necessary, swabbed with a mild bleach solution.

● Nylon shower curtains can be machine washed if you prefer.

Rust

HG (see My Directory) sell a rust remover.

Stains on enamel

A splash of biological washing liquid added to a tub full of water goes a long way to removing rust/lime stains on enamel.

DEALING WITH PESTS

PEST SIGNS

I have been urged to give you an easy recognition chart so you can identify which pest is invading your house and clothes. I know this sounds helpful and I do wish to help, but I doubt whether it would make a great deal of difference to you which breed of moth is eating your clothes. You just want to act as quickly as possible and find an appropriate solution. Usually this will mean calling in the professionals.

MOTHS

Unless you are on the qui vive you might not spot a moth problem until it is too late and your prized garment has become a colander chewed away at critical points.

However, if you check out your wardrobe each spring and autumn, you might just catch the pests in the pupae stage. Moth pupae look for all the world like tiny pale shreds of wool nestled down into your tweed, alpaca, lambswool and flannel. They adore and feed off wool, but will try silk and superior blends if pushed.

If you brush these pupae off briskly, using a hard brush, you may be just in time to stop them making holes. Follow up by a blast of moth deterrent, such as Doom, and/or hang outside in the sun. Moths like dark, smelly, dusty and airless places.

MICE

Mice are quite easy to spot, even if you never catch sight of the tiny creatures, as they leave little droppings – like black rice grains – along their 'runs'. Mice breed so prolifically that you should call in the local council pest control at once. A cat may help – mice back off at the smell of cats – but don't rely on this. Some cats are lazy! I am afraid poison is the only certain solution.

The pest-control officer will give you the childproof, pet-proof poison containers, but for follow-ups you might need to go private.

RATS

Rats scare us silly and are carriers of umpteen diseases. Their droppings look like those of mice, but are bigger dark pellets up to 1cm (3/8in) long. However, you are just as likely to spot rats by the damage they do, chewing through wood and plaster, not to mention food.

Rats are a serious health hazard, so report your suspicions or finds as soon as possible to your local pest-control department. Where feasible, block up any entry sites (missing bricks and gaps under doors) and take the experts' advice seriously.

Most cats are not quite up to dealing with adult rats; this was a terrier's job when rat catchers cruised rat-infested areas. A good ratter could become a local celebrity in the nineteenth century!

COCKROACHES

As a rule, you can spot cockroaches as soon as they appear if you know what you are looking for. You may be consoled by the fact that an infestation of cockroaches doesn't mark you as a slut. They are particularly attracted to terraced housing and, as we all know, there is a lot of this about. Summon your pest control immediately. Cockroaches often lurk in the works of second-hand fridges – dark, warm, dirty.

ANTS

You might be able to cope with ants on your own by tracing the ant run back to the entry spot, filling it with ant poison and monitoring the outcome. To date, I have been cool and calm about ants, but I have spotted a few racing about my worktops. The experts warn that if you ignore the first appearance of ants, you could in be for a massive invasion. I must do something soon!

WEEVILS

These are very small beetles and can arrive on your kitchen shelves via imported foods such as pulses, flour and spices. If you open a kitchen canister or food pack and find the contents jumping, dispose of them immediately.

CARPET BEETLES

I once stashed a tin trunk under a bed on top of an old Chinese rug and when I moved it a few months later, I found the rug pile had been given a crew cut by carpet beetles. As I have a lot of pile rugs, this was sickening. I had the whole space professionally sprayed, but it was very expensive.

Like most invasive pests, carpet beetles work in dark quiet spots – so the rug under my bed was ideal. You can guard against them by vacuuming regularly under beds, sofas, pile carpets or rugs (they don't care for matting) and by occasionally moving your furniture around. A spray insecticide will also help, but cleanliness is the first priority – don't leave areas of carpet untouched for months on end.

SILVERFISH

These do sad damage to books, especially old books, chewing irregular holes and doubtless contributing to that musty smell that lingers around old book stacks.

They like leather bindings and the smell of animal glue. If you include books in your annual/bi-annual deep clean – clapping two books together to expel the dust, what Dr Johnson called 'buffeting'– and keep your shelves reasonably dusted, these pests should not be a problem. Use a soft cloth to gently clean any old books you may possess.

I wouldn't advise using insecticide on the books themselves, but you could spray the shelves before putting the books back.

FLEAS

For animal fleas see page 94. If you don't keep pets, these may be another flea species. Signs, as you might expect, are red itchy bites on the skin.

Contact your local pest-control department. They should hurry round, since fleas multiply alarmingly. Usually they will spray your premises with a pesticide that not only kills fleas but their eggs and larvae, the next flea generation. These sprays may vary in toxicity – ask for information if you are worried.

Meanwhile, it does no harm to use a branded pesticide – these come both in spray and powder form – on bedding, sofas and chairs, following the manufacturer's instructions.

Calamine lotion, applied liberally, helps soothe itchy bites.

NOTE: flea attacks are often most virulent in second homes, after an absence, when the creatures – maybe animal fleas here – breed and get ravenous.

DIY methods are better than nothing in this situation. OK, you contact the local pest control, but by the time they can make it you may be off and away again.

BEDBUGS

The shame of nineteenth-century slum homes, these were pretty well phased out of UK inner cities until the increase in foreign holidaying has resulted in sporadic outbreaks – often in hotels – where travellers, unbeknown to them, have imported them concealed in their clothing.

Bedbugs are tiny when dormant, only becoming visible when they latch on to skin and suck blood. An unsettling thought, but hardly a normal problem as yet. Call your local pest-control department for advice, and to book a visit.

FLIES

Endemic pests at certain times of year, usually late summer and autumn. DIY methods seem adequate and applicable here. Sticky fly papers look horrid, but are effective fly catchers. A blast of anti-fly spray is a deterrent, but don't use this around food.

Check your fridge to make sure flies haven't sneaked in; they can and do. If you have a larder where you store cooked food, keep the food covered. Use plastic lidded containers, or those old-fashioned muslin covers weighted with beads which every household kept on hand in the pre-fridge era.

Raw meat and fish are especially attractive to flies and a flying visit can lead – as I found when I tried curing a ham myself – to a maggoty horror story.

PIGEONS

Dubbed 'flying rats' by their detractors, I have only found these a real problem in the tiny, walled backyard of a shop in Notting Hill Gate. Pigeons flocked down into this space, covering windowsills and paving with sticky bird lime, feathers and the odd broken egg. Clearly no hungry cats around.

All the council could come up with was to screen over the entire space with wire netting. We made a stab at this, with the result that determined birds forced their way through any gaps, then found themselves trapped and usually committed suicide in a panic. A cat was not an option here. The experience fuelled my antipathy to pigeons.

I have been told by old-time builders that coating ledges and window sills with limewash (as you see on fruit trees sometimes) is a pigeon deterrent, since the lime is caustic enough to burn their feet warningly. An air gun or a catapult might be effective too, but this is not my bag.

FOXES

Once a rural problem, now increasingly making their way into suburbs and inner cities, foxes have been spotted in Spitalfields, the heart of city commuterland.

These animals are handsome, cunning, and predatory. Foxes maim and kill for the sheer bloodlust of the exercise, decapitating a whole roost of hens in one go, given the chance. They will happily kill your chickens, pet rabbits and smaller rodents such as guinea-pigs.

I'm not blaming the fox, but one sure as hell wants to keep them off home territory. Easier said than done. My hunch is that a large dog – a hunting breed preferably – is the most effective deterrent, patrolling a suburban garden at all hours, especially during the night, when the foxy breed get out and about. Fierce barking may frighten the foxes off; cross fingers the two don't meet head on. Also, tedious but necessary, you should make sure your fences/hedges/walls are fox proof.

If the problem has escalated already – I have seen a foxes earth, vixen and cubs romping, in a North London garden – you will need to take expert advice, foxes being, I need hardly remind you, a hot political issue. Phone the RSPCA.

HOUSEHOLD TIPS

Whence, or wherefore – I ask this in all seriousness – our passion and craving for Tips? Have you ever tried them out? Having delved deeply into 'Tip' literature, from Mrs Beeton and *Enquire Within* up to the present day, I can report with some confidence that:

● Most tips don't actually work. Try using cigarette ash with a drop of oil on 'white rings' on your polished furniture?!

● Some *do* work (ie, dropping a denture-cleaning tablet into a cloudy vase) but it costs more than malt vinegar, and what if you aren't a denture wearer? And what is so brilliant about polishing your jewellery (or your bathroom mirror) with toothpaste, when a dunk in Silver Dip or a spot of meths will do the job more effectively and cheaply?

● Most tips are lazily recycled as clever wheezes (like the one about rubbing scratches on furniture with half a walnut), but no one seems to have tried them, or figured out why they might or might or not work, for sober, scientific reasons. Yes, a smear of oil (linseed might be the best) will tone down a nasty scratch, but it won't level up the surface. Whereas an application of wax – and this comes from the *National Trust Manual of Housekeeping* no less – will do just that, without the bother of buying walnuts. And you probably already have it in your *batterie de nettoyage*.

It is mostly, though not only, women who keep the Tip Industry alive. I watched, with mounting irritation and incredulity, a video of BBC's Trade Secrets, where aproned sweeties raced about with walnuts, toothpaste or dentifrice tablets like a bunch of amateur conjurors, thrilled when their tip worked on camera. I concluded, sourly, that it is the 'hey presto' bit that appeals, not whether there is any foundation in fact or practice. Furthermore, don't run away with the notion that if it was shown to work on telly, it must be a winner. I have done enough TV work myself to be sadly aware that the team are not too bothered about veracity so long as the shot looks good on camera and the team can pack up and get home without running into overtime.

I thought I had found an ally in the 'tips are bullshit' field when someone sent me a copy of *I Hate to Cook* by Peg Bracken, published umpteen times in the 1960s on both sides of the Atlantic. I enjoyed her iconoclastic approach and I quote:

'... I have been, for the last dozen years, rather intimately involved with household hints,' she writes. 'During this period more than 10,000 of them have sifted like counterfeit pennies through my fingers. I therefore feel I speak with a certain modest authority when I say that most household hints are pretty terrible.'

Then Bracken, having done a nice demolition job on the competition, comes up with 73 hints of her own, the cream of those 10,000 counterfeit pennies, promising 'they all work'. I read on excitedly, in high hopes. Could these 73 out of 10,000 – like 0.0007 per cent, I hazarded – be the real stuff?

Sadly not. A few were really good: turn the sprinkler on to your washing if it's dried out before ironing; vacuum your dog clean to remove loose hair (if the dog agrees!); clean windows vertically inside and horizontally outside so that you spot the bits you missed, etc.

However, I am never going to keep a soft powder puff in the flour bin to dust cake tins (disgusting thought), though I might manage plasticine to bridge the gap when candles are too small for their holders. As for sticking strips of adhesive tape on family shoe soles so that they don't slip on polished floors … what adhesive? Double-sided sellotape? Elastoplast? And while it is a smart idea to use an embroidery hoop to keep fabric taut while you deal with a stain, surely a boiling water treatment goes against all the received wisdom about stain removal?

A TV series that applied some investigative rigour to the Tip scene really could be interesting; surely it is time for some debunking and demystifying? Maybe we would be left with some workable suggestions we might never have thought of for ourselves.

This book, as you may have gathered by now, does not major on tips, certainly none of the 'flush out your toilet stains with a can of Coca-Cola' variety. You will find some seeded through the text, and boxed for recognition, but they are really no more than little nuggets of common sense.

DOING IT THEIR WAY:

WORKING MOTHERS

Running a home in tandem with a full-time job is demanding. Juggling the priorities of work and young children, even when a husband/partner is available to help out, is exhausting and relentless. Therefore, it is only to be expected that spending time with one's children in the evenings and at weekends takes precedence over housework. The wonder is that working mums do seem to summon the energy to tackle domestic chores in a purposeful way, with necessary – and appreciated – support from their partners.

I talked to two women, Beth and Anna. Both are mothers of young children and have full-time demanding jobs. In both cases, their partners play a crucial role in holding the domestic structure together; collecting a five-year-old from school, and doing the weekly shop on the partner's day off. Even so, both Beth and Anna sounded bone tired – admittedly I spoke to them towards the end of the working day. I think 'conflicted', that fashionable word, probably describes their state of mind; balancing the two sides of a working mother's life is no picnic.

Anna is married to James, who works in education and has a relatively flexible time sheet. They live in Clapham, and have a five-year-old daughter, Tamsin, whose school day starts at 8.15 and ends at 3.15; pivotal times in the couple's daily schedule. This dictates that they eat an early supper *en famille*, washing up supper things straight away, and breakfast at 7.30 so that James can drop Tamsin at school on his way to work.

Anna then has 30 or 40 minutes to clear away the breakfast things, make a quick dash at general chores like vacuuming and tidying, before getting herself ready to leave for work at 8.30. Every minute counts here: 'I can hoover the downstairs room very quickly because it has a fake wood floor with rugs,' she says. (Hoover is a misnomer here, the machine is a Miele cylinder model as recommended in WHICH?; see page 79).

Anna and James do not have a) a cleaner, or b) a dishwasher. 'The money I save not employing a cleaner just about covers the cost of a holiday,' Anna explains. However, she has toyed with the idea and admits she could be 'easily persuaded'. The dishwasher (such a must-have in many young professional homes) she dismisses as unnecessary for a family of three. James, as well as delivering and collecting Tamsin from school, usually does the weekly shop, on a Thursday (avoiding the weekend crowds), and enjoys ironing, which Anna hates.

She has thought about ordering staples on the net, but lives so close to a major supermarket it seems a bit pointless. Instead the couple 'top up' on the weekly shop as needed. They eat 'fairly simply' – pasta, soup, roast vegetables, though curry is her speciality. Anna buys meat from a family butcher in Clapham: 'I'm not wild about supermarket meat.' This is the couple's main concession to current food concerns.

If Anna has a niggle about the domestic set-up it is that familiar womanly fuss about what men usually dismiss as mere detail. 'I like it to be cleaner than my husband – I find chaos harder to cope with, and I find it irritating when surfaces are not wiped down.' Interpreted, this means that Anna has to be the one who races about with a sponge cloth clearing away daily detritus. At five years old, Tamsin is too young to be mother's little helper, thought she has her own cupboard downstairs for stashing her stuff, which she does on the whole, without too much parental prompting.

Beth and journalist partner Steve have a 20-month-old son, Sam, who is cared for by a childminder during the day. They live in two flats joined together to give a sizeable five-bedroom home. A cleaner comes in for five hours, once a fortnight, to vacuum, dust and wipe down surfaces. Steve, 'who is more fussed about tidiness', makes up any shortfall.

Because his work hours are more flexible, Steve also does most of the shopping and almost all the cooking. He enjoys cooking and is pernickety about hygiene – plastic board for chopping meat and wooden for vegetables and herbs, etc.

When the couple moved in together they argued about which possessions should be kept, and which should be chucked out as clutter. 'Mostly about kitchen stuff,' Beth recalls, 'also books and prints; we both fought for our prints.'

According to Beth this clutter clash regularly occurs when 30-somethings, each with their own backlog of possessions and different tastes, move in together. Where they are at one is about having board floors with rugs instead of matting 'because of all the disgusting stuff that collects underneath'.

Like Anna and James they do not have a dishwasher, although for different reasons. 'I don't like that chalky stuff it leaves on dishes and then think of the arguments about who unpacks it – just another thing for him to get anal about,' Beth says. This getting anal is the downside of living with New Man. Still, for someone as laid back about housework as Beth, there must be distinct compensations. There are two domestic chores Beth really enjoys. She loves doing the family washing in the washing machine, and – this is surprising – she gets a kick out of bed making. 'I love changing sheets and towels every week. But I make it a bit easier for myself by changing the sheets one day, and the duvet covers the next.'

Ironing? She hoots incredulously. 'Maybe once a month or so I might do a bit of ironing so that I don't get taken for a bag lady.' It is also fortunate for Beth that not many toddler outfits need ironing today. She also avoids dry-cleaners because 'they leave clothes looking exhausted'. I visualise the couple dressed in jeans, spankingly clean jumpers or T-shirts (washed at lowest machine setting) and leather jackets; the sensible daily uniform for most busy working people today.

Beth hasn't given much thought to time savers like shopping on the net. Steve does the big shop – being a cook and foodie – on his weekly day off. She tends to pick up any fresh items needed – bread and salads – on her way back from work. Beth is lucky that her place of work is within walking distance.

Her resolution for 2002 is to 'double up'; an eminently sensible idea which I have scouted in this book. So far she has got to 'two sets of bathroom things, so I don't have to trail up and down stairs for cleaning materials'.

I leap in with my own suggestions – scissors, sellotape, etc – and our conversation winds up capping each other; Stanley knives, stamps, elastoplast …

My two interviewees flag up interesting similarities, and some burgeoning trends in their demographic group: a much more even sharing of domestic responsibilities with their partners, health and hygiene concerns (board floors/fresh organic food), and a disinclination to be rushed into consumerism: no dishwashers and the use of local shops and stores. It is a no-frills attitude: yes, washing machine, yes, vacuum cleaner, no dishwasher for a small family that is not into entertaining – and thoughtful about where they spend their joint incomes.

Neither Anna nor Beth come within nodding distance of the old-style 'housewife', though Anna, with her early morning blitz with the vacuum cleaner and her dislike of 'sticky surfaces' comes closer than Beth, her friend and colleague. But then Beth has a regular (albeit fortnightly) cleaner as backup as well as a bit of a paragon in Steve.

The important thing is that both couples have arrived at a modus vivendi which works for them. Far from ideal: both women would love more time off (another day) even if it meant less money. But as the full-time workers in both partnerships, they provide the security until such time as James gets his business going or Steve makes it big in music.

LAUNDRY

I learnt the ABC of laundering, which is only common sense, over many years coping with the needs of a household with young children, helpless husbands and a fluctuating budget. I have hand washed thousands of terry towelling nappies, trampled sheets in the bath (kids enjoy helping with that) and tramped with bulging bags to an unbeautiful laundrette in extremis. I can iron a shirt and fold it into one neat oblong in four minutes, and lightly starch and iron an heirloom tablecloth to a professional standard. I picked up these skills, some more skilled than others, either because I had to, being skint, or because I wanted to, finding a creative pleasure in restoring a bedraggled garment to its crisp, flouncy first intention. So you could say, I'm a proficient washerwomen. So far so good.

My problem, which millions of busy women will have no trouble understanding, is training up one's regular, or occasional, household help – or partner – to cope with the ABC of laundering efficiently.

A succession of au pairs over the years, usually female and Eastern European, has shown me that teenagers and 20-somethings from around the world have all been raised (with a few notable exceptions) in complete ignorance of basic laundering common sense.

The word 'damp', for instance, seems untranslatable. Just try explaining to a Hungarian (with barely 100 words of English) the reason why laundry to be ironed – shirts for starters – should be just damp, while a neatly folded stack of T-shirts in your cupboard should not.

FORWARD PLANNING AND SORTING

Laundry never seems to be a problem for the young and footloose; they wear non-iron clothes and haunt launderettes, or take it home to mum at weekends, or, if yuppies, patronise a posh laundry.

All this changes when kids arrive, especially when they get to school age, needing their school kit ready to wear on Monday morning and then again during the week. You need time to get the wash under way (first thing Saturday morning), allowing more time for drying and ironing before the Monday morning clamour.

Unless you have a quiver full of school-age kids, most of their kit – shirts, knickers, etc – can go in with a load of other whites and washables, thus saving time, energy and money. Start early, hang out by midday and then iron on Saturday evening or Sunday morning. This lets you steal a march on the week. Really grimy stuff can be given a pre-soak using biological washing powder or liquid. If that doesn't hit dirty collars and cuffs hard, try a rub with a stain soap (Bio-tex is good before the wash).

Get your children to stash their dirty washing in either the communal basket, or their individual one – a bag can substitute. The important thing is they bring it to your washpoint in time to get it all under way on Saturday morning, or even Friday night if you feel up to it. If they weasel out of this small duty, they don't get clean clothes for Monday. Be firm!

SORTING THE WASH

I assumed that everyone was familiar with the basic rules: whites with whites, coloureds with coloured, and dark fabrics with dark fabrics. Well, that is a simplistic approach – and assumes all the coloureds (the dodgiest lot) are colour-fast. The younger generation in my household has proved me wrong here, not my fussy daughters but my insouciant stepson who just bungs the lot in – Paul Smith shirt along with cheap socks and pants bought in Thailand – then moans when it all emerges dun coloured.

Long experience – even without consulting every garment label – gives a shrewd idea of what will wash well, or what may bleed, crease or shrink horribly. If you are new to the wash game, check those labels carefully.

● Natural fibres – cotton, linen, silk – usually wash safely, although using the coolest setting and taking the completed wash load out speedily is a safeguard.

● Anything which is a natural/synthetic mix can misbehave. (I once shoved a part wool, part acrylic cardigan in the wash and it shrank to doll size. It should – though the label didn't stipulate – have been rather carefully hand washed.)

● Some woollen or wool-mix items (socks and most kids' jumpers) are designed to be washed in a machine – but on a cool setting.

● You would be mad not to wash special cashmere, alpaca or angora, etc, by hand (see page 179).

Colour runs

Where one coloured item has leaked over a load of whites, wash again using Colour Run (available from supermarkets). The coloured item shouldn't have been in the wash in the first place, of course. But while Colour Run will get whites white again, it won't remove dye leaked on to coloured fabrics, or rather it will bleach the coloured fabrics to near white.

WASHING MACHINES

Simon Kirk repairs and services washing machines in an area stretching from the East End of London deep into Essex. He averages eight calls a day. One of these was mine, when the machine refused to spin with a load of washing swilling about inside.

As we all know, there are fast talkers in the appliance-repair trade. You know the type: picked at random from the Yellow Pages; arrives hours later than promised; shakes his head dubiously; has to keep running back to his van for more tools or parts; charges £60 for starters/call-out fee and ends by suggesting the machine is past its sell-by date.

Simon Kirk, on the other hand, arrived almost on the dot, sorted out the problem in half an hour and charged me £45. What endeared him most to me was his willingness to explain what had gone wrong. 'Nine times out of ten there's a blockage,' he said, pulling out the filter tray where, sure enough, a 5p coin and a pea-sized glass 'jewel' nestled in half an inch of unappetising grey sludge.

It is a pathetic admission that I had never realised that there was a filter tray, nor how to clear it, nor had I perused the owner's manual. It seems there are a lot of people out there like me. Reading user manuals is famously one of those little jobs one puts off till a rainy day, or the machine plays up. How rarely is a user manual a good read? Or even intelligible? They often read as if translated from Japanese.

Blockages may be caused by any of the following: coins, keys, socks, bra wires (very common these days of underwired boobs), even tissues. It behoves you to go through the wash (pockets, pockets and more pockets) like a keen cop doing a body search.

What happens is that the foreign object hits the fan, slowing it right down or stopping it dead and since the fan drives the pump – acting like a ship's propeller – the system either struggles on feebly or gives up altogether.

Here are some tips for a longer machine life:

● Clean the filter at least once a month. (Mine is a discreet little drawer down in the bottom right-hand corner, but yours may be located elsewhere.)

● Once a month, set the machine to its highest temperature wash programme and toss in a cupful of soda crystals. Nothing else. This will flush out the system beneficially.

● Don't pack the machine too full as this strains the works.

Other frequent problems could be that the rubber door seal has been torn or worn out. Or the carbon brushes need replacing. This is really a job for a skilled operative.

Simon reckons the life of a washing machine averages two to three years. 'People don't realise that 85 per cent of a new machine is plastic. Ten years ago 85 per cent was metal which is clearly stronger.' His own machine is an Indesit, but he was cautious about expressing a preference. 'Ten years ago or so people thought German machines were a good bet because they were solidly made. Now Bosch machines are made in Spain. Creda machines are owned and made by Hotpoint. They keep the brand going because of customer loyalty to Creda.'

He thinks the real innovation of the Dyson washing machines is not the push-me-pull-you action, but the much larger tub. He is sure other manufacturers are poised to follow suit. This does not mean the machine gets bigger. 'There's a lot of spare space in there. I can't think why they didn't think of it before.'

Another advance would be to cut down the number of washing programmes. 'Most people use three programmes: cool, warm and hot. So why have 25 programmes to choose from? I'm not exaggerating – ring your friends and you'll find they only use three programmes.'

Pre-wash fans tend to be senior citizens. 'They are really fussed about getting everything really clean, and they don't mind spending time over it. Your usual family today just wants to get the loads through and out of the way as quickly as possible, so they may use only the warm or cool setting because the cycle is faster.'

Washing machines in the UK tend to be front loading (though top-loading models are available) whereas top-loaders predominate in the USA and Australia. This is because homes in both places tend to be larger, with utility rooms as a given. In the UK we try to tuck our washing machines away under a worktop so front loading is a requirement. Top loaders spin faster, it seems, but use a lot more water. With water bills rising as fast as floodwater, this is an important factor to take on board.

As for the choice between washing liquid and washing powder, Simon chooses powder. 'It floats and dissolves in the water, where the liquid may congeal at the bottom of the drum and cause blockages.' 'But powder is messy,' I objected, remembering snowfalls of powder and a drawer so gloopy it wouldn't fully open. 'Chuck the powder straight into the drum with the wash. That's where you want it.' Powders are also less likely to cause skin rashes and other allergic reactions.

Gizmos and gimmicks such as the Washsaver (see next) or Persil's Revive aroused scant enthusiasm compared with an ingenious invention he saw on a TV consumer programme which dispensed with the need for soap or detergent altogether. 'It thinned the water, you see, so it passed through the clothes freely and sort of dissolved the stains and stuff.' So why wasn't this on sale everywhere? His northern accent took on a wry tone: 'Well, the supermarkets wouldn't want to upset Lever Brothers and all the other manufacturers, now, would they?'

THE WASHSAVER

The Washsaver is a bright pink plastic gizmo, slightly resembling a mini lifebelt but with corners. Its maker claims that by adding this to the drum, with every wash load, the amount of detergent needed is 'significantly reduced'. It works along the lines of the old-fashioned wash board – the ridged board which washerwomen used to get a purchase on while scrubbing out stains – adding a bit of resistance to the washing machine action, that rub-a-dub muscle, which a washerwoman's powerful arms and washboard supplied. Dyson's new washing machine attempts to solve this problem with its push-me-pull-you action. The Washsaver is a very mini, vastly cheaper stab at the same thing (see My Directory).

Does it work? I have thrown my Washsaver in with scores of wash loads (the makers claim it will last 500 washes), cut my washing liquid by half and the wash came

175

out fine. Possibly the tea towels were even cleaner?

The honest truth is that testing such claims rigorously is well nigh impossible. It's a bit like taking mega doses of Vitamin C to ward off a cold. The cold doesn't disappear overnight, you still sneeze and sniff, but the catch is you don't know and can't tell whether it would have been worse without the Vitamin C.

The catch with the Washsaver is similar because you don't have two washing machines and two identically soiled loads so a strict comparison is impossible. However, it does seem to be the case that reducing detergent by 50 per cent is a viable option, and gives satisfactory results.

WASHING POWDER, LIQUID OR WOOLITE?

Simon, my washing machine expert (see page 173), favours powder over liquid: it dissolves more thoroughly, and gives a cleaner wash. But if you have started with liquid, stay with it – mixing liquid and powder is inadvisable. If you must change, try Simon`s tip – run washing soda through the empty machine first on the hottest setting to clear the works. Woolite is really for the hand wash (see page 178), an extravagance used in the machine.

FABRIC CONDITIONERS

Fabric conditioners put up a brave show on the shelves, but I would only use them to cut

Dilemma: wash or dry-clean?

In my experience, the majority of clothes one buys today have a label inside (which you should always consult prior to purchase) stipulating whether dry-cleaning is necessary. This is often a blanket safety precaution on the part of the manufacturer and thus quite unnecessary in many instances. One can see where they are coming from as it is easier to advise dry-cleaning, albeit more expensive, than trust the customer's common sense when it comes to appropriate laundering procedures. There are plenty of idiots out there (usually young males!) who will cram all their sweaters and socks into one wash load, regardless of whether it is cashmere or wool-rich mix being dealt with. To them wool is wool and there is no way they are going to stand over a basin squeezing woollies by hand in soapy tepid water.

static when washing a load of synthetic fabrics. Thorough rinsing is a better – and cheaper – way to get fabrics soft again. Fabric conditioners should not be used with silk or towels.

WATER SOFTENERS

When to use water softeners, such as Calgon? I think there is a case for using these a) where your water is exceptionally hard, but only for special items – fragile, old or expensive fibres and fabrics, christening robes, cashmere, antique silks, etc, which you should be washing by hand anyway. I don't use water softeners myself – yet another product to remember to stock up – and my wash comes up pretty good though I live in a hard water area – Central London.

A recent stay in San Francisco – where the water is divinely soft – certainly showed up a noticeable difference when it came to washing glasses – ie, no smears or residue – but the clothes wash came out pretty much the same as it does here.

However, I am told that adding Calgon to your wash will help clear limescale off the washing-machine element.

NATURAL FIBRES

I tend to work on the assumption that all natural fibres – wool, cotton, linen and silk – are washable, though this rule-of-thumb gets a bit wobbly when non-colourfast dyes enter the picture. With pricier garments this is unusual, but can occur when, for instance, you are washing a pure cotton fabric which has been tie-dyed, or a hand-painted silk. When there is any doubt, try a corner first in cold water. If this seems OK, follow by hand washing in tepid water with the merest squidge of Woolite or pure soap flakes (see page 112)

Ninety-nine per cent of the time, you can safely hand wash any items made from natural fibres in tepid water, squeezing rather the rubbing, rinsing in clean water at least twice and wrapping in a clean towel before hanging out to dry. The worst that can happen here is that the item shrinks just a little if woollen, or leaks a little colour as you wash, or goes a little floppy (often the case with linen). (See page 179 for starching advice). At best, it will come up smiling, in which case add it to your wash load next time at a cool setting and keep all pale and dark colours separate. It is not just that you are saving money: natural fibres generally

Washing towels

If towels emerge like cardboard, you may be using too much detergent, or rinsing insufficiently. I usually find a good shake when dry limbers them up again.

look fresher and smell sweeter given a wash than swirled about in a cylinder full of dry-cleaning fluid.

Cheap, colourful imports of printed cotton and muslin are the fabrics to approach with caution, though even here standards of colourfastness have improved considerably and most fabrics are pre-shrunk due to pressure from retailers. What can go wrong is that some of the colour leaks into any white areas of the print.

FIBRE MIXTURES

These are a risky proposition unless clearly labelled washable. Some slithery synthetic fabrics such as rayon wash as easily as pure silk. However, fabrics containing Lycra emerge a little tighter from the washing, which is fine unless you have gained weight meantime! With the more complex mixtures, involving unknowns such as polyamide, you may be safe washing if the predominant fibre is one you know, ie, a natural fibre. It is certainly worth a try if the item in question is a cheap and cheery number and where the cost of regular dry-cleaning seems absurd by comparison. However, with anything a bit 'designerish', it is best to play safe and opt for dry-cleaning.

In all my years of ignoring label instructions, I have only had four failures. A Jean Muir frock in viscose jersey shrank to the size of a baby dress. The pretty coloured stripes on a woven ethnic shoulder bag bled irredeemably, and two tops, one in stretch lace, and the other in an irresistibly soft open knit wool/synthetic mix just stretched and stretched till the sleeves and hems reached my knees.

Too late did I realise that I should have practised what I preach, rolled them in a towel first, and then dried them flat.

WASHING CASHMERE

The secret is 'cold water and Woolite'. This comes from the horse's mouth: ie, the formidable stallholder at Spitalfields Sunday Market, who does a brisk line in vintage cashmere knits. Her woollies, beaded cardis, and checked golfing pullovers couldn't be more varied in style and provenance (trade marks like Pringle and Lyle & Scott are currently the most sought after), but they are in peak condition, due to her simple treatment. Moreover, they are all beguilingly cheap. I tried her suggestion. It works.

WASHING DELICATE ITEMS

Some items need special care if they are to survive the rough and tumble of a washing machine. I have an old Victorian hand-knitted white cotton bedcover which I am most attached to and – which being white – needs fairly frequent washing to keep it looking pristine. The knitted blocks are quite tough, but it is the crochet work joining them up that is fragile. Stuffing it bodily into the machine at its lowest setting (30°C) leaves a lot of gaps or splits in the crochet, and too much mending for me to cope with. Instead I now stuff it into an extra-large pillow case, using safety pins to keep it tightly closed during the wash. This stops the coverlet thrashing about and straining its weakest links. I would advocate the same precaution when washing anything bulky but fragile such as patchwork, Durham quilts or lace tablecloths.

Anything really fragile, but not bulky, such as an antique christening robe or a Victorian peignoir covered with lace, is best washed by hand. But the above-mentioned bulky items are just too difficult to deal with when soaking wet so machine washing is the best compromise I have found. Watch out for safety pins coming adrift and blocking the machine (see page 174).

I often put silk fabrics through the machine, on the coolest setting, with half the usual quantity of detergent, wiping a stain remover like Bio-tex soap over greasy shirt collars, etc, first.

Same procedure for everyday woollen items – blankets, thick jumpers – checking labels first. Anything at all special I handwash in cold water, with Woolite.

It is maddening to be told that thorough rinsing is what makes the difference to the softness of woollens, but it is quite true. Rinse till the water stays clear was the old maxim, and that still holds good, especially in hard water situations.

STARCHING

If you like linen clothes, try starching. Starched linen not only looks elegant, but it stays shapely longer and sheds crumples and stains better. It is a three-minute transformation job which will give the most banal linen shirt and pants the crisp, floaty chic one envies on catwalk models. And it is ridiculously easy. However, it is only for use on linen or cotton.

USING HOT-WATER STARCH

Hot-water starch (don't bother with the spray stuff) is a fine white powder, closely related to cornstarch, and is sold by Boots or under the trade name Robin.

To make up enough starch to stiffen two or three garments:

- Put 1.5 litres (2½ pints) water in a kettle and bring it to the boil.

- In a big bowl or pail, drop 30ml (2 level tbsp) of starch powder, add 30ml (2 tbsp) cold water and mix to a smooth paste.

- Pour on the boiling water and stir until the mixture thickens and goes transparent (like cornstarch in a Chinese stir-fry).

- Thin this down with approx. 2 parts cold water to 1 part hot starch mix, stirring to blend smoothly. Dunk in your clothes wet from the washing machine, one at a time. The first garment dilutes the mix further.

Paddle them about to make sure they are evenly coated. As you take each one out, wring or squeeze excess starch back into the receptacle.

- Hang out as flat as you can manage. When dry they will be as stiff as cardboard. Damp well with your spray bottle, roll loosely in a towel and iron (using a hot iron) as soon as possible.

Starching leaves a semi-sheen finish after ironing. If you don't want this I recommend you iron the item on the inside. Ironing reduces the board-like stiffness to a wearable crispness.

NOTE: Other fabrics (cotton, muslin, voile and lace) also benefit from starching lightly. It is a great pick-me-up for droopy ruffles.

DRYING

A tumble dryer is undoubtedly a blessing when there are babies and children to cope with – Lydia, my latest granddaughter, seems to get changed two or three times a day – or if you live in a flat without a drying space. I used to have a dryer until I discovered that all the teenagers used it to dry a couple of items apiece, mooching about the place (in one case, wrapped in a bath towel) until jeans, T-shirt, socks and Y-fronts were ready for an evening's clubbing. When scolding and warnings fell on deaf ears, I decided it was time to take action. The tumble dryer went outside the front gate with a note saying 'it works, help yourself'.

Instead, I bought a whirling clothes line and set it up in my diminutive back yard and it is in use almost the whole time. Carrying baskets of washing to and fro and pegging it out takes longer, but clothes have a sweet tang drying outside, even in the polluted air of the inner city. One local hazard is curry-making day when some 50 Balti and curry houses fill the air with turmeric, leaving distinctly yellow patches where it settles on my washing. I have to sniff the air; if it smells of curry, I make sure the washing comes in as soon as possible, even if it means draping the kitchen with damp clothes and sheets.

I know housewives in the past kept an anxious eye on the weather on wash days, rushing to gather it in if rain threatened. I am afraid I just see it as a free rinse. Even rained on, the stuff dries, though it takes longer – something my au pairs find hard to believe. Anyway – as I catch myself repeating for the thousandth time – slightly damp clothes makes ironing that much easier and more effective. 'Damp', though, is a highly subjective term, as I have discovered, which translates with difficulty. The ebullient Jana never got the hang of it, and I would find neat piles of soggy T-shirts and underwear awaiting distribution around the house. Jana recognised the word all right, she just couldn't get her head around the concept, or tell the difference between a damp and a sodden item. In the end I gave up and just shoved the soggy items in the airing cupboard, figuring that Jana would get the message only when she had a baby of her own to care for; as any parent knows, a significant watershed. When I told her this she giggled cheerfully, and not long afterwards departed to set up house with a handsome Sardinian she met working in a sandwich bar.

DRYING PROCEDURE

The hardest point to get across – and I am talking about my own family, as well as au pairs, all 20-somethings – is that there is a skill in pegging out washing so it dries taut, smooth and hardly in need of ironing. Girls pick this up if you keep pegging away (ho ho!) but young guys seemingly never. Where a girl will tune into the wash cycle, and get the stuff out on the line promptly, the bloke breezes off, letting the creases and crumples cook in overnight. When reminded, he will snatch it up and fling it over the line any old how. It pains me to see these corrugated items – pants twisted like barley sugar, bunched-up T-shirts, even prized dude designer shirts – stiffening contortedly outside my kitchen window. If I am feeling generous, or need the space, I try to retrieve the situation, but I doubt they even notice.

Pegging out your washing for best results is not rocket science; in fact it is crashingly obvious once you get a feel for it. Basically, the more smoothly an item hangs on the line, the flatter and less wrinkly it dries, so less ironing. There are certain little refinements, however: more to do with not putting extra strain on the drying garment or leaving peg marks in unwelcome spots.

- All items to be pegged up should be given a good shake first, to return to shape. Pull puckered seams taut, close zippers or flies. Smooth out trouser turn-ups, chunks of embroidery or drawn threadwork on bed linen. This saves ironing time.

- Plastic hangers are useful for drying jackets or long frocks, but bear in mind the stretching propensities of 'wet weight'. If in doubt, roll in a towel for an hour or two before drying outside.

- Hang shirts by the tails, not the neck or yoke. Hang side by side with enough overlap so one peg secures two shirts, but be generous with pegs, folding the two fronts across, and pegging in the middle.

- Hang pants by the waistband, stuffing pocket linings back inside.

- Bias cut clothes are best towel-wrapped first, to guard against stretching. Dry on shaped hangers if you can.

- Towels, pillowcases and tea towels can be pegged loosely by the corners, not stretched flat, to save space on the line.

- Peg socks in pairs by the toes. Saves sorting and missing socks.

- Double sheets, duvet covers and tablecloths dry quicker if pegged by hems on their long sides, so the air can blow through. If this takes up too much time, hang by the short hems, but make sure they don't trail near the ground, especially if you have dogs – some of them find flapping laundry an irresistible temptation.

- Hot sunshine does a great bleaching job on white cotton and linen, but it can yellow white silk so dry inside out.

- Shake up fluffy clothes or blankets once or twice during the drying time to fluff them up more. Shake towels too once dry to get them soft and fluffy.

- Your best knits (cashmere, angora, pashmina) deserve the towel treatment. Drying flat is always recommended but, lacking space, I end up pegging them too, by the hem, preferably after pulling and coaxing them back into shape. Wool mixes, as in a loose-knit sloppy Joe, can stretch alarmingly, so are best dried flat.

Bringing it inside

If you can snatch clothes off the line while just damp, you make ironing easier and quicker. But this means you have to stick around waiting for the right moment and you would need to get stuck into the ironing straight away. Anyway, damping with a spray bottle is no problem. However, don't pile your washing into your basket any old how. Fold everything loosely and stack so ironing doesn't feel like wading into a choppy sea. It has taken years of exhortation to persuade my family that the time saved by stuffing dry clothes pell-mell into the basket is lost when it comes to getting the creases out again.

IRONING AS THERAPY

What is so slavish about ironing? People keep telling me the one job they keep putting off is ironing. It is so boring, they moan. My most hated task is packing and unpacking. I accept that we all have our Achilles heels when it comes to routine tasks. However, there is an attitude problem here.

My way of taking the grind out of ironing is to cut it to essentials: don't *think* of ironing jeans, cotton knits, T-shirts or underwear. Many of these feel crisper and look fresher unironed anyway, and if they are pegged out to dry with finesse (see page 182), they only need shaking out and folding before stashing away. The same goes for tumble drying. Here the trick is to catch them at the end of the cycle, but before they have creases cooked in. Then shake out, fold and air if needed.

Those items I do iron, however, I give the full works. This includes anything linen, silk, cotton, rayon or crêpe. Shirts must be ironed – women's and men's both – likewise any garments that are at all special. Here, taking extra care and going for a professional finish will make both them and you look and feel sleek and snappy, and prolong their life.

Get comfortable

The first requirement for an easier ironing session is to make it as comfortable as possible.

Gerald Fox, a young designer friend, dispatches his ironing over the weekend. With the radio tuned to a favourite programme, the odd tea break and a stack of hangers, he finds it a breeze. This also saves him real money compared with, for instance, a City chum who sends all his shirts to a laundry at an average cost of £25–30 per week. Gerald would rather spend the cash on a weekend cycling around Provence. 'I'm quite proficient at ironing, and I quite enjoy it now. I don't see what people make such a fuss about,' he says.

Gerald, I need hardly point out, has the right attitude. If ironing must be done, and unless you live in drip-dry or shell suits it can't be dodged, then make it a positive thing. Radio is better than TV as companion for this because it is hard to concentrate on the job with one eye on the box. Plus you need a decent basic kit, as follows.

THE IRON

Steam irons sound like the answer, stomping out creases in a puff of steam. The downside is that they need re-filling with deionised water in hard water districts, otherwise the lime deposits gradually gum up the works. I have tried de-scaling tablets claiming to rectify this, with only partial success. Remembering to keep a bottle of deionised water handy doesn't sound like a big deal, but one does forget and it is also an extra cost.

I fell for the bravura showmanship of a steam-iron salesperson in a London department store, and walked out with an elaborate piece of equipment: a steam iron umbilically connected to its own water tank which plugged into the electric socket with another few yards of flex.

What I failed to pick up on – hypnotised by the way she transformed a crumpled tweed jacket by snorting steam over it in a few magic passes – was that this invention needed not only ionised water but a constant supply of special filters to keep it in good shape. I bought several filter packs along with the iron, discarding them as recommended when they turned orange, which they did quite rapidly. When they ran out I re-ordered by mail. However, the next time I tried to re-order I was told that this particular steam iron model was no longer stocked and regretfully this included the filters. Did I want to take the matter up with the manufacturer in Switzerland? Call me a wimp, but I didn't feel like devoting hours to chasing up filter packs for what was probably already an obsolescent steam iron which had already cost me somewhere in the region of £160.

I reverted to a modestly priced steam iron, recommended to me by WHICH? (see page 79). Moral: don't let yourself be suckered by pricey variants or updates on a crashingly straightforward domestic gadget.

Heat, steam and damp

Irons work by applying heat and pressure to just-damp fabrics. The most beautifully ironed clothes I can remember – smooth, crisp and immaculate – were ironed daily in China during my childhood using a couple of crude flat-irons filled with a glowing lump of charcoal.

Lim, the ironer-in-chief (also our cook) tested the iron temperature by spitting on the base, knowing precisely from the degree of sizzle when it was right for heavy linen or fine silk. The smell of burning charcoal, hot metal and damp cloth was rich, complex and memorable. Not for nothing did so many émigré Chinese set up as laundrymen in the New World. I like to think that my own fussiness when I do a big ironing session harks back to Lim's masterly control over his basic equipment.

The bottom line is that the simplest electric iron will do the job efficiently so long as the fabrics to be ironed are not too creased (which means taking a little thought when drying) and just damp enough to create steam under pressure from a hot iron. You don't have to be Chinese to iron skilfully, but you do need dampness. Lim's washing was fetched in by the washing amah at just the right state for good ironing; this was his refined skill.

We add dampness more crudely by spraying the fabrics to be ironed. I use a plastic spray bottle filled with clean water, an hour or two ahead of my ironing session. I bundle the clothes up loosely and wrap them in a damp towel, which sits in one of those plastic laundry baskets in my laundry venue. Another ruse is to give the clothes a spin in the tumble dryer with a wet towel.

iRONING BOARD

Light, folding aluminium ironing boards, which can be set at a range of heights, are pretty standard today. I find the ready-made ironing board covers available, often with a curious metallic finish, rather unsatisfactory. I prefer a soft, squidgy cover which I make myself from a couple of thicknesses of old blanket with a smooth top cover of old sheet fabric. With a pocket to fit over the point end of the board, and a few ties that go underneath to hold it taut this only takes an hour or so to run up on a sewing machine and seems to give better results. Failing a sewing machine, try using safety pins, judiciously applied, to hold it in place.

Folding boards can be hung up on the back of a convenient door with the help of a cotton reel screwed in place, or a couple of large, right-angled pot hooks.

Ironing while standing up brings more pressure to bear, but ironing from a sitting position is far more comfortable.

HANGERS

An ideal ironing location would have a rail handy to take hangers (I hook mine to the cornice of an old linen press); a clean empty table top for folded items and a plastic basket to accommodate the rest of the clean clothes that are not being ironed.

If you have a large family, a table long enough to stack up each member's clothes separately imposes a welcome sense of order and completion. Most likely it would be the kitchen table, in which case you need to set a deadline for collecting the stuff and putting it away.

Padded hangers

Wire hangers are fine for summer clothes, but they don't do anything for tailored jackets or stretchy frocks, which end up with funny pointy 'shoulders'. Clothes stay put on padded hangers.

It is easy to make your own. You will need:

Wooden clothes hangers
1m (1yd) flameproof wadding
Sewing thread
Scraps of fabric (or knit sleeves from discarded clothes)
Bias binding (optional)
Ribbon for bows and/or lavender bag (optional)

● Begin by wrapping the wood hanger in wadding, binding in place with thread.

Hanger tip

Twist rubber bands around the ends of hangers to stop clothes sliding off.

● Cut two fabric rectangles (half the hanger length – more if you fancy a shirred look) and then machine down the long side and one short side.

● Slide the tubes over the wadding so the open ends meet in the middle. Catch them together with a few stitches.

● Finally, if you wish to cover the hook, wrap it with bias binding. Trim with bows and a small lavender bag if you wish.

Covering a wooden hanger

1 Wrap the hanger in wadding and bind with sewing thread to keep it in place.

2 Make two fabric rectangles to cover the wadding. Sew up three sides, leaving one open.

3 Slide the tubes over the wadding, stitch together at the centre, and bind the hook if you wish.

IRONING REFINEMENTS

Radio

A radio, as mentioned, is basic in my view. You may prefer music on CD, but I find the human voice, in all its styles and embodiments, makes time speed by while engaging one's mind in not too demanding a fashion.

Sleeve board

Really a mini-ironing board, this speeds ironing small areas like yokes, sleeves and pressing jackets. These used to come attached to ironing boards, but these days I make shift with an old cushion pad, which I can bunch up to fill a tailored shoulder, though not a sleeve.

Spray bottle

A plant spray bottle works well (see page 185). Label it clearly and keep filled with clean tap water. (Hedonists can use lavender-scented sprays for bed linen: lavender is claimed to give sweeter dreams.)

Repair kit

Superwoman stuff, but not to be sneezed at. A small basket, or drawstring, containing shirt buttons, sharp pointy scissors, needles and thread handily placed means you can do the stitch-in-time-saves-nine bit: replacing shirt buttons, securing bra straps or catching up loose hems in short order. The tedium of such small repairs is outweighed, I swear, by the huge and perhaps absurd triumph at having booted them out of mind.

Pressing cloth

Any old square of torn-up sheet will do here. Wet but not dripping: dip in water, then wring out. Use this for pressing tailored garments, flattening obstinate creases.

Spray starch

Maybe I am incompetent, but I find these give spotty results and seem to lead to scorching. Nothing beats old-fashioned hot-water starching, in my view, for fancy table linens, dress shirts and those designer linen outfits which mysteriously seem to lose substance through repeated washings (see page 179).

Stains

Sometimes stains you hadn't noticed appear on tailored clothes needing a quick press. Always deal with these before pressing, as heat can make them immovable. Identifying them – egg, candle wax, wine, gravy or biro – is a priority (see page 192).

IRONING – THE TRICKS

Ironing is such an ancient skill, and one taken to such professional levels (by couturiers and tailors as well as laundries) that there are, as it were, recognised procedures for going about it to give the best results in the shortest time. Shirts are the obvious example. Shirts should be ironed so the 'show' parts – front, collar, cuffs – emerge crisp and creaseless. Back, yoke and sleeves matter less, for men, though women who slip their jackets off need to be fussier.

Ironing a shirt

Assume the shirt is just damp, either because you caught it at the right moment or have sprayed it beforehand.

● Iron the sleeves first, then the cuffs on both sides.

● Next the back. If it's a button-all-the-way-down shirt, open the shirt out flat. If it doesn't open all the way, slide it over the board to get at the back.

● Iron the yoke next, over a sleeve board, or by sliding it over the pointed end of your board; one half, then the other.

● Iron the front next, pressing hard enough to flatten the buttonhole strip and dodging the iron prow between the buttons.

● Last, iron the collar, wrong side then right side, trying to avoid a run of tiny creases along the collar edge – spraying if

necessary. These creases are the result of trying to flatten a collar by ironing laterally from side to side in one movement. Iron from the centre outwards, nosing the iron inwards to follow the slight bias in a collar. Fussy it may sound, but the collar is the showpiece – the giveaway – of the exercise.

All things being equal – hot iron, damp fabric – ironing a shirt should take approximately four minutes. (Apparently Martha Stewart takes three.)

To hang, or to fold?

Still-damp shirts need airing before putting away or they will smell mouldy. This can be done either on hangers, in a warm room, near a radiator or folded in the airing cupboard in a neat stack.

Wire hangers are OK for hanging shirts provided you button up the top buttons, though shaped plastic or wooden hangers are better as they mimic the hang of a shirt on your back.

Folding a shirt (see next page) is best if you have more drawer or shelf than hanging space, and is useful practice for packing shirts in a suitcase. Laundries use pieces of thin card to keep the shirt front taut, but with a couple of trial runs you should achieve a stack of neatly folded shirts with unblemished fronts and collars.

Folding a shirt

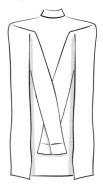

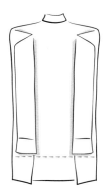

1 Place the shirt front down and fold the sleeves and part of the body to the back.

2 Fold the sleeves back over the folded body and smooth flat. Fold the shirt tails up.

3 Fold up the bottom half of the shirt and sleeves. Turn the shirt over to the front and smooth flat.

Ironing linen

Linen needs a section to itself because (a) it is becoming such a designer fabric and (b) getting it right makes all the difference between an item you enjoy wearing and a limp rag, which sags and bags in all the wrong places.

In an ideal world (not the one we live in) all linen would be lightly starched in hot water starch, before ironing. This is worth considering for your most loved clothes. I find much designer linen gets progressively softer with washing, which suggests it arrives with a super-added dressing. Softness is fine with pyjamas, but can leave you feeling dressed in damp hankies when it comes to shirts, dresses and pants. Only

starching will remedy this, restoring crispness and enough body to resist creasing longer (see page 179).

When ironing linen, always turn the garment inside out as ironing on the right side makes the fabric shiny. This is especially noticeable on dark colours. Ironing inside out also encourages you to flatten out the seams, which makes all the difference to the hang of the item, pants and pencil skirts especially. Seams are always pressed flat in classy tailoring. Twisted or wrinkled seams can wreck the shape of any garment. Pockets also need to be well flattened to avoid a sinister bulge just where you don't need it. Mingy, overstitched seams look better smoothed out and stretched as you iron from the inside. If you need to smooth out creases at the finish, use a damp cloth on the outside, airing the item till quite dry.

Embroidered linen

Usually this means table linen, which tends to look nothing unless starched. A bother, yes, but worth it for those show-off occasions when resplendent napery sets the tone impressively, even if it is only once a year. Starching also provides a protective coating to the fibres so that wine and food stains wash out more easily.

Iron embroidered linen (or cotton) on the wrong side, over an extra layer of softness, such as a folded sheet, pressing firmly and smoothing out the embroidery carefully as you go. Try not to stretch it, or you end up pulling the cloth out of shape.

Other fabrics

One hundred per cent cotton is a cinch to iron: it only needs to be slightly damp and can be ironed on the right side, though a little attention to seams on the inside can be a help here too. Cotton mixtures – polyester and lycra, etc – often feel friendlier and look better unironed. Rayons (coming back into fashion) and crêpes are best ironed on the inside, with the iron setting as recommended on the clothes' label. If in doubt, use a lower setting than on linen and cotton and test a small section first. If a low setting doesn't do

the business, press with a damp cloth and a higher setting.

Bias-cut or stretchy fabrics

It is easy to pull these out of shape when ironing. Bias-cut fabric needs to be ironed on the 'straight', ie, with, not against, the weave. To establish this, pull the item and where it gives or stretches is the bias. Where it doesn't is the straight.

Stretch fabrics are usually best unironed, if a cotton-lycra mix. You want them tightish, and your body heat will get rid of creases. Hanging them up in a steamy bathroom will help smooth them out. Alternatively, this is one brilliant use of a steam cleaner (see page 116): hang the garment up, play the nozzle up and down a few inches away from the surface and you can see the creases fall out. Steam treatment is best for all pile fabrics,

Cleaning and pressing ties

Men's ties are the devil to clean: use dry-cleaning fluid on cotton or face-cleaning pads. Most ties are silk or silk substitute, and should never be ironed flat. Slide a pad of Kleenex, kitchen role or loo paper inside to round out the tie and steam lightly, no more. Remove pad when dry.

including devoré. At a pinch, pass the fabric over the spout of a steaming kettle.

Fancy lingerie

Sexy bias-cut satin nighties and camisoles cling more suavely when they are ironed on the reverse. I don't usually bother with bras and knickers, but if you aim for perfection, iron over a damp cloth. This takes care of lace insertions, pin tucks and other frou-frou.

Pressing

This is the way to sharpen up tailored garments of wool, wool mixtures, tweeds and cashmere cardigans. It is also a safety measure for any item you are unsure about ironing, since the damp inhibits scorching. You can either use a steam iron over a dry cloth, or a non-steam iron over a damp cloth, with the same results. Pressing between trips to the dry cleaner means fewer visits and also you don't look like a sad sack meantime.

A valet, or a gentleman's gentleman, would have pressed a suit after every wearing. Men's suits do need fairly regular attention, but so do pencil skirts. Pushed for time? Just press the most crumpled areas; around the crotch of trousers and the waistbands of skinny skirts. Skirts are easy; slide over the board and press the crumpled areas flat. Trousers need to be dealt with one leg at a time stretched flat on the board and pressed until smooth. You can press trouser creases in at the same time. A moment's attention to the knee area (which bags in wear), flies or zip, pocket and waistband; four minutes?

Suit jackets wrinkle across the back and around armholes and elbows as you would expect. The back is easy (just lay flat), but sleeves are a pain if you don't have a sleeve board, and armholes throw up access problems. A blast of steam from a steam cleaner would be neat if you have one. Otherwise, flatten along the sleeve, press the armhole by bunching a towel or pillow into the space and do your best. Never press a suit/jacket collar folded over – ie, as you wear it – open out and press flat.

For a professional and de-luxe pressing job, cover the whole item, flattening pocket flaps, jacket front, the lot. Seams sag and even Saville Row fabrics bag. Pressing tightens up the fabric, restores resilience to the wool, cuts the shine and sends it all back to… well. maybe not square one… square two?

Reviving hats

Hold dented or crushed felt hats in the steam from a boiling kettle (or steam cleaner) and watch them spring back into shape. Steaming also revives pile fabrics, eg, velvet and velveteen.

CLEANING FEATHER AND DOWN ITEMS

Ideal Dry Cleaners in Devon runs a cleaning service for eiderdowns, pillows and duvets at competitive prices: £5 for feather/down pillows, £13 for eiderdowns and £14 for duvets. They are linked with the Eiderdown Studio (see page 218) and thus offer a mint of expertise. There is no collection service but they do mail order (see My Directory).

While I had the experts on the line, I took the opportunity to check out some basic facts about cleaning feather/down pillows, eiderdowns and duvets. These are some of the tips they gave me.

● Although tumble drying an eiderdown can fluff up the filling it is generally better to use a launderette machine as a domestic tub will be too small for the job.

● They use solvents for cleaning feather bedding to get rid of dust mites, etc, but assured me that the solvents have completely evaporated before the items are returned to you. They not only clean the filling but blow it back into new cases.

● Can down/feather fillings be home washed? The answer is yes for pillows, which are small enough for a domestic washing machine to cope with. Wet feathers are massively heavy, which rules out washing either duvets or eiderdowns. Tumble drying a pillow is feasible to fluff up the filling, but the expert's view is that you will be paying more in electricity than getting it cleaned professionally! I recall reading somewhere that you can restore fluffiness manually by shaking the pillow, hanging it in the sun and shaking it several times during the drying period.

STAIN REMOVAL

Red wine splashed on your pale linen sofa cover, ribena down the front of a small daughter's party frock, or a squiggle of felt pen on the bosom of your snowy silk shirt – these misadventures do happen and are a stiff challenge to your sang froid. Undoubtedly, stains are a pain for everyone.

If you move fast, most stains can be eradicated.

However, this is not always so easy. Stripping off the sofa cover your guests are happily seated on is liable to damp the party spirit and make the red wine culprit feel ten times worse. Nor does the ribena show up until your offspring returns from the bunfight. And who actually takes a spare top to work? Nonetheless, especially with natural fibres, there is always a good chance of success with stain removal, even if you can't get to the problem straight away. At least, you will always feel better for trying.

I have the impression that stains and how to remove them is not a subject that preoccupies people today to the extent it did 100 or even 50 years ago, when you could expect any household manual to devote several pages to the subject. Even *Superwoman*, published in the 1970s, gives stain removal a whole pharmacopeia and pages of advice, but then Shirley Conran is, as she explains, a dry cleaner's daughter. Some of her favourite remedies, it turns out, are now blacklisted as carcinogenic, while others – sodium sulphite, sodium sulphate – are unlikely to be stocked these days by your local chemist.

Somehow, the bother of assembling your own stain-removal kit and familiarising yourself with the procedure involved in their use is just too much hassle, especially now that there are so many ready-to-go commercial preparations claiming to do the

After dinner return to quite another drawing-room, and sit next to yellow-satin lady with iron-grey hair who cross-questions me rather severely on my impressions of America, and tells me that I don't really like Chicago, as English people never do, but that I shall adore Boston. Am just preparing to contradict her when she spills her coffee all over me. We all scream, and I get to my feet, dripping coffee over no-doubt-invaluable Persian rug, and iron-grey lady, with more presence of mind than regard for the truth, exclaims that I must have done it with my elbow and what a pity!! … Iron-grey lady takes the initiative and calls for cold water – hot water no good at all, the colder the better,for coffee.

Diary of a Provincial Lady, E M Delafield
(Macmillan, 1930; Virago, 1984)

Stain removal rules
- The one cardinal rule when it comes to stain removal is NEVER USE HOT WATER as this is likely to fix a stain immovably.
- The second rule is to try to accurately identify the stain – a smudge of tar needs different treatment from a smear of boot polish.
- Choose natural fibres in the first place, because these are more forgiving of stain removal procedures than synthetics or mixes.

same thing. I compared my own experience of these with that of the professionals and the consensus is that they deal with some stains really well (biro, for instance), others less successfully; but they are well worth buying and trying.

However, everyone seems agreed on the emergency drill for dealing with stains, worth knowing because disasters still happen and first aid in these situations can make a big difference.

- Speed is of the essence. Fresh stains respond better than old ones.

- Blot up as much of the stain as possible immediately, using Kleenex, loo paper, kitchen roll or whatever is to hand, keeping a fat wodge behind the stain to absorb your treatment.

- Next, use cold water on a sponge, cloth or cotton wool (depending on the circumstances) to soften the stain, wetting and blotting simultaneously, and changing your absorbent pad repeatedly. The aim is to draw out the stain without flooding it over a wide area. Easier said than done, as I know. Flooding a red wine stain with white wine (popular myth in my experience) works less well than cold water. Nor does salt help – another old tip that fails.

- Once you have mopped up the worst, anything that can be soaked – ie, a loose cover, washable clothing – should be dunked in a basin or bath full of cold water to help float and disperse the stain, harmlessly. At this point use a nail brush and a drop of biological washing powder or liquid to scrub at the mark, vigorously. If you have Bio soap on hand, try this too. I am a firm believer in friction, marvelling at the way Asian women did such a great job with stones and river water.

● When it's as pale as all this action can achieve, resort to the washing machine, on lowest setting. Hang out to dry. Faint stains look worse wet than when dry.

I am aware that this is a drill that won't fit all situations – upholstered furniture, for instance, leather desktop, suede pants, rugs and matting. However, the principles – soften, blot, scrub – remain valid for all liquid stains – ink, fruit juice, red wine and blood. If you catch these fast, you have a good chance of paling them to insignificance.

The problem comes when the stains have 'set', like blood-spotted sheets. Soak these first in a salt water solution: cold water, any old salt followed by a scrub. Next try a biological liquid or wash powder, in a pre-wash situation. Dry in the sun if possible. On 'whites' these stains should gradually disappear.

I tend to resort to the commercial stain busters as a second line of attack, if my first aid remedies haven't come good enough. I use them if the stain looks really obdurate, even after the wash and dry, in the hopes that some chemical ingredient may do the trick. It makes sense to try them out on a seam or invisible place first, to check they do not harm the fabric.

Work inwards

Shirley Conran's 'Top Tip', which I pass on gratefully, is to encircle the stain with the treatment and work inwards with the solvent. If you work outwards you simply risk spreading the stain more widely and will fetch up with a large pale splodge rather than a small dark spot.

You can sometimes soften old, immovable stains by sponging with glycerine, leaving it to soak in and float off the mark, before washing, or following up with another treatment. A diluted solution of hydrogen peroxide (read the label instructions) is a safe and efficacious bleach for 'whites'. This is what I use on, say, coffee stains on a white silk shirt, which still showed up after my emergency treatment, laying the stained area on a towel, and spotting it with the bleach. Even if all this sounds too arduous, too technical, and your instinct is to rush to the nearest dry-cleaners, it is worth knowing that you have made their job easier by dealing with the worst of it immediately, where possible, and when it counts.

Sometimes, sadly, your best efforts are counter-productive. I managed to get biro scribbles on the cuffs and front of a red suede jacket. They were not eye-catching, but I thought I would use my commercial stain buster on them – it did soften the scribbles, but it also leached the red colour from the suede, so it looks worse, more conspicuous than the stains themselves. With stains, some you win, some you lose.

SPECIFIC STAIN TREATMENTS

The following remedies include some proprietary stain removers, some of which work beautifully and others not so well.

Red wine

Folk wisdom tells you to throw salt on the stain immediately to soak up the worst. Another school of thought advocates pouring white wine over the red. I have tried both approaches. At the time, neither made an appreciable difference to my red Chianti stain. On the other hand, when I later scrubbed at the stain using a spot of clothes-washing liquid and cold water, the stain disappeared completely. It could be that either salt and white wine prevented the full implantation of the stain in the fibres.

If possible, stuff a pad of kitchen roll or a clean rag under the stain at the time in order to contain the stain and prevent it from oozing outwards. The moment you can, whip off the cover or tablecloth, etc, and scrub the stain in cold water with a dab of clothes-washing liquid making sure you don't soak the whole item. Rinse in cold water.

Finally, leave the entire item in a cold-water bath, to which you have added a few capfuls of biological washing liquid. Alternatively, you could stuff the item into the washing machine on the pre-soak setting with a reduced amount of washing liquid.

Then put it through a cool wash the following day and with luck your wine stain should have at best vanished, and at worst be barely visible.

Blood

Soaking in salt water is the traditional remedy, and this will usually even dissolve old stains if scrubbed at regular intervals. Should it be a large item such as a sheet, soak the relevant areas in a large bowl of salted water first – it is a good idea to stand this in the bath. Once you see the stains begin to soften, use a bristle brush to scrub as you would with those red wine stains mentioned above.

Finally, give the whole item the biological pre-soak and cool wash. This procedure should get rid of blood stains, but should traces remain it is always worth trying the oxalic treatment (see below).

Felt-tip, ballpoint or biro pens

Here, the branded products, namely Stain Devil and Supersoap, do actually work. However, do make sure you have the right one! Follow the instructions carefully; spot with stain remover till you see the marks dissolving, then wash as instructed.

Coffee and tea

As you can imagine, these are hard to shift since both were used as 'antiquing' dyes (in solution) for new fabrics which needed 'ageing'. Therefore, it is important to deal with these as soon as possible, soaking in cold water to which you have added borax (to soften both water and stain). Even rapid sponging with plain cold water will help. Do not be afraid to scrub because, as we all know, friction can do wonders. If we are talking natural fibres, repeat washing and hanging out in the sun will gradually reduce stains to invisibility. Oxalic acid (a strong bleach – see below) can be used as a last resort, but only on natural fibres intended to be white.

Grease and cosmetics

Men's ties, in particular, pick up greasy fallout, conspicuously on the bit below the knot. Dry-cleaning usually delivers back a wizened rag.

Alcohol is the most effective grease solvent. Although meths is wood alcohol, the purple colouring renders it unsuitable. It may sound odd, or extravagant even, but try spot cleaning with vodka, neatly applied on a cosmetic pad. Vodka is about as pure as alcohol gets, in the UK at least, and most people I know have it on hand! It is best to stuff the tie first with a roll of kitchen paper, so as not to flatten or warp it, then swab with a cosmetic pad moistened (certainly not dripping) with vodka on the dingy bits. It should also help with smears of foundation – but not lipstick.

Lipstick

This is a brute (especially now that lippy is more a stain than a coloured grease). Having tried various solvents (unsuccessfully), I moved on to a proprietary product, Bio-tex Supersoap, and it worked like a dream. A light scrub in tepid water after a smear of Supersoap, and the lippy stain is completely washed out. All two-timing males should keep a pack of Bio-tex in their briefcases!

Sweat

More of a man's thing (at least in my experience). Some men sweat copiously, discolouring underarms on shirts, even after they have washed and applied anti-perspirants. I suggest you try a mild bleach made from 20vol/6 per cent hydrogen peroxide (from chemists) diluted 50:50 with cold water. Test a corner first to see if the colour is affected. If not, swab on the actual sweat stains, leave for half an hour, then give the garment the bio/cool wash treatment (see above).

Shout

This does an excellent job on food stains, as well as baby poop, as I discovered recently in a Sicilian restaurant, when my partner splashed a seafood sauce all over his pale tweed jacket while greedily chasing up the last spoonfuls of the best fishy broth ever.

While we were taking stock of the damage, the proprietor raced up with a spray can of Viava (Italian brand name, as this was all happening in Sicily) and began squirting it on to the stains. `No problem', he insisted, 'leave a few minutes, then I brush it, and you will see, no marks, nothing.' The valeting operation took another half hour, what with more squirting and harder brushing, but sure enough the jacket emerged looking perfectly clean and respectable, able to join the evening passegiata without attracting disapproving glances.

I ran Viava to earth in a backstreet shop and found it was a product of Johnson Wax. When I called Johnson Wax UK, their marketing person told me that Viava was the Italian name for a cleaning product sold in the UK under the name of Shout. I suggest you keep a can of it on hand.

Fruit and vegetable stains

These are also tough to remove as many fruits – blackberries and elderberries, for example – were originally used as dyes. *Superwoman* suggests glycerine, left for an hour, to 'float' the stain away. This is worth a try since glycerine is cheap, and widely available from chemists. Follow this with the standard pre-soak using bio washing liquid.

Paint

I have always found methylated spirits, rubbed on and off (use an old towel underneath as a pad) works effectively on drips and spots of emulsion or acrylic paints. You may need several applications to clear the paint completely. Use your fingernails to pick off loose stuff first, then try the meths, leave a few minutes to soften the paint, then rub with an old towel.

For really hard old paint stains, emulsion or oil paint, the best recourse is a dab (use a brush) of paint stripper. Today most brands will deal with both types of paint. It is important that you leave the solvent in place until you see the paint softening, then rub with an old towel and finally wash and scrub at the spots by hand. Don't leave it too long: paint stripper has a powerful caustic action and will attack the fibres of your fabric. So keep an eye on it and move fast.

So far, we are only talking about paint stains picked up as you brush past a newly painted surface. When the unthinkable happens and a pot gets knocked all over your floor or carpet, keep cool and think quick.

● Grab a metal spoon or spatula and a bowl to scoop up all the liquid you can.

● Use kitchen paper (a whole roll if necessary) or an old towel to mop up anything remaining. If you can slide rags, newspaper or kitchen paper beneath the spot, do so.

● Then dribble on the solvent in a cautious fashion (meths for emulsion and white spirit for all oil-based products) starting at the outer circumference and working in towards the middle; mopping fast with a towel or rag as you go.

● When complete, leap in with detergent or carpet shampoo, etc, adding a dribble of washing soda, borax or ammonia – basically all water softeners – if you have them. Wash and wash, mop and then rinse, then rinse again, mop, mop, mop!

If you caught the damage quickly enough, you should escape with slight discoloration – and this you can probably live with.

Gravy

I use this word loosely to cover any number of cooking splats and juices, which may contain anything from Worcestershire sauce to tomato purée, saffron and turmeric. I often hang damp clothes on the Aga rail to dry off and try to ensure that I remove them before embarking on the cooking process. However, some of my sous-chefs have been known to forget this precautionary measure. As a result, my silk shirt gathered a bright yellow splodge on the collar; could be either saffron or turmeric (both are traditional dyes). In desperation, I tried all my stain removers. No change. I then recklessly dripped a touch of Cif on the stain, with the result that the stain paled slightly. Finally, in a flurry of impatience, I dunked the shirt into tepid water and proceeded to scrub away with just a little drop of washing-up liquid – applied neat – which got rid of, say, 90 per cent of the stain. Furthermore, this has pretty well disappeared over subsequent washes.

Fortunately, if you get to the stain in time friction – washerwoman rub-a-dub-dub – is pretty reliable. Perhaps the ultimate last resort – but have you ever sent your clothes to be washed in South East Asia? Here rub-a-dub-dub is a tradition, on stones by the riverbank, yet it all comes back immaculate. Perhaps too much tough love for 'delicates', but how often do you splash gravy on your Agent Provocateur or Janet Raeger underwear?

Rust

This is the devil to shift and tends to turn up on old antique garments or crocheted white bedspreads. Start with lemon juice, then try a solution of oxalic acid.

LEATHER AND SUEDE

LEATHER

Most clothes, bags or shoes are made from soft, thin hides. I might start with saddle soap (see page 131) for a basic clean up if the item looks dingy and discoloured: like that '30s ostrich bag that you picked up in a thrift shop, a '60s snakeskin waistcoat or some mad platform boots! When cleaning scaly skins such as alligator, snake or lizard always apply the soap so that the scales are smoothed down as opposed to ruffled up. Alligator and crocodile hides are immensely tough and can come up a treat even if the rest of the bag or case is a shambles. In some cases, it may be worth getting the item re-fashioned to give it a new lease of life.

New leather clothes or the fashion items mentioned above are best treated with Properts Hide Cream (see My Directory). This will keep the finer, softer leathers supple and burnished in a low-key way. Its use is dead simple: apply with a soft cloth, leave to penetrate for a while and then gently rub to a sheen with another clean and soft cloth.

Scotchgarding might be a further option with pale leather which shows every drop of rain (although these usually vanish as it dries) but it seems superfluous with a dark leather garment. Leather has its own inbuilt weatherproofing. After all, why do bikers choose it? Nevertheless, should a leather garment get really soaked, make a point of drying it out slowly at room temperature. Drying it over a radiator or other heat source will stiffen the leather, which in turn can lead to cracks. Stuff boots, bags, etc, with scrunched-up newspaper or kitchen roll to ensure that they keep their shape.

Patent leather

Twenties flappers used plain old Vaseline to keep their patent shoes and bags from cracking, as well as adding a dazzling shine. It is still the business for patent, better **than neutral shoe cream, and – well buffed – is less likely to rub off on your clothes.** However, you might wish to cover up cracks or scuffs first with shoe dye or, on black patent, Indian ink.

SUEDE

Complete turnabout here because suede has a nap, or raised surface, and this makes it much more vulnerable to wear and weather – as we know to our cost. That peachbloom texture which makes it so sensuously appealing is also pretty fragile. It makes sense to give extra protection where possible and a spray finish such as Scotchgard is a rapid solution. It won't, alas, prevent the nap wearing away but it will reduce staining and stiffening caused by rain, pollution and other nasties.

There are super-tough and practical suedes on the market today which can be put through the washing machine (Boden do jeans) but I haven't tried them, and this wonder hide does not seem to have become standard.

Cleaning suede

It may be the nap needs reviving rather than the suede needs cleaning. Start to work on this with a rubber suede brush, gently rubbing it round and round on the darkened flattened areas. Next, try a fine wire brush applied in the same manner but never too forcefully or you could find yourself rubbing away the nap altogether. If the suede still looks dark and discoloured, your next move is to apply suede shampoo, per instructions, rubbing the nap again with your brushes once dry. It is best to shampoo the whole

item or you may end up with lighter patches.

Alternatively, try steam cleaning suede to lift out dirt and raise the nap. However, don't soak the surface – two light goes is better than one saturation.

In my book, suede dyes are a last resort which can even out or alter the colour but you do risk losing the bloomy texture en route.

SUEDE OR NUBUCK?

You need to know the difference here because what works on suede (suede shampoo) can mess up anything in nubuck, removing colour, stiffening the hide and spoiling its texture. Nubuck, also called 'velvet calf' is much more common than real suede, which has a deeper 'nap'. Nubuck is cheaper too – not that a nubuck garment, cushion cover, bag, etc, is necessarily cheap if it has a designer label.

I bought a zip-front designer (Clements Ribeiro) jacket in a second-hand clothes shop for £75, reduced from £800, or so I was told. I assumed it was suede and started cleaning it with suede shampoo, on a 'test area', luckily, since the patch I worked on leaked some colour on to my sponge, dried stiff, and looked no cleaner.

Could it be nubuck? I tried spraying the jacket with Meltonian nubuck cleaner, which uses no water, and to my amazement it came up a treat, brighter, several degrees cleaner, and almost 'as new'. All this without any further complications, other than brushing lightly with a suede brush when dry. Since a professional cleaning job cost almost as much as the jacket, secondhand, I thought this was good news worth passing on.

The problem remains: how to tell the difference between real suede and 'velvet calf'? Ask the sales assistant or the shop manager, who should know, if it is an expensive item. In my case, since the jacket was secondhand, the shop owner could be forgiven for not knowing – on the other hand I do recollect her advising a good brush rather than suede shampoo, so maybe she had an inkling. It is a great little bargain though, now clean and sparky, so I'm not complaining.

WATER-BASED PRODUCTS

I tend to shut off when a shoe-shop sales assistant tries to persuade me that I need a special polish, brush, or water-proofer for my already extravagant purchase. But I am glad I listened to the guy who sold me a Coach handbag in San Francisco, and convinced me that it needed the Coach Leather Cleaner and Moisturizer as well. In for a penny, in for a pound, I thought. Now I am a convert. They clean well, protect leather against weather, handling, etc, but best of all, the products leave no stickiness and do not affect the colour or finish of the leather.

Coach bags are stocked by Harrods, who also retail their Leather Cleaner and Moisturiser at about £5 each (see My Directory).

DOING IT THEIR WAY

ALEX POLIZZI

Alex (short for Alexandra) Polizzi is one of the two daughters of Olga Polizzi, Olga being designer/sister to the hotel chain entrepreneur Rocco Forte. Alex is what one might call professionally domesticated. Besides taking turn and turn about running Tresanton, the chic Cornish hotel venture she shares with her mother and sister, she is often rushed of to the latest Forte hotel to add her nous and experience.

In her 20s, Alex is strikingly handsome with dark bushy curls and wide grin which add up to a distinctive style. Watching her do the maître d' routine on a packed dining room in both a friendly and highly efficient manner, casual but on the ball, is a lesson in how 'front of house' should be managed: a light touch masking professional skill and self-discipline. A Forte family trait perhaps, but not always one that persists into the third generation.

I first spotted Alex early one summer morning doing a Cinderella on the terraces of Tresanton. She was scrubbing down the teak tables and chairs solo. I then next observed her inside the dining room giving a couple of young Aussie waitresses a quick brush-up on how to lay, not the tables but the tablecloths. 'All the creases should point the same way, it looks better,' she said, firmly but smiling. Here, I thought, is a chip off the old block; running a hotel with style and intelligence is very much in her genes.

Although Alex adores her job, she is quick to mention that she read English at Oxford before entering her uncle's hotel scene. 'My mother always told me to get it in quick about the Oxbridge bit, so people couldn't run away with the idea that if I enjoy catering I must be thick.'

Alex has been on hand to groom and tweak six hotels in the chain. Although these include the glamorous locations of St Petersburg, Rome and Florence, she assures me it is no holiday. 'It's an incredibly hard life,' she says cheerfully. 'I'm on pretty much between 8am till 12 or 1 the next morning.' With 28 rooms and a busy restaurant at Tresanton there is a lot to see to. In the afternoon break she occasionally nips down to her mother's boutique of clothes and jewellery, Onda, to do a stint behind the counter.

Since the takeover of the Forte hotels by Granada (fiercely resisted by the family) netted them many millions, Alex certainly doesn't do this job for money! Her explanation is simple: 'I am a perfectionist. If I see a T-shirt folded untidily it bothers me.' (Or even tablecloths with the creases pointing in different directions.)

Her mother, quoted in the hotel's press cuttings book, puts it differently: 'It is strange that both my daughters have caught this mad catering bug. Maybe it's in the Italian genes. Italian women do have that thing of wanting to give service, of wanting I suppose to look after people.'

Nature maybe. but also nurture. Olga trained her daughters up from an early age. 'We used to serve at her dinner parties, and she sometimes reduced us to tears over laying the table correctly. We all know how to cook and make a place look beautiful.' As Alex herself says, 'people only grow through criticism and pointers. The hardest part of my job here is to teach people there is value in repetition … Some of my friends think I'm wasting myself, my degree and all that, but I have always thought it was the most interesting job in the world.'

She admits to being no good at multi-tasking; 'I can only do one thing at a time and right now I want to concentrate on Tresanton. I've had enough of doing openings, and this place needs me.'

REPAIRS AND RENOVATION

The Japanese have a word, *sakiori*, to describe the art of recycling old, tattered items of indigo-dyed fabrics, either patched into quilts or torn into strips and woven into sashes or floor coverings. Why throw out a worn item of a handsome fabric when with imaginative, patient stitching, it can enter a new phase of existence, honoured all the more for its previous history? This frugality is not seen as evidence of poverty, or meanness, but as showing respect, an attitude of mind far removed from the consumerist extravagance of the late twentieth century which, with hindsight, looks pretty gross.

Signs are, however, that the zeitgeist is blowing from a different quarter now. As the world out there feels scarier, home and family regain their centrality, cocooning is a buzz word, domestic crafts – knitting, patchwork,

canvas work, even dressmaking – are coming back into favour as a new generation discovers the satisfaction of making, creating or recycling alongside 'staying in', home cooking and quiet evenings in front of the box. In the USA young guys, normally into computer games or gory action movies, have become fascinated by Norm, expert joiner and star of a hoary public TV series called 'This Old House', where he quietly demonstrates how to plan, cut and put together a bookcase, kitchen units, even, Lord save us, an inglenook. Raised on the cutting edge of IT technology, this new audience is riveted by Norm and his cool, seemingly casual, ability to construct permanent fixtures in the home out of a pile of sawn timber, screws, glue and paint. The novel drama of this guy actually making it before your eyes almost beats baseball, so they tell me. The appeal of Norm, as I see it, has to be that he re-introduces the notion of DIY, a whole mastery of materials and their potential to an audience so accustomed to ready-mades, flat-pack, pre-package, that his projects seem magical, astonishing.

If this has me laughing up my sleeve, ironically, it is because like Norm I grew up with DIY, right across the board. I learned by doing, hands on, and found very little that was impossible, given patience and determination. Needlework came easily, paint finishes took longer, and skills such as carpentry, wiring, plumbing I had a bash at, with partial success only. But, my goodness, the triumph and satisfaction of getting something right, operational, convincing, was mega, always. I do believe we all have a maker inside us, bursting for release, at any level – carpentry, needlework, decorating, whatever – and giving this creative urge an outlet, an aim, a project, puts you in touch with an undiscovered part of yourself which is as exhilarating as it is therapeutic.

I recently came across Fine Cell Work, an extraordinary and imaginative project where long-term prisoners are taught to do needlework – mostly what we call tapestry – to the highest standards, with a share of the profits to look forward to. Most of them are men, they mostly never used a needle before in their lives, but their handiwork is superb, and some of them have discovered a designing skill they never suspected was in them. But what shouts at you from their work – cushions, rugs, patchwork – is the discovery that using time productively is altogether different and superior to killing time as a couch potato.

I must have introduced hundreds of people to the rudiments of decorative paint finishes under my paint guru hat, and I always found their delighted astonishment at discovering they could do it, making the mark or brushstroke happen, immensely rewarding. If you had seen a group of stroke victims jubilant to find they could still control hand and eye sufficiently to execute a stencil, I think like me you would have recognised a profoundly therapeutic value in just 'making' things.

What this preamble is about is preparing you, dear reader, for many incursions into re-cycling, refurbishing, make-do-and-mend, which you may not be familiar with, but which I guarantee – well almost – will lead you into fresh fields and pastures new.

ELBOW PATCHES

I have rediscovered the excellence of elbow patches. If you associate these with Professor Higgins or rustic toffs, think again! It is often one's favourite garments, designer jackets or cashmere woollies, which go at the elbows whilst remaining perfectly sound elsewhere. First aid in the shape of neat elbow patches can extend their wearable life considerably. They could even be a fashion statement, especially if you choose cheeky contrast colours.

Woollies and cashmere

Here, my advice is to put like with like: ie, cut patches from another knit and sew them on the wool so stretchiness and washability are not affected. My favourite cashmere jumper was seriously out-at-elbows and I couldn't find a sacrificial woolly to cut up so I bought a pair of cashmere/wool socks for under a fiver, plus a skein of darning wool. Since the jumper cost over £100 and the repair took all of 20 minutes, I feel this is a tip worthy of note.

Oval or egg-shaped patches are the traditional solution for elbows as these cover worn or holey spots without interfering with the fit and comfort of the sleeves. Make sure that the patches cover the worn spots generously. Should cutting ovals be a problem, start with a circle and then gradually slim down the sides.

Stitching patches on a knit is straightforward enough. Slip your hand into the sleeve and hold it stretched out, pin or baste the patch in place and then oversew with small neat stitches all the way round. Use a darning needle and wool for stitching and make sure that you don't pull the stitches too tight. If you are nervous of pricking your hand, you could stretch the sleeve out with something along the lines of an old-style darning mushroom: perhaps a small bowl or saucer?

Jackets

Shiny elbow areas on my beautifully cut black Cerutti wool jacket were a sad discovery. Since the jacket goes to the dry-cleaner periodically, like with like was not the solution here. Instead I bought ready-made black elbow patches in mock suede, cut them down (most commercial patches are intended for men's clothing and are proportionately huge) and stitched them down with strong black thread. The said jacket has been dry-cleaned twice since with complete success.

Should you need to patch a prized jacket that has sleeve linings, take care that they do not get stitched in and cause the sleeve to twist uncomfortably. Being a fairly expert stitcher, I manage to avoid this. If you are not, I suggest you unpick the lining at the cuff, roll it up beyond the patched area, sew the patch in place and then roll the lining down and re-stitch inside the sleeve cuff. A professional repair service would probably unpick the sleeve seams so that the patching can be done on a flat surface by machine. However, I doubt many of my readers are prepared to go to quite so much trouble!

DARNING

In an era of 'wool-rich' socks, cheap enough to chuck without a twinge of guilt, darning skills seem on the way to obsolescence. All the same, a neat darn can have its uses. I darn moth holes in clothes too distinguished or comfortable to jettison, and once in a while I have lavished fine darns on hand-embroidered table linens bought for a pittance in antique textile fairs or boot sales. I have a weakness for old embroidered linens into which so many hours of patient stitching have gone. The older they are the more likely to be a bit 'faulty' in trade parlance. Often they have been minutely darned already and I enjoy testing my skills against that long-dead needlewoman. Of course, on a fine old linen these darns show, but I think they add rather than detract. A well-executed darn shows respect.

Where darning skill is raised on to a higher plane altogether is in 'invisible mending' (see below). A cigarette burn on your cool, new designer suit? Or, as happened to a young man I know, a small but conspicuous slash on a gorgeous Valentino jacket? This was his very first big label extravagance, a dream fit and sales bargain to boot. Heady with clever shopper euphoria, my friend caught sight of one of those wicked little tags, attached by a plastic thong, to the left pocket. He tugged. It laughed at his show of strength. Feverish with impatience he snatched up a razor blade, and well you know the rest! His hand wobbled and there right in front of him was a sharp wound in the Valentino silk wool mixture. To get this 'invisibly' mended, by a professional, cost him roughly a third of what he paid for the jacket. Had he been a bit clever at darning the incident would have closed with less angst and self-reproach.

Anyone with keen eyesight and steady hands can darn. It just takes patience. Essentially, your stitching mimics the weave of the textile in question. Use a closely matching thread: wool for wool, linen on linen; and in the 'invisible' mending situation, the very same fabric snipped from a side seam or hem and patiently unravelled. Your equipment is simple: a darning needle with an elongated eye, suitable thread and a pair of sharp scissors.

Once upon a time, a wooden darning 'mushroom' was a staple of every family sewing basket, smoothly carved and specifically designed to make sock darning easier. Snuggled into a sock with a grievous 'potato' of a hole, it held the hole stretched open while the darner needled across the surface, vertically and horizontally. These days, the nearest equivalent seems to be a wooden 'pusher' sold in kitchen supply shops. They cost a few pounds and consist of a smooth wooden hemisphere attached to a stubby handle.

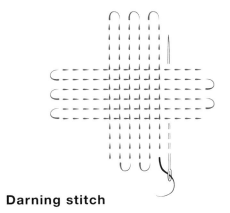

Darning stitch

Moth holes

In my experience, these usually appear on prized woollen garments in nastily conspicuous places: smack centre front, under the arms and round the seat or crotch. Moths seem to go for wool plus a spot of protein, such as a drop of gravy, egg yolk or bodily secretions such as sweat. Moths have always been with us but they do seem to have multiplied of late and nearly everyone I speak to has horror stories of moth damage running into hundreds of pounds. Prevention is better than cure (see page 161.)

Cure means darning, not the full-on darning of sewing manuals, but a subtler approach using fine thread and gently closing the moth hole.

● Work from the inside of the garment but refer regularly to the front to make sure that you have not ended up with a lumpy scar instead of a smooth, next-to-invisible suture. The aim is to bring the edges of the hole together as close as possible.

● Then, by deft tiny stitches you secure and flatten any protruding edges and bits. Leave a little 'give' as you darn, especially on stretchy fabrics such as wool knit and jersey; ie, don't pull the thread too tight.

● Finish by pressing with a damp cloth. Result: only your worst enemy can spot the repair, and you don't feel like Raggedy Ann.

Superlative darns

Full-on darning needs to be meted out to old, exquisite or heirloom stuff. Such repair work addresses those odd little holes caused by time, cigarette ash or candle wax. Where an old fabric has worn along fold lines there is not much you can do. However, small holes can be darned, adding useful life to the piece. It is slow and finickity work but justified if the cloth belonged to your great-grandmother or is so lovely you want to use it on special occasions.

The closer your darning thread matches the original fabric – linen, damask or cotton – in fineness, fibre and colour, the better your work will look in the end. It calls for TLC. Don't rush it. One delicate darn a night, feet up in front of the TV will do the trick far more effectively.

THE STITCH THAT CHEERS

Your average mass-produced clothing range today is high on style and cut but skimpy on finish due to the interest in keeping prices competitive. Seams gape, hems suddenly unravel and buttons pop off. If you keep a skeleton sewing kit in key areas – utility room, wardrobe or your bedroom – this is not an insuperable problem. A stitch in time …

The 'finishing' I am referring to is more structural. For instance, how many jackets, coats or dressing gowns are supplied with a sturdy loop for hanging them up? Lacking these, your clothes get slung on a hook and end up with curious pointy excrescences around the back of the neck.

Facings are another weak spot. I have some linen pyjamas, excellent in all respects but for the facings. Traditionally, these were stitched down to make the jacket sturdier and easier to iron. Mine are flapping loose, get twisted and are a bother to press. I am not suggesting you spend hours adding dressmaker touches to your cheap and cheerful garments. However, a morning dedicated to upgrading your favourites will prolong their life and keep them looking good.

You will need a sewing machine plus the full sewing kit (not a stitch in time one). This needs to include reels of thread in a good range of colours, black tape for loops and a length of chain if making hanging loops for really heavy coats. A pair of fine-nosed pliers for cutting short lengths of chain will come in useful. Invisible – ie, transparent – thread is handy for stitching up hems if your hemming is less than exquisite.

Button storage

Every household needs a button box or glass jar. This is where you keep those cute little packets that come with clothes containing a button or two and a length of matching thread. It is also the repository for all the buttons you thriftfully remove from shirts, duvet covers and other items on their way out. A sharp craft knife, or scalpel, does this quicker than scissors. Mrs Wonderful would keep like with like: shirt buttons in one jar, fancy ones in another and so on. Recycling buttons may strike you as OTT, but you would be amazed at the time it saves when you get down to mending, and a surprising number of buttons today are of high quality: ie, real mother-of-pearl rather than plastic.

Hanging loops

Thread your machine, fold your tape sides to middle, and machine down the centre to make a tough 'bootlace' a couple of metres long – the extra will come in handy.

To make a loop chop off a 5cm (2in) length, open out each end slightly then stitch the ends down firmly using a tough thread – button thread is best – at the back of the neck just below the label.

A short length of chain (hardware shops sell brass chain for sink plugs) is the best loop for really heavy outdoor garments such as tweed overcoats. To get a short piece use fine pliers to open up a link so that you can slide your piece off. Then simply stitch down the end links using button thread and being generous with your stitching.

Neither tape nor chain are suitable for fancy garments such as silk dressing gowns. I suggest you use satin ribbon here.

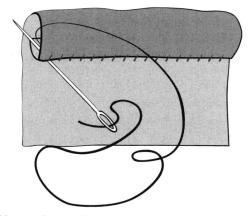

Hemming stitch

Hems

Most hems – trousers and jackets as well as skirts – are held in place today by a flimsy transparent machined thread. Because it is fragile, it easily snaps and because it is machined, once a length unravels, you can soon be drooping all over the place. In an emergency, double-sided tape is a big ally. (Failing that, I have known people to use staples, but not only will they show up, they will most likely ladder your tights or nip your skin.)

Getting it done professionally

Here are some standard prices for repairs done by the professionals. These come from a cleaning company in London,SWI.

- To shorten trousers: £9.50
- To turn up skirt hems, or re-stitch: from £11.50.
- To patch, visibly, ie, on jeans £9.00.
- Invisible mending – from £20.00
- To shorten sleeves, ie, a man's jacket sleeves, with their buttons and button holes – from £18.

There will be cheaper alteration services in less posh areas, but not much cheaper, I suggest. The point is: do it yourself and save a considerable sum.

To re-stitch by hand is no big deal. All you need is a needle, a reel of thread (matching polyester is best; transparent will be kinder to uneven stitching), scissors and pins. You can even do without pins if you tack the unstitched length first, using big stitches and holding the hem taut. Once positioned hemming is easy.

Take quite big stitches, but only pick up a thread or two of the main fabric – the visible side – and don't pull the hem stitching too tight or it will pucker. Start and end with a few little extra overstitches to stop it undoing itself. Anyone who takes a hem to be repaired by a professional is a wimp!

Facings

Pyjama facings are best tacked and then machined down in a thread that matches the fabric – white thread at a pinch. Pull threads through at each end of the seam, knot and snip off and then pull out the tacking.

Flapping facings on tailored jackets need to be hand sewn invisibly so that the facing is anchored to the jacket front down its entire length.

Herringbone stitch is good to employ because it has some 'give'. If you pick up only a thread or two of the jacket front as you go along, this reinforcement will not show in wear. Keep the herringbone stitches quite large – 1cm (3/8in) approx – and don't pull the thread too tight. You will be pleasantly

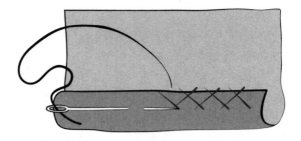

Herringbone stitch

surprised at how much more together your garment feels after this minor attention.

Zips

Zips are another weak spot in the 'finishing' of mass-produced clothing. A heavy-duty metal zip giving out on a favourite pair of jeans is a familiar annoyance. However, it shouldn't be the signal to chuck them away. Safety pins may save the day, but wait until you need a quick pee in a station toilet and you may think differently! Examine the zip closed after washing. Usually one zipper 'tooth' has gone missing. In some cases you can deal with this (especially if it is low down) by stitching firmly just above the missing 'tooth', thus making a new starting point.

However, if the zip has gone because the jeans are really tight (sexily tight), you may be faced with a replacement job.

● The first move is to unstitch the existing zip. This can be done most rapidly using a scalpel, but go cautiously as zips often involve heavy-duty stitching and you will need to open the waistband up slightly to remove the top end of the zip.

● Next, take your zip to a store that specialises in what used to be called haberdashery and match it in length, colour and solidity.

● Line up the new zip with the old stitching lines and tack it in place tucking the top ends under the waistband. Re-stitching by machine is straightforward if you have (a) a machine and (b) the special foot which allows you to stitch close to the zip teeth and (c) know what you are about.

● Failing all or any of these, the simple answer is to stitch the new zip in place by hand using tough thread (or standard thread doubled) taking small stitches and back stitching every two or three stitches for strength. Pushing a needle through tough denim is easier if you wear a thimble – third finger, right hand.

Replacing a jeans zip is not a fun job agreed (so many lines of stitching and such tough fabric) and a handstitched zip won't look quite as before. However, if it gets your beloved second skin pair back into circulation, it must be worth a try.

The other zip problem I have encountered is quite different. It is a skinny plastic zip in a pair of stretch pants which keeps snarling up (OK, they are tight but that is what stretch is supposed to be about!) This is because the zip is only held in place by two lines of machining, the outer edge not being secured. Overstitching the outer zip edge, both sides, to the seam beneath solves this problem. A second row of machining would be even better.

Waistbands

A flimsy, unsecured waistband has an annoying tendency to ride up in wear – you find these on a lot of skirts and pants. One thickness of fabric is meant to be folded down out of sight. To achieve this, simply catch the edge of the waistband down to every seam it crosses with a few stitches.

Pockets

Pockets are often so poorly stitched that the seams give way and your small change, credit cards, etc, drop through a hole. To access and repair in tailored and lined garments you will need to unpick the lining quite extensively. Along the hem is usually the best point of attack. Pull out the pocket lining and, either by machine or by hand, stitch generously along the seam line. Then re-hem the lining in place using long loose stitches and matching thread.

SHOE REPAIRS

Fashion shoes – pretty but not too expensive – can usually be kept wearable with a visit to a heel bar, as it is the heels that take punishment. By the time the soles wear through you probably want to chuck them anyway. However, there are shoes, especially boots, you paid more for and expect to give you longer wear. Sending these to a fast-fix shoe repair service can return them clunky, subtly mis-shapen and oddly heavy. OK, they keep your feet dry, but the elegant fit and balance – a rare find in a mass-produced shoe or boot – has been irretrievably wrecked.

This happened to me with a pair of fancy western boots I splashed out on during a brief visit to Calgary, Canada – 'stampede city'. I wore them so hard the stacked heels wore down dramatically and holes appeared in the soles. I dropped them in to a local cobbler. They came back so thickly re-soled and heeled the cool and shapely line had vanished; they looked and felt more like wellies. I keep them for my country walks.

Once bitten etc … My next boot extravagance, little lace-up ankle boots which fitted like handmade, I took to the most expensive shoe repair service by my reckoning: Jeeves in London. A heels and sole job cost over £40, about a sixth of the cost of the boots, but the pain of shelling out so much cash turned to relief when I found the boots as light, elegant and perky as when new. A crude repair would have been a false economy as I would not have enjoyed wearing them and they would have been relegated to the back of my wardrobe. They are into their second wind, the uppers a little creased and scuffed, but the perfect fit which first attracted me (badly fitting boots are cruelty to feet) remains brilliant. Three years on, that posh repair job feels more like a Best Buy.

If ever you light upon one of those pairs of shoes or boots that put a spring in your step because they fit like a second skin, never chafe or give rise to blisters or bunions, and look sharp – my advice is to go for the top repair job. It will be cheaper in the end. Jeeves, a London-based dry-cleaning and shoe-repair service, has several branches, and all their work is done to the highest standards with prices to match (see My Directory).

BEDDING REPAIRS

REPAIRING SHEETS

Sheets invariably wear gauzy thin down the middle, which you can see when you hold them up to the light. The next thing is a tiny tear, where a scrabbling foot has been pushed through, then in no time a huge rent develops and the sheet gets torn into rags – always useful.

If you need sheets more than rags, the time-honoured move here is what my Argentine granny, Evelina, called briskly 'sides to middle'. Evelina, of the eagle profile and snapping black eyes, was a queen of 'make-do-and-mend'. This was partly to do with sitting out wartime privations and post-war austerity as well as her earlier unpampered married life on the pampas with a large family and a tight domestic budget. Evelina would catch a sheet at the wearing-thin stage and rescue it with the 'sides to middle' operation. The sheet emerged smaller (doubles became singles and singles became cot sized) and there was a seam down the centre of your bed, but it would be good for a few more years. We felt lapped in grandmotherly solicitude and as a result slept just fine.

Reserve 'sides to middle' for your 'best' sheets – linen certainly and special cottons – but I wouldn't bother with mixed fabrics. The latter are hardly worth saving and make lousy rags as they are linty and non-absorbent. I am sure that Evelina never encountered a cotton/polyester fabric during her lifetime and would have certainly turned it down with a snort if she had!

Sides to middle

This process is largely self-explanatory, but there are a few subtle refinements that are worth noting.

- First, slit the sheet down the middle – don't tear it. Then trim off the threadbare sections on either side but be careful not to do this in too radical a fashion.

- Now, turn your attention to the sides – are they machined hems or selvedges? Selvedges are no problem but stitched hems need to be unpicked using a seam-ripper, a tiny plastic gizmo (a bit like a crochet hook) with a built in sharp cutting blade. Old machining will sometimes yield if you pull sharply, but use the ripper to start things off. The reason for unpicking these hems is to make a neat, flat seam down the middle (see page 216) without losing a precious cm of sound cloth. This will require two rows of tacking and two rows of machining with a little hand-stitching to tidy up the ends. A flat seam

Sewing a flat seam

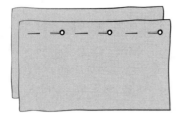 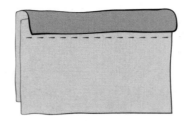 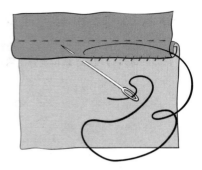

1 Place the two raw edges together, with one 1cm (³⁄₈in) lower than the other. Pin a seam line 1cm (³⁄₈in) below the lower edge, then stitch.

2 Fold the top raw edge over the lower raw edge as closely as possible.

3 Open the fabric out flat. Press the fold down flat, pin, and hand or machine stitch to make a flat seam.

should be approximately 1cm (³⁄₈in) wide and lie quite flat when stitched down. If done well, it will outlast the sheet.

● All that remains is to tack and stitch down by machine the outer edges of the sheet to make small, neat hems. As we are talking about somewhat worn fabric where a sharp pull could cause a horizontal split, I recommend tackling the hems first.

Maybe it is sentiment, or a touch of Evelina in me, but I find such thrifty repairs both honourable and touching. Give me a sides-to-middle sheet any day in preference to a linty, drip dry cotton/synthetic mix fabric

where every patch of rough skin snarls on the fibres and makes you feel like a dinosaur rootling sweatily in a temporary lair.

HOT-WATER BOTTLE COVERS

A last use for shrunken woollies? Not strictly bed linen, but in the same department. Hot-water bottles seem to be gaining ground on electric blankets as an eco-friendly way to take the chill off bedding. They are even friendlier with a woolly cover. It is easy to make your own.

Use an empty hot-water bottle as a template. Lay flat on an old jumper, allowing a 2cm (³⁄₄in) clearance, and cut round – cutting two similarly shaped pieces, but

Hot-water bottle cover

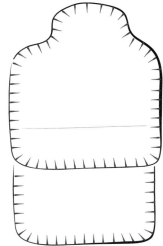

giving one extra length. This is to make an overlap, as shown above

Place the two pieces right sides together and machine or hand sew round, using a loose stitch to allow for the stretch of the fabric. Turn the right way out and blanket stitch all around in a bright contrast wool. *WARNING:* replace hot-water bottles regularly, preferably each year. Fill with hot tap water rather than boiling water from a kettle.

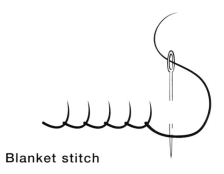

Blanket stitch

EIDERDOWNS, DUVETS AND PILLOWS

It may surprise you, but not everyone today is a duvet fan. You may not be aware that there are fashions in bedding. I recall an eloquent piece by Jonathan Glancey in the *Guardian* Style section calling for the return of tucked-in bedding – sheets and blankets – for which he foresees a revival. Well, maybe. There is something luxurious about climbing into a neatly made bed, the top sheet folded down over a warm and weighty sandwich of blankets with hospital corners. Yes, I know that bed-making is a slog, contraindicated for dodgy backs. Still, for restless sleepers, or a special weekend guest, an exception might be made?

This brings me to the subject of eiderdowns, because the proper finishing touch to an old-style bed must be one of these old-fashioned precursors to the duvet. The sight of one of these plump, billowy jobs, floating on top of the tidy bed, is irresistible. In addition, thanks to the vagaries of bed fashion, eiderdowns can now be picked up for next to nothing in thrift shops, boot sales and brocante fairs. If the filling – usually feathers and/or down – is lumpy, try putting the eiderdown through your tumble dryer on a warm setting in order to loosen and fluff it up. (The older an eiderdown, as a rule, the better the quality, as it will be filled with down rather than chopped feathers.)

For a more radical cleaning of eiderdowns, duvets and pillows alike, see below.

Recovering eiderdowns

Very often the original cover of an eiderdown will either be fragile, patched and mended or too retro (dusty pink taffeta or maroon chintz) to be a visual treat. Re-covering, for a quality down-filled item, is a viable option and a means of restoring it to use in a fabric of your choice. The Eiderdown Studio in Devon, established now for almost 20 years, specialises in recovering eiderdowns. They also do valances, bedspreads and bolsters – a whole bed wardrobe (see My Directory).

To recover a single bed size eiderdown (110 x 160cm/3ft 7in x 5ft 3in) the charge is about £73 in your fabric and for a double size (165 x 175cm /5ft 5in x 5ft 9in) £123.40. Send for their catalogue to review the various options, such as piped or frilled edges, same fabric both sides (ie, fully reversible) or one of their backing fabrics on the underside.

Cleaning eiderdowns
See page 192.

CUSHIONS

Cushions are good news for anyone wanting to revitalise a room that is looking a bit tired, or bland. Cushions are the safe way to test out colour combos because they are too small to overwhelm, though large enough to have impact. Also, they add comfort in portable form, softening the angles of sofa arms, or plumping out deficiencies in a saggy armchair. I suspect a lot of women collect cushions the way they collect handbags, a foible which has not escaped the notice of retailers. Cushions to go – in a dazzling range of colours, fabrics, textures – and prices –

It may also be noted that after the bread had been baked and removed from the brick-oven feathers and dum [down] that had recently been plucked from fowls were placed in the oven while still hot. Baking the feathers killed all the insects that might be in them and also ensured that they would be dry and not mat when they were used. After they had been baked the dum and feathers could be stored for years before being used in pillows and mattresses.

Ask the Fellows Who Cut the Hay,
George Ewart Evans
(Faber & Faber, 1956, 2e 1977, 1999)

are a profitable part of any design range, catering to that 'impulse buy' tendency so hard to resist.

FILLING

The trouble with the budget cushion is the filling, or 'pad', a lump of foam, granules, or prickly feathers which refuse to mould themselves to the small of your back, or the back of your neck. The ideal cushion has a filling of pure down, or feathers and down – a quick shake returns them to plump perfection.

These are always expensive, ready made, but are not that difficult to make for yourself if you keep your eyes open. Look for old bed pillows going cheap because the filling has gone a bit lumpy, or the cover is stained. A duvet may be too big for a washing machine, and heavy besides, but a pillow can be put through a cool wash with a mild washing liquid – such as Woolite – and either fluffed up in the tumble dryer (cool setting) or hung on the line and shaken at intervals to loosen the stuffing and plump it up again.

It can then be re-covered as is, or if you fancy square cushions, one of the shorter sides can be unpicked, the filling pushed down and a new seam made, by hand or machine, to close it. Be warned though – this can release clouds of feathers or down – you need to move fast, pinning first to control the filling, then tacking before closing.

CUSHION COVERS

Covering – or re-covering – cushions is so straightforward and requires so little fabric, anyone with a sewing machine can handle it confidently, and this way you get the uplift of colour and texture at a fraction the cost of a designer cushion. Be your own designer.

My most successful cushion covers ever were made from curious but attractive pieces of loosely knitted fabric I lit upon in an Oxfam shop, striped in subtle colours – pink, beige, white, grey. I realised, on closer inspection, that they were relics of the post-war austerity years, made up of war-time garments in stretchy rayon carefully cut into narrow strips and knitted up on huge needles to make … what? Tiny rugs? Whatever their original purpose, they stitched up into brilliant cushion covers, splendidly soft and floppy – I don't like small, firm cushions so much – and washed like a dream.

More cushion cover ideas:

● I sometimes buy old textiles and trimmings that catch my eye: embroideries, scraps of cut velvet, antique fringe or bullion.

● If antique is not your style, try the remnants counter in a department or fabric store.

● Absolutely the most cutting edge cushions I have seen recently: dark grey flannel with bullet shapes in low relief.

MENDING CHINA

A generation ago, china mending was a job that appealed to women with artistic leanings and time on their hands. Not so much the fiddly part of sticking the pieces back together – though that came into it too (see below) – as fancy restoration; painting over the cracks and touching up the decoration so cunningly that only a dealer could spot the mend. However, the intention was not to deceive but to make pretty again.

Nowadays the emphasis has shifted, possibly in line with the curatorial dictum that restoration should always be visible. Therefore, broken antique pieces held together with copper rivets have more appeal and value than the same item taken apart and invisibly mended.

Old cracks pick up a lot of dirt over time which can detract from the ensemble, but these can be paled to insignificance using the following method:

● Apply a poultice of kitchen paper, damped with water and then spotted with household bleach. However, do go cautiously: the bleach will not affect the enamel-like decoration one finds on old Chinese floral pieces, but it could attack gilding, or transfer ware, where the decoration was printed and the over-glazing is less robust. Test a morsel first.

● Keep the poultice confined as closely as possible to the crack, pinching it to a worm-like shape.

● Leave for several hours and finally rinse off thoroughly.

● An alternative approach, if the background is largely white, is to dip a fine brush into a strong bleach solution and paint it into the cracks. Leave for a while and then rinse.

THE STICKY BIT
Superglue

I only use the range of superglues on the most straightforward breaks, such as cracked teapot lids or jug and cup handles which have snapped off cleanly. Though such mends stand up pretty well to use (I would wash the piece by hand, not soak it for too long and avoid the dishwasher), I personally wouldn't trust a superglued handle on a full teapot. Nor a superglued mend on a water-filled vase. In the first case heat and weight would bother me, in the second the constant soaking of the glue.

A superglued fracture is next to invisible and any excess can be pared off with a Stanley knife blade. I don't need to warn you about proceeding with care; use cotton buds to apply the stuff if you are a scatterbrain.

Araldite

For more complex repairs, where a piece needs to be re-built from fragments, I tend to use Araldite two-pack adhesives – adhesive and hardener – which need to be mixed and applied following the instructions scrupulously. I find the adhesive flows better if the pieces are slightly warmed first, although you need to rehearse the process, because warmth will make it harden faster.

● Start by gluing together the smaller fragments, or a small fragment to a larger one, so the final coming-together join is made as straightforwardly as possible.

● Apply hand pressure to force the pieces tightly together, if you are using the fast-dryng version of Araldite.

● The slow-hardening version – handier if the mend needs adjusting fractionally – can be bandaged together with sellotape.

● A tray of sand is useful if the piece needs to stand at an angle during the hardening process, but take care not to get the sand in the mend.

● Surplus adhesive can again be pared off with a sharp blade, but keep it away from gilding because it will usually pare this away too.

TO MEND OR NOT TO MEND?

A mended item of china will never be quite the same, its resale value – if you are interested in that sort of thing – drastically reduced, and its useful life restricted to avoid putting too much stress on the joins.

I would not use a mended piece, whatever the glue manufacturers say about the mend being stronger than the object. However, if it is decorative and you love it, and the thought of chucking it away feels obscene, a neat, careful mend will return it to some sort of circulation,

But it will need TLC to keep going. Don't let your cleaner, for instance, flick it with an impatient duster, still less give it a well intentioned dunk in the sink. Mended decorative items – blue and white china, for instance – will survive longest hung on the wall or displayed on dresser shelves for visual impact.

Refurbishing gilt frames

A smear of gilt cream (available from art shops), applied with a fingertip, is the quick way to disguise bad chips on gilt picture frames. It comes in many different shades – choose the one closest to your frame.

REFURBISHING WOOD

FLOORS AND STAIRS

Now that wall-to-wall carpet has been shown to harbour such an alarming mulch of invisible allergens, there is a decided move to bare all. This may uncover anything from old parquet to stained concrete.

But more often than not in houses of a certain age, not to mention mansion flats, you will be looking at deal planking: narrow boards sprinkled with knots, and almost certainly patched here and there when the house was wired up or the flat was converted. The stairs, treads and risers may be made from a superior grade of softwood, to stand up to endless passing feet.

Assuming you have done a rescue job on this bare wood the following question arises: how to protect the surfaces and unify them visually? The most attractive solution I have found, and used, is a traditional Scandinavian three-part treatment which goes by the quaint name of Trip Trap (see My Directory for stockists). It leaves softwood a cool, greyish white shade, infinitely preferable to the stary yellowish tone you get if you apply varnish or wood seal. And unlike the range of varnish stains available it leaves the wood pleasantly matt. It wears off gradually in heavy-duty areas over a year or two, but this is quite acceptable because the treatment actually 'lifts' or 'leaches' out much of the yellow in the wood itself. It leaves the wood a 'driftwoody' shade, which may darken a bit as the finish wears thinner in much-trodden areas, but without a return of the yellow tone.

It would take too much space to detail the instructions here. They are explained in many languages (including English) on the Trip Trap kit, three plastic kegs of different liquids, which need to be thoroughly shaken up before use: 1, lye (the leaching agent); 2, the soap; and 3, the wax finish. Allow a weekend for completing the process – mostly time waiting for the particular ingredient to do its stuff.

You will also need:

a large paint brush
squeegee or sponge to apply 1
mop and bucket to mop off the
    yellow colour before applying 2
    with sponge or squeegee; and the
    same (well rinsed) to apply 3

To clean the Trip Trap surfaces from time to time use a mop with water and a tablespoon, per gallon, of Flash not mentioned in cleaning products. When the finish looks a bit shabby, it can be refurbished (after cleaning) with 4: another jerrycan of Maintenance Wax from the same firm, in the same fashion.

STAINING WOOD

Wood stains come in a wide range of shades of brown from pale honey to dark 'Jacobean' oak and in two formulations: water- or spirit-based. Both are equally effective. In my experience, the spirit-based stains penetrate faster but the solvent content may not be acceptable to you or your family. The water-based types are safe in this respect, but tend to 'raise the grain' slightly, although this can be smoothed out with careful sanding using a fine grade abrasive paper once dry, rubbing lightly along the grain.

Both types of stain will instantly alter the colour of a clean, dry wooden surface. The skill comes in selecting the right colour for the job. If stripping down a Windsor chair reveals that the legs are of a much paler wood than the rest, you will want to stain the legs to match. If none of the swatches seem close enough, do remember that you can intermix different shades as long as they are the same formulation – ie, spirit-based mixed with spirit-based and water-based with water-based. You might arrive at a mid-tone golden brown by adding a little dark oak stain to a lot of golden pine, or a dusky mahogany by adding a little Jacobean oak to a basic mahogany stain.

Remember that it is safer to start with a slightly paler shade than you want (test on an offcut) because each successive application will strengthen the stain colour considerably. Any finish you apply – varnish, wax, shellac – will also deepen and strengthen the stain colour. Although it is as well to know this, I don't think you should lose sleep over getting an exact match, unless we are talking about a valuable antique, in which case you might be better off with professional help.

Staining floors

You might, on the other hand, be looking at staining an entire floor of patchy deal to posh mahogany. I did just this within my own house. To begin with, the overall colour looked unified and rather impressive. Given three coats of semi-gloss oil-based varnish (a bit of a performance this as each coat had to be applied last thing at night to avoid footprints) the initially rich and glossy finish looked fine for several months, but imperceptibly at first, the varnish and stain started to wear through in heavy traffic areas, so my faux mahogany stairs turned piebald, in a patchy way, worn right down to the bare pine in places. Touching up with more stain, more varnish, on the bare patches helped visually but the result was less satisfactory than the original finish, applied when the whole surface was clean and absorbent.

In the end, I decided the upkeep of my fake mahogany stairs and floor was too much trouble and stripped and sanded it all off again (which took much longer than staining in the first place!) and went for the eighteenth-century scrubbed-planks look on the stairs, and painted black-and-white squares on the landing. The lesson I draw from this is that stains are not really suitable on floors that take a lot of foot traffic, although it remains a viable option for a spare bedroom or round the perimeter of a living room where the floor is mostly covered by a large carpet or rug.

Do not skimp on the varnishing because this is what protects the finish; at least three coats with adequate drying time in between. Acrylic varnish, which comes in matt, semi-sheen and gloss, is most people's first choice because it can be applied with a roller and dries amazingly fast (you can walk on it after an hour, though you should allow longer for it to harden before re-coating). Furthermore, it is colourless, or 'water clear' as they say. It is not, however, as durable as an oil-based varnish, or the two-pack coatings as used to finish bar counters. The snag with this last is (a) the smell and (b) the longer 'curing' time – a week to ten days – during which time the room is off limits.

Method

Surfaces to be stained must be cleaned to bare wood and completely dry.

● Tip the stain (stains if you are mixing colours) into a shallow bowl to make access easier, and apply the stain with clean, bunched-up rag. (I find a torn-up towel works well, not the deeply looped kind as the loops may catch on splinters, but a beat-up, old, drying-up cloth.) Wear rubber gloves to protect your hands.

● Dip the rag in the stain, start rubbing it on along the grain, moving fast and spreading it over as wide an area as you can manage. No problem with a small area such as a chair leg. Larger surfaces should be covered as fast as possible.

Cleaning paintbrushes

Treat classy paintbrushes respectfully to prolong their life. Brush off as much loose paint as you can on newspaper, then use a scrubbing brush and a spot of washing-up liquid under a running tap to clear the bristles, for both water- and oil-based paint. Scrub from the handle down the bristles. Dip in a weak solution of water and hair conditioner. Shake well, then dry flat, shaping the bristles.

Initially, they will look patchy but this can be taken care of by a second application. Avoid rubbing at one spot until the colour darkens and you have to keep up this intensity of colour right across the surface.

● By the time you have applied the first coat, you will have learnt how to even out the colour, by rubbing more lightly on the dark spots and picking up more stain on the lighter ones. It is a gloriously simple application once you acquire the knack.

● Let the stain dry (check the instructions) – and then varnish. Repeat the varnishing at least twice on floors and once on furniture.

EXTERNALS

Keeping a building in good repair is an ongoing task so do yourself a favour by checking out the exterior of your home on a regular basis. Any weak spots – fallen slates or tiles, loose finishing or crumbling mortar – could open the way to structural damage that always proves much more expensive than a small repair. In our unforgiving climate, one thing leads to another – leaky roofs means wet timbers, which mean stained or sagging ceilings or wet/dry rot (the home-owner's nightmare). And all this because the sun was shining and you thought you could safely forget about that fallen tile or slate?

The following list focuses on the most likely house repair problems.

ROOF

Check the state of your roof on a fine spring day. Fallen slates or tiles should be replaced as soon as possible by a reputable roofer using the same materials. Also check loose flashings, cracked asphalt, crumbling mortar on the chimneystack, clogged drainpipes, missing or cracked coping stones on parapet walls.

You don't need to be a quantity surveyor to spot potential trouble areas. However, I do admit that some roofs are more easily accessed than others. If a check-up involves swaying off a triple extension ladder, chicken out and call in a tradesman. Word of mouth is the best recommendation here. I need hardly add that there are some cowboys in the roofing trade who are not above taking advantage of your and my ignorance in this area. Any roofer who suggests a quick fix on the lines of waterproofing sealant sloshed over the tiles, slates or whatever is almost certainly a cowboy. Ask any architect. Once this 'sealant' fails, which it surely will, you are stuck with a complete re-roofing job instead of a spot repair.

To be on the safe side, get three estimates. Do not necessarily go for the lowest price. What you need is experience and professionalism. I know of no infallible tests of these. Signs to look out for would include attention to detail, understanding of existing structure and materials (such as re-pointing old brickwork with an appropriately soft mortar), a clear spec of works to be done, and a clear start and finish date. Spring is the obvious moment for an inspection, to check what the winter weather has been up to, but it might be wise to do a follow up after violent storms and gale winds throughout the year.

GUTTERS AND DOWNPIPES

Late autumn is the best time to check these out, after leaf fall and the birds have flown. Rainwater should sluice freely from your roof via guttering and downpipes. Blockages (leaves, birds' nests and creepers) can create a dam effect: trapped water building up to the point where it rushes down outside walls, sneaking in through every crack and springing a leak in a ceiling two floors below.

Basically, this is a simple clearout operation that you can cope with yourself if the heights are manageable, or there is – as in much period terrace housing – a solid parapet wall. For the record, I once had a freak leak caused by rampant wisteria together with a mystery wodge of cloth – previous roofers' oversight?

DRAINS

We are not talking here (I hope) about blocked sewage pipes, strictly a task for the experts, armed these days with sophisticated TV cameras, screens, rods and pumping equipment. I refer only to outside drains under downpipes, which often get clogged up with fallen leaves and other rubbish. This should not happen if they are provided with covers or grilles, but it is a simple matter to check that they are clear and operational. A square of chicken wire, held down by stones, will help to keep them clear of debris.

Water backing up and overflowing indicates a blockage. Prodding with a stout stick or working away with a sink plunger can sometimes clear this. If this fails, seek professional help.

MASONRY

External walls, of whatever materials, are under pretty continuous attack from all fronts: inclement weather in the main, but also some localised causes including leaky downpipes, crumbling mortar, or protective coatings (pebbledash or render) which have come away in a patchy manner, allowing rain to penetrate behind. All of these can and should be dealt with promptly by a reputable builder to avoid further damp problems.

One outward sign to take seriously is where old brickwork springs a crack *across* the bricks. There may be all sorts of reasons for this, from minor (hard mortar used to repoint soft old bricks) to serious and structural, but professional advice is called for. The same goes for bulging walls, though these are seen as less alarming. Everyone's heart sinks in these situations, understandably. Visions of escalating costs, disruption, builders' chaos, scaffolding – oh my God! But it won't get better or go away. Listen to the professionals, think it through, and get on the case. This is my heartfelt advice.

EXTERIOR FRAMES AND DOORS

These take a beating in our climate with the worst damage inflicted towards the bottom of window frames, sills and doors. Rainwater pools here, and alternating frost and/or hot sunshine further degrade protective coatings such as paint or waterproofing treatments. Once the base material is exposed – bare wood or metal – the damage is accelerated: wood goes soft, cracked or spongy; metal rusts; and inadequately seasoned timber swells up to the point where casement windows don't close.

Refurbishing any of these surfaces is within DIY scope and is best done in summer when the wood or metal has completely dried out.

Cleaning paint rollers

Paint rollers (the roller heads only) emerge like new from a washing machine cycle. Use a little clothes-washing liquid and clear the filter drawer afterwards.

- The worst hit surfaces should be rubbed back to bare wood or metal.

- Metal frames should be cleared of rust because it works its way up through paint. Use metal primer on these.

- Sealed wood frames which have swollen can be planed back cautiously once dry, and re-sealed.

- Prime, undercoat and repaint all wood surfaces; or for wood seal and recoat it.

A quick fix might simply deal with the damaged areas, but once you start, the likelihood is you will feel inspired to carry on over the entire window.

Exterior doors usually stand up to weathering better, being made from stouter, well-seasoned timber. I find that mine survive two or three years before needing repainting.

FINDING HELP

CLEANERS

Are you looking for a cleaner? Now that all those genteelisms, such as 'cleaning lady', have been banished, cleaner it is. This is logical since many aspirant cleaners turning up at you door in answer to an ad or call to an agency may well be men, students or resting actors.

On the whole, men are accepted as part of the cleaning team, being stronger and musclier. However, they haven't got a much of a chance with Christine Griffiths, who has been running Clean-In-Dom (short for domestic) very successfully for the last ten years. 'Men? Oh, we've got men phoning up – students and such, but I don't often take them on. We're all women here, family, friends.' she announced whilst turning up the volume to drown a chorus of female shrieks and rude noises. Apart from the ties of kinship and friendship which bonds Christine's 25 cleaners together, there is a strongly pragmatic belief that only women really know how to clean; it is in their bones. Unlike men, they don't need to be shown or told how to follow a cleaning routine.

The routine starts in the kitchen and Christine rattled off the list of jobs – 'wiping down worktops, tiling, cooker, mopping the floor, dusting shelves' – with practised fluency. She then proceeded to go through all the rooms and crannies of an average house or flat. The team don't take on office-cleaning jobs. Clean-in-Dom operates throughout the East End of London:

Docklands, Hackney and Bow. The charge is £8 an hour; the going rate for London's up-and-coming areas rather than swanky residential districts such as Knightsbridge, Kensington and Chelsea. 'There's a lot that charge a good bit more,' says Christine.

Too right. The gentrification of the East End, together with the whole shift eastwards of the metropolis in terms of commerce, transport and housing, has made cleaning jobs newly appealing to women living in or around the area because it means they can find part-time work within easy reach of their homes and their children's schools. Unlike the Cockney char of folk memory, these are mostly young women fitting in a few hours a day during school hours to boost the family income or provide themselves with some independence. References can be provided, says Christine, although it's apparent she isn't often asked for them.

Unlike commercial cleaning teams, Clean-in-Dom cleaners expect the client to provide cleaning materials and implements. Most of the group work solo, though Christine does acknowledge that they enjoy working in pairs 'for company'.

I find it interesting that the wheel has turned full circle and that the East End is once again a recruiting ground for cleaners. The difference now being that these women are in a much stronger position than their grandmothers, who had to make long journeys across London for cleaning work in Kensington and such salubrious vicinities. Folklore records them as grumpy, tough and indomitable old gels and certainly this is what they needed to be. Think of the hours of travel, the corns and bunions, not to mention the tough nature of the job.

Now that cleaning has become a much sought-after service industry the work has acquired a certain status. Demand outruns supply and thus today's cleaner can afford to be picky. They want to work near home for starters. They may never strike up a relationship with their clients and may communicate only via scribbled notes on the kitchen table. My guess is that they prefer it this way. A straightforward business type of relationship – excuse the pun – is cleaner.

WHAT DO THEY COST?

After calling round a whole swathe of cleaning services, from small local outfits like Clean-in-Dom to London-wide outfits such as Andersons and Betterclean, the picture that emerges is full of anomalies.

- At the time of writing, prices vary considerably, from the £8 per hour quoted by Clean-in-Dom to the £18.50 per hour quoted by Andersons. However, these are London prices. Chances are you will find cheaper quotes if you live outside London. What you will find is a reluctance to quote a straightforward rate per hour on the part of the larger agencies. They explain this in various ways, mainly differing job specs and the vagaries of client requirements. Many outfits prefer to quote for the job.

● Andersons offer a 'general clean' service or a 'fortnightly blitz' for a two-bedroom flat for £46 plus VAT (this includes 'light ironing, ie, four men's shirts').

● Betterclean charge £70 upwards for a similar Light General Clean.

● Some agencies (mainly those working from vans and in teams of two or three) will supply their own equipment and materials; others like Andersons expect you to provide these, as their cleaners will usually be travelling by public transport. The reason that their price per job is lower than Betterclean's, or any comparable 'team working from a van', is that it does not include such invisible costs as petrol, parking, or van maintenance.

● For what Betterclean call an 'intense general clean' – the price can shoot to £80–130 upwards for a two-bedroom flat. This does not include windows (£50 minimum call-out charge), carpet clean (minimum £45) or upholstery clean (minimum also around the £45 mark).

Security

All the companies I spoke to were evasive about references and interviews; in fact they seemed surprised that I asked about these at all.

If security is a priority for you, for whatever reason, the safest bet in my view would be to sign up with a lifestyle management operation such as ten^{uk} (see page 258). which buys you the security of knowing that all personnel they subcontract have been thoroughly checked out, references followed up, and performances carefully monitored.

Giving a total stranger admittance to your home, in your absence, is inevitably a worry. Avoid agencies that tie you down to a three-month contract with one-month notice. The mind boggles at what a cleaner under notice might get up to during their final month. You don't want to have to change all your door locks every time a cleaner doesn't work out.

Some agencies, Andersons for instance, are 'fully insured' … 'to put your mind at rest'. I personally think you would need to check out their insurance liabilities, especially the small print, before your mind was fully at rest. At the best of times, insurance claims are a long drawn-out hassle. Claiming against an agency's own insurance strikes me as a grey area, strewn with pitfalls for the unwary.

FINDING YOUR OWN

I realise that the foregoing does not offer much comfort to a typical working couple, living in a two-bedroom flat, in desperate need of a regular, reliable cleaner. The fact is the most reliable, experienced cleaners prefer the steady employment provided by an agency to freelancing. ten^uk, the lifestyle management company (see page 258) confirms that 'finding a cleaner' comes top of all the requirements on their members' lists. A sharp downturn in the economy could change all this. In the meantime, here are some suggestions:

● Word-of-mouth, as with so many other areas of modern life, still seems to be the most promising source of reliable cleaners. Ask around locally, since most cleaners prefer to work on their own patch. If your are new to the area, you may need to work harder: get to know your neighbours; chat up your local publican and shopkeepers. If this fails, consider running an ad in the local paper, or freebie magazine. However, make it tempting, a bit above the going rate for your area.

● Try papers such as Loot, Friday-Ad, or Talking Pages for cleaning firms in your area. If you can locate the equivalent of Clean-in-Dom, a small family-and-friends-based outfit, I would choose this in preference to one of the bigger agencies, whose prices seem exorbitant. I would dearly love to know how much of the agency fee fetches up in the cleaner's pocket. Many cleaners on agency books today are immigrants. This may be perfectly above board, but it does flag up the possibility of dodgy practice: ie, exploitation and paying below the minimum wage.

● Try to secure references and then follow them up, or failing this, try for an interview; preferably both, but today this is probably wishful thinking. Don't expect a motherly old gel. More likely you will get a young mum with kids at local schools able to fit in a few hours cleaning on a daily basis. However, do be prepared: cleaners are a rainbow-coloured lot these days.

● Even if you have given the agency a written spec of your requirements, make an extra copy for the cleaner in order to avoid any confusion. Put her/his name at the top (correctly spelt) and yours at the bottom. I think small courtesies help foster a good working relationship; don't gust but don't be too formal or chilly. If you get lucky and hit on a capable, reliable and good-hearted cleaner, you will be a fortunate person, with a valuable ally on the home front.

● An au pair (see page 234) could be a workable alternative. Though not in a two-bedroom flat.

● Finally, you might consider crawling out of bed on Sunday morning and doing the work yourself. Maybe just a temporary measure? Investing in a steam cleaner (see page 116) will allow you to catch up on the professionals. Look at what you save as you zap the dust mites and cleanse the stains and grime from carpets, upholstery and windowpanes: remember the aforementioned minimum charges. Lets round it off at £300 per fortnight (my maths isn't too great). This is shaping up at around £600 per month or £7,200 per annum!

If that strikes you as the piffling sum you spend on magazines and make-up annually, you probably won't be reading this book. Furthermore, if you prefer to live in squalor … well, you won't be reading me either!

PROFESSIONAL CLEANING – WHAT DO YOU GET?

When calling round a range of domestic cleaning services one of the issues that arises is that there are varying degrees of clean. A 'regular clean' or light clean is the cheaper option and will involve vacuuming all rooms, mopping down hard floors, dusting (including shelves, door and window architraves and cupboards) and wiping down worktops, bathroom units and the cooker top. In other words, basic maintenance so all looks spic and span.

The heavier-duty clean (more often a one-off than a rolling programme) will stretch to clearing cupboards, cleaning the insides and their contents and replacing these in an orderly fashion, window cleaning, shampooing or steam-cleaning carpet, moving furniture to clean underneath and washing down paintwork. Cleaning windows and shampooing or steam cleaning upholstery and soft furnishings is usually carried out with an additional charge.

Most companies send out a printed outline of what you can expect for your money. Of course, whichever type of clean you opt for, you will need to add your own requirements to the specification if you have special needs such as washing down the dog basket or getting the tiling grout steam cleaned. These needs should be discussed, priced and signed off by your agency contact person beforehand. Don't be shy of raising such questions: these are worldly wise folk – been there, seen it, done it all.

The bottom line in these situations is 'how long?', in the sense that Cleaner A might complete the specified routine in two-thirds of the time it takes Cleaner B. A tough nut to crack.

Assuming you have sorted out your requirements with the agency, it is best if you can be there on Day One in order to guide your cleaner round the place and point out your priorities and preferences. (Perhaps your partner is allergic to chlorine bleach or your swanky stainless steel hob must never see the rough side of a Brillo pad.)

Failing the guided tour, make sure you write out your own additions to the spec and send a copy to the agency in addition to leaving one out on the kitchen table (cleaners tend to start in the kitchen) for your cleaner to peruse. Even if you haven't done a run through yourself, which I recommend (see page 121), you will soon have some indication whether the job is being done well, thoroughly and to time. Cleaning is now such a sorted and profitable service industry it is unlikely that you will be disappointed in terms of value for money.

Complaints

Most of us can spot a real sloven. Should this be the case, get right back to the agency with itemised complaints. If, like the curate's egg, the results are good in spots, go for the tactful approach first. Perhaps you could leave a pleasantly worded note on the table suggesting where she/he might spend more effort, reminding him/her about the areas overlooked and stating that these are important to you. Round it off by asking if they also have any problems? Maybe the vacuum cleaner is blocked or you haven't provided their favoured cleaning materials? If the situation doesn't improve, you need to do a clean, swift cut, more in sorrow than in anger, call up the agency or give her/him their notice, with a small cash sweetener, to take effect immediately.

With jobs chasing cleaners these days it doesn't do to get too stroppy unless you have real cause. On the other hand, if you are paying decent money – at least twice the minimum wage – you are entitled to claim that the work is not up to standard. Maybe a word to the manager of the agency will do the trick or maybe they will offer you another cleaner from their books. However, do try to avoid getting blacklisted as the client from hell!

AU PAIRS

A time comes in most households with young children when the beleaguered mum, run off her feet trying to cope with an avalanche of pressing needs and demands, feels that she is being eaten alive. Like the mythical pelican. She thus tearfully decides that she must have help around the house, with the kids and the shopping. Simply just some help, another pair of hands and feet to delegate some of the many domestic tasks to.

Where money is no object, a live-in nanny and a cleaner might be the ideal solutions to your domestic problems. A more affordable option is a live-out nanny on duty from nine to five – and maybe you could share the cost with another nearby family with children of a similar age. However, even with such a reshuffle, the extra costs add up to a formidable slice of the family budget, somewhere between £15,000 and £20,000 per annum (see page 240).

It is therefore hardly surprising that the majority of families opt, as they have done for 30 or 40 years, for an au pair. The basic definition of an au pair is a young person, wishing to improve their command of English, who is prepared to offer help around the house when you need it for a prescribed number of hours per day in exchange for a modest weekly stipend (called 'pocket money'), board and lodging plus enough time to attend a language school and socialise during evenings and weekends. You need to offer them a safe, friendly family environment which can reassure their anxious parents back home. In return, they offer you help and muscle with household tasks and child-minding. Perfect synergy? Yes, if you are lucky.

SELECTING AN AU PAIR

Au pair agencies (see My Directory) work hard to ensure a good match, emailing photos, CVs and warm recommendations from teachers, local worthies and school friends. Nonetheless, due to UK agencies teaming up with their counterparts in the country of origin, increasingly this is a blind-date situation and you can often find yourself committing to an applicant you have not met in person. It is devilishly hard to decide on the basis of a CV, smudgy photocopied mug shots and enthusiastic letters and references which candidate is likely to suit you best.

Phoning up (a phone number comes with the bumf) tells you a little more. You will be able to tell whether their English is 'fair' as they all tend to claim (but 'fair' in my experience can mean anything from just competent to barely there) and whether they sound cheery and upbeat or moody and fractious. Invariably, they express fondness for children, dogs and insist they are good at – if not keen on – housework.

You need to spell out clearly your idea of their duties, how many hours a day they are required to fulfil, how many babysitting evenings, what free time they can realistically expect and how much you are prepared to pay. About £50 a week for five hours a day is the current rate for a full-time au pair, but there are descending rates for 'part–time' au pairs (three hours per day) and summer au pairs who hope to brush up their English over the school/university holidays and are thus a whole different ballgame.

It sounds straight-forward, but in practice these phone interviews are not much help unless your criteria are very clear, you are prepared with a list of questions and are patient enough to cope with constantly busy phone lines and bursts of unintelligible speech when you do get through. Not to mention a few porkies from the interviewee. Unfortunately, you won't know they are porkies (helping mum with the housework and ironing since they were little is the common one) until they arrive on your doorstep and evince consternation when you suggest the day might start with washing up or hanging out the washing, or any of the other household duties it is reasonable to expect.

Should you be fortunate enough to interview an au pair in person, you have to be aware that the young person could be over here because some other family took him/her (there are now male au-pairs too!) on, sight unseen, and is only looking for a new placement because he/she is not happy in the original family. Ask about this, and find out the reasons if you can. Better still, phone up the previous employer. However, go carefully here, as this harassed mum may not even anticipate that her au pair is planning to do a runner and could react with hysterics or a stream of vituperation.

Talk to your potential au pair first. The other possibility is that the previous employer

> The phone was answered.
> 'Millie's All Staff-Agency,'
> said a nice female voice.
> 'I want a live-in mother's help please,' said Lucy Elliott.
> And she thought, I want a very ugly one. Unlike Craig …
> 'We have a Dutch girl,'
> said the voice. 'Available at the end of the month.'
> 'Is she pretty?' snapped Lucy Elliott.
> 'She's from The Hague,'
> said the voice,
> as if that was an answer.
>
> *Mrs Fytton's Country Life*, Mavis Cheek (Faber & Faber, 2000)

has had it up to here and cannot wait to get shot of him/her for reasons which she may be delighted to pass on and may well affect your decision to offer the young person the job. Talk about walking on eggs!

AU PAIR EXPERIENCES

Over the years, I have taken on something like 15 au pairs, 14 girls and one young Hungarian man. Of these, two were absolute gems, both Czechs, intelligent, co-operative within the household and got on with everyone. Moreover, they were reliable and responsible and a general pleasure to have around. They were both called Radka. Radka I, a teacher of English in Prague, was spectacularly helpful to me, intuiting my needs without being told, almost embarrassingly diligent, shy and reserved but blessedly free of attitude. Radka II was a tall, dreamy girl who played the flute and taught music in a home for handicapped children. She has now married a young Englishman she met whilst working in a London sandwich bar. What made the Radka's different? Simple answer, they became our friends. Of the others, I would say that most were reasonably helpful around the house once they got the hang of their routine. They enlivened the household, and on a good day they were nice to have around.

When an au pair does a bunk (some do for all sorts of reasons) my first thought isn't 'damn, there goes the agency fee!' it is more like 'Oh my God! I am going to have to go though the tedious training spiel all over again.'

It gets so you hate the sound of your voice droning out the household rules and habits for what seems like the umpteenth time to a young person making an attentive face but patently only taking in 20 per cent at any one time, even when you speak slowly, and nicely with a friendly smile fastened over your gritted teeth. It is tedious enough laying down the law to the younger members of your own family, but at least they speak your language. Spelling it all out to a teenager or 20-something with a rudimentary vocabulary, who will merrily trundle the vacuum cleaner around when it is clearly not picking up is a serious test of tact, tolerance and diplomacy.

You need to remind yourself that these young people are unskilled, probably homesick, struggling with an alarmingly complex, idiomatic language, and really just wanting to pack in a bit of fun, get by in their 'family' and meet an attractive member of the opposite sex.

Nevertheless, sometimes the smile freezes, the nerves snap and you blow it. The resulting atmosphere can usually be dispelled by a heart-to-heart with the young person concerned. But to your family, the situation reads differently. Your partner/ husband, encountering this fresh-faced, smiley girl at breakfast – and freed up from the tiresome domestic detail of wash loads forgotten, vacuum cleaners driven to collapse and your computer bill rocketing up with mysterious emails – cuts short your dreary report with a broad hint that it is all your fault as this is a perfectly amiable and helpful girl who laughs at his jokes, copes with the kids and stacks up the breakfast things like a whirlwind. So what are you moaning about?

It can turn into a good cop/bad cop situation with yourself, as necessary interface, always cast as the bad cop. This is bad for morale, I need hardly say. You may find your own children, especially the older ones, siding against you too. My own lot, in their early teens, were enchanted by Austrian Katrin, a lesbian punk, who filled them in on the gay rave scene at Heaven, then *the* place. However I had to cope with her on Monday mornings; stoned, hung over and deeply dazed and confused.

WHAT GOES WRONG

Au pair agencies will fill you in with the basic requirements and formalities of engaging an au pair. What they are less upfront about, not unreasonably, is their private understanding of what the au pairs are looking for from the arrangement, and fore-knowledge that some family arrangements are not going to work out for the following reasons, which I feel competent to divulge.

Country life

Don't expect an au pair to settle in if you live in the deep country, however beautiful the scenery, adorable your kids and easygoing yourselves. Most au pairs these days come from Eastern Europe and are spoilt for beautiful countryside. Instead what they are really seeking is the whole urban experience: bright lights, raves, clubbing, shops, sex and romance – or at least a host of social opportunities. If you live in a remote area, they may sign on for two years and do a runner after three weeks.

In this instance, your best bet might be to take on an older, male au pair who is likely to be more studious, serious and anxious to improve his English (teacher, architect or a doctor?). Perhaps lots of conversation and free English coaching will compensate for the scarcity of social opportunities. Young blokes find it harder to get placements, so this is a buyers' market.

Most Eastern European and Turkish men have done military service, which means – so I am told – that they are dab hands at ironing and other domestic tasks you might not expect a young man to know much about. Agents tell me that clients have quirky reactions to the notion of a male au pair like 'I couldn't possibly ask him to wash my daughter's knickers'! Husbands/partners are also less keen. However, in some situations it could be a good solution, pals to your teenage boys for instance, and they are more likely to undertake – even prefer – heavier tasks such as cleaning windows.

Needing independence

In order to retain an au pair it is important that she/he has some independence worthy of their status as young adults. It is helpful if the au pair has his/her own room on bedsit lines rather than a straightforward bedroom. A separate TV is not a bad idea as both of you might welcome some time on your own.

Feeling exploited

Au pairs may leave because they feel exploited. You can usually trade some babysitting time against working hours. Alternatively, pay for babysitting on top of the weekly stipend. Most au pairs are eager to pick up extra cash so you might mention the babysitting possibility to your friends.

Learning English

In order to keep an au pair happy you need to accommodate their desire to learn English. Signing on for an English-language course is to be encouraged, as it means they will make friends as well as improve their English.

Loneliness

A lonely au pair is bad news. Check that transport is available and the course hours fit in with your routine. Some au pairs simply can't afford course fees. The enterprising ones find part-time work in pubs or sandwich bars, etc, which is, strictly speaking, illegal but a great help with language skills. You might be able to rustle up casual jobs for them yourself; mowing lawns, car washing amongst your friends and neighbours. Extra cash is always welcome and it gets them out and about.

Duties

Work out, and write down, a weekly rota of duties and go through this with the au pair in question, making sure that she/he understands it all. Stress that this in only an outline and that you will all need to be a bit flexible and see how things work out. A sensible young person from a familial background will realise that this is the best approach, but some au pairs can be touchy about their rights, seeing it as a formal job specification. Then you find you have overlooked a vital item, like putting out the refuse bins on a particular day, and the au pair gets stroppy and quotes your work list back at you.

Boundaries

As hosts to an au pair you are in a 'loco parentis' situation to some extent. You need to discuss with your husband/wife/partner where you draw the line: whether a boyfriend is or is not permitted to stay the night, for instance. Some people rule 'this out absolutely; others take a more liberal line: OK if the snogging and bonking are discreet, you approve of the boyfriend and deem the relationship to be reasonably serious.

This situation arises with one's own children, but the difference here that a young foreigner may not be streetwise enough to differentiate between a decent bloke and cynical chancer. How you resolve the problem must depend on your own reading of the situation as it arises.

Once, when a portly and prosperous Sikh gentleman rang the bell and asked me to introduce him to the young ladies of the house, I had to do some pretty fast thinking! Someone was sending out the wrong signals if a respectable middle-aged man had gained the impression that I was running a bawdy house. With two young daughters (nine and twelve) my first thought was to put him squarely right about that. Politely, but with a touch of hauteur, I explained that this was my own house where I lived with my family and that he must be mistaken about the young ladies. He protested that a young blonde lady had leant out of an upstairs window, smiling and waving at him, but I could already see his confidence oozing away, so I said firmly 'No, sorry' and closed the gate on him. Even though Eva was 'only having fun', she didn't protest much when I told her to go.

NO KIDS?

Not every au pair wants to look after children. I have been employing au pairs well after my own children have grown up and moved out and I know other people who do the same. Usually dog-walking takes the place of child-minding, an exchange which suits some au pairs very well, ie, studious older women/men who want extra free time to learn some English. Wages stay the same, as do domestic duties, except that an hour a day out of the nominal five hours is spent walking the dog in the nearest park or green space. What they lose in family life they gain in independence.

To offset the more impersonal relationship, however, the odd treat becomes more important: a play, concert, restaurant meal for example, and it helps to suggest that he/she brings a friend along if the budget will allow for it.

MOTHER'S HELPS AND NANNIES

An altogether different scene from the au pair situation. The cost rises steeply, though the girls work longer hours. Think £180 per week upwards, not inclusive of food and board. On top of that you will need to employ a cleaner two or three times a week in order to underline the fact that cleaning is *not* included in the girl's job spec, though if you talk to her nicely she may throw in a little 'light housework': unloading the dishwasher, hanging out the washing or food shopping. This might cost a further £50 per week at London rates for cleaners (£8 per hour). So you will be looking at disbursing around £10,000 per annum minimum, exclusive of food and board. And that is for an unqualified mother's help (ie, no training in child care), who may or not be able to drive – she is not required to.

These are not pampered young persons, but young women looking for a not too exacting job which pays them enough to have a good time while they are broadening their horizons with travel. Almost without exception they come from Australia, New Zealand or South Africa because this disposes of any language barriers. The fact is that they can afford to be choosy because the 'market is so tight at the moment' (agency speak for demand outrunning supply). The girls I have met over the years struck me as sensible, lively with a breezy, not to say brash, way with them that goes down well with their charges.

MOTHER'S HELP

The crucial distinction here is that a mother's help works along side mum: ie, she is not in sole charge of the children. She will usually be in her early 20s. She is expected to work a 12-hour day from Monday to Friday. This generally includes two nights of babysitting. She is not expected to provide references or hold a driving licence. She may come from a large family and have an easy rapport with young children and a knack with a baby.

Remember, alongside means alongside. It is down to your own savvy and instinct in the last resort. Is she open, jolly and looks you in the eye as you talk? Or does she frown, chew her nails, seem a touch 'chippy', and toil up the stairs rather than bounce up them?

Crude as it may sound, I would steer clear of neurotics. How to define this? If she makes you feel uneasy, you start apologising, talking too much or trying to put her at ease. Should this be the case, she is probably not the girl for you. This is a real poser and it seems odd that there are so few guidelines to making the right choice in such an important area of your life. If you are undecided you might like to try one of the following suggestions:

● Meet the kids. Children can be uncannily perceptive when it comes to good or bad vibes.

● Have a close friend come along, casually dropping by as it were, for some quick feedback.

● Have her meet your partner. OK a cute face goes a long way, but most men who can afford to take on a mother's help will be reasonably sussed when it comes to job interviews.

● Suggest a week's running-in time; 'see how it works out', is the polite formula. Check with the agency that a lesser fee is charged for this. However, beware that you may lose the girl if she feels under scrutiny, threatened and has lots of other families to see. But maybe that tells you something?

Don't let paranoia run away with you, but don't, on the other hand, rush into a decision before it feels right. Finally, with untrained and possibly inexperienced girls, your real safeguard must be the agency definition of a mother's help 'working alongside mum'. So do that.

NANNIES

Nannies tend to be older. Their qualifications vary from full-time work in a nursery or day-care unit to full-blown nannyhood, with a NNEB qualification or its equivalent. (NNEB stands for National Nursery-nursing Examination Board, but has been replaced by a BTech qualification.) As you might expect, pay increases with qualifications.

Another factor in determining their salaries is whether they are live-in or live-out nannies. A live-out nanny works shorter hours: eight to ten hours daily, five days a week, but is paid at a higher rate, roughly £300–350 per week (at the time of writing) in order to cover her cost of living. With tax and National Insurance, and if applicable, the London weighting on top, the cost can really mount up. Live-out jobs are highly sought after as the employee can retain independence.

Live-in nannies earn £220–270 per week and are more likely to accept jobs outside London. Babysitting is not part of the job as it is with mother's helps. You must acknowledge that babysitting would be an additional expense at the going rate for your area. The live-in nanny's hours may be more flexible, but do handle this aspect with tact – one of the commonest gripes is being expected to work too many hours.

Remember that weekends are their free time, although a nanny who is getting a fun experience (such as a holiday en famille in a glamorous place), along with the job, may be more flexible.

In contradistinction to a mother's help, a nanny prefers to be in full charge of the children and one of their most frequent complaints is that mum is breathing down their necks, interfering, getting in the way of what they feel is their wider experience, not to mention professional training.

Speaking as a mother rather than a nanny, I can see pitfalls lurking here. Working mums will be better able to delegate but will undoubtedly experience pangs of resentment or, frankly, jealousy if a nanny seems to be too popular: the baby acts up if she is not around or kids keep going on about 'nanny says this, or does that' and run to nanny first with their cuts and grazes or their quarrels and spats. You must expect something like this because babies and young children will bond with the person who cares for them in a routine way, five days of the week, and it is healthy that they should. It would be much worse if they were to take against their proxy mum and scream when they spot you leaving the house.

So be generous in spirit, tolerate some divided allegiance and make the best of your family time – evenings, weekends and holidays. A nanny is a bird of passage – usually signs up for a year – and a smiling, kindly and trusty young woman is a jewel to cherish if your work life is fraught with anxieties and responsibilities. It can be painful to pass the care of a youngish baby into other hands while your own maternal hormones are still in full flood, but if you have no option, make the best of the situation. Ask your nanny's advice about screaming jags, bed-wetting and eating fads, and accept it, gratefully reminding yourself that while nannies come and go these sprogs are yours for your lifetime.

As with mother's helps, it is vital that both parties 'click'. Both the nanny and yourself will have filled out full job specifications. You will have detailed your requirements: driving licence, OK with pets and a clear outline of the workload you expect her to fulfil. In turn, the nanny will have detailed any problems she may have such as allergies, dislike of pets, smoking or even tall houses with many floors! A good agency, recognising the importance of client and nanny hitting it off, will often suggest a trial week, with a charge of £50 if the situation doesn't work out for either party.

WHITE KNIGHTS VS. COWBOYS

How many cowboys have to pass through one's life before lighting upon Mr Wonderful? I am talking about the builder or electrician who turns up on time, completes the job within budget and up to scratch, and tidies up behind himself daily.

It is a solemn fact that honest, qualified and reliable tradesman are fast disappearing from the world of work, or at least from the middle-income stratum of work opportunities which used to keep many a chippy, sparks or tosher fully employed in his own locality. The good old guys, who have either died or retired, are too often replaced by bumptious opportunists with a 'can do' line of chat. Others may have the requisite skills but there is an insurmountable language problem which gets in the way. There are also those lovable hippies who mean well, jump at the cash, but have a fatal tendency to peter out before completion.

To a large extent this seems to be the fault of a society, or education system, that has not set a proper value on craft or technical proficiency. As a result a whiff of 'tradesman's entrance' snobbery lingers on and thus downgrades skilled specialist manual work in the eyes of the very young people it urgently needs to recruit.

My guess is that, given intelligence, training and aptitude, a young person starting out in any of the areas mentioned could soon be in a position (if that is what they want) to run a successful business. Unlike many other industries such as interior design and catering – where you need capital and PR to get noticed – a skilled reliable operator in the 'manual trades' only needs good recommendations to become sought after, booked up and make big bucks. Demand has seriously outrun supply.

In Germany, this destructive downgrading of 'manual' as against 'white collar' skills seems hardly to exist. Streaming of students into further education on either academic or technical levels is not viewed as a big put-down but rather as a realistic assessment of where your talents lie and how they can best be developed.

The well-intentioned levelling exercise in the UK to up the status of polytechnics to universities seems to have been counter-productive. The old snobbery lingers: it is simply not cool or trendy to study woodwork, electrics or plumbing. However, social stereotyping can shift dramatically – it wasn't so long ago that working as a sous chef was seen as a lowly job. Now, thanks to TV chef programmes and smart lads like Jamie Oliver, it is well oversubscribed.

An Oxbridge product myself (Girton, Modern Languages) I was once told by a graphologist that I had missed my vocation: architecture. At the time, as an aspiring hackette, I took this as a put-down as I didn't rate architects in those days. On later reflection this was perhaps a highly perceptive observation.

My life seemed to come together and my aspirations connect with enjoyable work when I wrote a manual on painting and decorating. I discovered the enjoyment of mixing paint and glaze colours, experimenting with 'finishes' and doing a decorative number on my own rooms. It was certainly far preferable to journalism. My writing skills (sharpened no doubt by Cambridge and journalism) finally fused with a topic – albeit trade and manual – which I found fascinating. The timing was right – though none of us knew it at the time – and *Paint Magic* became the first best-seller to deal with paint. Before publication, 'Paint? What on earth can you find to write about paint?' was a baffled enquiry I met everywhere.

I mention this only to suggest that so-called manual trades and traditions are every bit as fascinating to write and read about as novels. More to the point, it only takes a book like mine or a television series such as Jamie Oliver's to dust off the snobbish prejudice that anything you do with your hands is menial, unsatisfying and uninteresting.

PLUMB AWFUL

If there is one domestic disaster that makes everyone feel an icy tremor up the spine, it has to be something connected with plumbing. For some reason, it always seems to happen over Christmas or on a Bank Holiday: toilet won't flush away, the sink refuses to drain or an outside pipe throws up a stinking, scummy puddle. You could be lucky enough to have a partner who understands such things, and is not too squeamish to set to work with a sink plunger and rubber gloves. However, it is funny how sink plungers vanish into thin air just when you need them.

More often you will be frantically chasing up a plumber and leaving messages on countless mobiles. If no one gets back to you, the most likely reason is that there is a serious shortage of reliable plumbers, and those there are are completely run off their feet. The Construction Council Industry Training Board reports that 29,000 new plumbers will be required over the next five years. This is clearly a pretty serious gap in the market. The smart lads who might once have taken up plumbing as a trade are now all trying to do something with computers. Yet there is proper money to be made in plumbing and there are smart gadgets such as rods which snake through pipes with cameras sending back images to TV screens, so it is not quite the mucky job it used to be.

And, as I said, there are rich pickings. My neighbour, faced with a plumbing emergency on a cold, dark winter evening, ended up paying close on £1,000 for the problem to be traced and dealt with. She groaned a bit, but paid up, which only goes to show that in a plumbing emergency we will pay through the nose gratefully, and regard the stalwart individual who successfully deals with our blockages as a white knight.

However, this is also an area where cowboys operate, aware that they have us by the short and curlies, given the general ignorance that reigns concerning how plumbing systems work, what causes blockages and how to deal with them. It is comforting to know that there is an Institute of Plumbing whose members must have passed a few hurdles in order to be accredited. When the Institute gets complaints about the work of accredited plumbers, they have the right to strike him/her off their list. Unfortunately, they are not in a position to force the plumber to return the cash, although they can put pressure on them to get back to the job and complete it satisfactorily.

From the customer's point of view, this is not an ideal situation, but an improvement over snatching at names over the net or in the Yellow Pages. The Institute can be contacted by phone or email (see My Directory). What this service offers is a list of names in your locality, anywhere in the UK.

Unless you know what you are doing, DIY interventions are highly risky, although some may be worth a try. Use your own judgement, but if in doubt, it is recommended that you call a plumber. The Institute list can be in need of updating: don't stick too close to home or your postal district.

DIY PLUMBING
Blocked sinks
The sink is the most straightforward appliance from a DIY viewpoint, especially a blockage caused by congealed fat plus gubbins – rice and tea leaves – in the pipework.

- First, try a plunger, positioned over the plug and worked up and down vigorously until you hear a gurgling noise – the blockage shifting – you hope. The sink being full is an advantage, since the pressure of the water is helpful.

- If plunging fails, empty the sink by hand. Stand a large bucket beneath the outlet pipe, unscrew the S-bend (this may send a cascade of nasties into your bucket), and, touch wood, the blockage will be cleared.

- Once the water runs away sweetly, you may safely follow up with a spoonful of caustic soda and boiling water (see page 110) to cleanse the system.

Outside drains

These may respond to the same somewhat primitive treatment as the blocked sink.

● Wear wellies as well as gloves and try the plunger.

● If that fails, shove a length of stiff wire – old coat hanger – up and down or back and forth to search for blockages, normally caused by leaves or litter.

I am uneasy about sending a dose of powerful caustic into these situations because if it fails, your plumber has an extra hazard to deal with. However, if you do try this, you must inform him that this is what you have done.

Blocked toilet

This is the baddie, bringing a flush to our cheeks as we gabble out the problem to the white knight. Even if you don't drop sanitary pads, tampons or condoms down the loo, can you ever be certain that someone else has not? But don't get too apologetic – for a plumber it is all in a day's work. They must have strong stomachs, and they also have rods and stuff to locate and deal with a blockage less unpleasantly.

● Of course, you must put the loo out of bounds as soon as a problem is detected (tape down the lid). Extra embarrassing evidence could just be scooped out and flushed down a still functioning toilet, or bagged separately in your domestic rubbish, as with pooper scooping. If nothing else, this makes it easier to look your white knight in the eye and negotiate a reasonable deal.

● You could try the sink plunger routine here, but on balance, blocked toilets are a job I would leave to the professionals. Enough said.

THE TOSHER

This is the word a lot of painters, even quite grand ones, use to describe themselves, among themselves (not for general circulation). With the current boom in building and refurbishing, painters and decorators are enjoying a knock-on effect, though this tends to vary around the UK. Depending on where you are located, you do have to phone around to find the person or team you desire. This is one area where membership of a trade association, such as the Interior Decorators and Designers Association (IDDA – see My Directory) is less relevant because so many toshers work freelance and can't afford the membership fees or the extra paperwork. Certainly, lack of a trade-association membership is no indication of lack of skill or experience.

Unusually, there are many female toshers who are attracted to the job by its creative side. They tend to opt for the more decorative paint jobs rather than the straightforward 'flat painter', whose job is to cover walls and woodwork fast with water-based paints, emulsions and acrylics.

Flat painters are the guys to choose for quick results using straightforward state-of-the-art media over large areas. Many of them work as part of a team for a decorating firm subcontracted by architects, designers or builders. 'Flat painting' is their expertise; they tend to look blank if you talk excitedly about colour wash, lime wash or trompe l'oeil. This is the province of the decorative painter whose daily rate will be higher and who will usually expect to start work on walls/woodwork already 'prepped' by a flat painter.

Do some research before deciding on a firm/individual as standards and estimates vary widely. You are on safer ground with a decorating team under contract since both parties should be insured against accidents (paint on the carpet) or faulty workmanship. With the decorative painter, you should ask to see his/her 'portfolio' of completed work, but do bear in mind that the photos tend to be snatched without proper lighting in empty rooms where furniture and fittings have not yet been replaced. Therefore, I suggest you view the images only as a guide as to whether your taste and colour sense coincide and whether the workmanship is sophisticated or sloppy. In both instances, flat or decorative, try to see previous examples of their work or call up previous clients for feedback. Here are some questions you might ask:

- Was the work carried out without unexpected interruptions? (Bear in mind that some of these are legitimate, such as waiting for the curing or hardening of varnish.)

- Did it come in within budget and on time?

- Did the painter/s clear up after themselves on a daily basis?

- How thorough was the groundwork – ie, sanding, undercoating and varnish? Are painted surfaces gritty and show 'runs' or drips? Is filler showing through?

- Is decorative paint/glazework tidied up round the ceiling, cornice or skirtings and properly varnished as protection?

How long?

The decorative painter's job is an unpredictable undertaking where all sorts of things can go wrong: cold weather delays drying, damp patches could be discovered or you may change your mind about a colour or a finish.

Try to agree a price for the job rather than a day rate. Make sure you have colour swatches or samples (A4 in size) before you commit because paint 'chips' are useless here – the larger the swatch the easier to visualise the final effect.

The fact that most decorative painters largely rely on word of mouth for commissions works in your favour. However, don't hang around all day 'keeping an eye' because this will make them nervous, but do talk through the project from time to time and raise any concerns or objections you have. Listen to their comments.

Sourcing painters

The back pages of the glossies such as *World of Interiors* and *Homes and Gardens* are full of small ads placed by decorative-painting individuals or outfits. The posher ones may have their own websites, flagged up in magazine articles.

Nonetheless, word of mouth is still the most valuable criterion. If you are impressed or charmed by interiors you happen on, get talking about them and you will usually find the client concerned is happy to put you in touch with the painter or designer in question.

In the case of the team job, you will be directed by your builder or architect.

Costs

Surprise, surprise, these vary according to location, size of job, general state of the economy (bullish or bearish), fashion, competition and such ineffables as personal liking. This is certainly the case with decorative painters, who do their best work for sympathetic clients in a supportive atmosphere. Broadly speaking, a flat painter will expect anything from £70 per day upwards, perhaps a bit less outside London. (Beware of a black market in the flat-painting scene with Eastern Europeans grabbed 'off the boat' by tough entrepreneurs and therefore willing to work for as little as £30. This is black economy labour paid in cash and is shamelessly exploitative.)

A decorative painter will expect more: £100 per day upwards. They will also charge more for highly specialised work such a polished tinted stucco, frottage or 'arty' projects such as murals and trompe l'oeil.

The contract: how not to paint yourself into a corner

If your team is subcontracted (by a designer, builder or architect), the contract will be taken care of by the main contractor. However, this doesn't mean you have to accept estimates you are unhappy with. You can ask to see a breakdown and argue the case. If you are employing a decorating firm off your own bat, more homework may be required. Ask about insurance, VAT and request a breakdown of costs: labour and materials, etc. In addition, do anticipate a contingency fee to be smuggled in, as part of the firm's profit, of about 15 per cent or more.

If in doubt as to cost, consult one or two more firms for estimates to compare. This will give you a more powerful position from which to negotiate. Don't be too picky as they may just stomp off!

I am more familiar with the small-scale decorative painter outfit and suggest adhering to the following procedures:

● For an initial fee (approx £60) a member will visit for a 'consult': ie, suss out the job, talk about your ideas and colour schemes, and agree to supply decent-sized swatches of colours and 'effects'. The £60 is wholly – or partly – refundable if the job goes ahead but is forfeited if not.

● Once you commit you will be sent a detailed estimate. You can, of course, still back out at this stage, not yet having proceeded to contract. You may also still be talking to other rival firms.

● You may still wish to 'negotiate' up or down, drop some items or add others and fix different dates for work to begin. Once you seriously commit to the details you will be sent a contract.

● You may want to check on the firm's insurance liability: How much is it? What does it cover?

● Once you have signed the contract you will be expected to put your money where you mouth is. Terms will vary. Small hungry firms may require 50 per cent of the total paid upfront before starting work. This is less exorbitant than it sounds as they will be working within tight margins and need to order up materials and have a reserve from which to pay their workers from Day One.

Bigger outfits may ask for 10 per cent on signature, 40 per cent approximately half way through the project and the remainder within 30 days of completion. Interest will accrue in the case of delayed payment. The smaller firm will also expect the remaining 50 per cent on completion or, in some cases, within 30 days.

If all this sounds beady, it is because all decorative painters know, like they know raw from burnt umber, that clients get tricky about the final payout once the project is completed. Once the initial thrill and gratitude have worn off and the client is back living in their refurbished space there is a risk that he/she will suddenly draw in their horns and drag out the final payment. This will result in a number of increasingly unfriendly calls from the decorating outfit.

If this fails you will get a summons to the Small Claims Court. According to a decorative painter I know, things rarely get to this state, but the threat of court action usually does the trick.

HUNTING MR WONDERFUL

The building trade is reputedly – notoriously even – more packed with cowboys than Stampede City at rodeo time. In just two months last year, 16,298 complaints were made by consumers against cowboy builders. 'All it takes is a barrow and shovel and you're in business,' says Keith Snook, the Royal Institute of British Architects' Director of Practice, though he hastened to add, in all fairness, that there are also plenty of competent firms who provide a reliable service.

How does one distinguish between the reputable contractor and the cheeky cowboy who leaves you in the lurch two weeks into the project or delivers such substandard work that you may contemplate suing. The trouble is you will then find the Consumer Contract issued by RIBA has no teeth when it comes to fly-by-night operations where payment is in cash to avoid VAT. Unfortunately, all too many householders are tempted by the chance to escape VAT charges and are unaware that this leaves them in a much weaker position when legal redress is concerned.

If you are in any doubt as to the reputation of a builder, your best bet would be to ask around in your locality and check out the recent work of the firm or outfit in question before going a step further. If you live in the countryside, there may be small local firms or jobbing builders who know their stuff but can't be doing with all the VAT form filling, though obviously you would ask for a written estimate. However, any of the official bodies trying to regulate the building trade will urge that you are out on a limb in this situation and will warn you that shoddy workmanship could end up costing you more than the savings on VAT.

It is safer all round to contact a building firm registered with either the Federation of Master Builders (FMB) or the Chartered Institute of Builders (CIOB). These two bodies are recognised trade associations whose members must meet strict criteria before being allowed to join. These include having both their business and craftsmen assessed. Both associations deal with small- to medium-sized firms and can put you in touch with one working in your area. They also provide Quotation Contracts, clearly setting out both parties' obligations. This will cost you 17.5 per cent more, but it offers you valuable protection. (Furthermore, both organisations have won a Crystal Mark from the Plain English Campaign; a fact of which they are justifiably proud and which one wishes every solicitor was obliged to emulate.)

Complaints

The high level of complaints against cowboy builders (currently running at approximately 100,000 per year) suggests that the situation is getting out of hand. The government has set up an anti-cowboy builder initiative called Quality Mark, designed to run them out of town. However, both the FMB and CIOB feel this is a paper tiger. Instead they have spent years lobbying for a drastically reduced VAT charge on building work and they cite French President Chirac's decision to cut VAT levied on 'repair, maintenance and improvement of domestic properties' from 20.6 per cent to 5.5 per cent in September 1999. Whereas UK home owners who have fallen for the no VAT promise are 'swindled out of £3.5 billion annually by rogue traders'. There you have it.

You could lobby your MP and sign up one of the accredited firms registered with the two afore-mentioned associations. Or you could forget about being public spirited and take a chance on picking a cowboy with a heart of gold and skills to match. Unlikely scenario!

Don't then come whingeing to Ian Davis, Director General of FMB, if it all turns nasty. His warning is unequivocal: 'However tempting it may be to save money by paying cash-in-hand to someone who knocks at the door offering to carry out building work at low cost, the result is often shoddy workmanship which will then have to be made good by a professional so that the work is paid for twice over … and remember, if you employ a cash-in-hand cowboy, don't expect to find him, let alone have the faults rectified by him!'

You have been warned.

SPARKS TALKING

Neil Roland came well recommended and efficiently replaced low-voltage ceiling lights which were on the blink with a new set. He is not a member of the Electrical Contractors Association (ECA), but has been running his own business, Pro Electrical Installations, for over four years. In that time he has worked both for big commercial companies and small 'prestigious' residential properties. Neil told me a number of things I didn't know:

- Low-voltage downlighting increases the risk of fire. A 50W low-voltage dichroic lamp can produce heat up to 200°C at the back of the lamp and can easily melt or ignite combustible material lying directly over it. Fireproof hats are now available and some authorities make them compulsory, especially in public spaces.

- Costs for an electrician? Emergency call-out rates are between £40–80 in addition to an hourly rate, plus parts and materials. Most electricians' hourly rates will be between £15–25 per hour depending on the type of work and overheads. Many of them will have fixed item prices for installation work plus materials. Try to negotiate on large jobs. However, remember that cheapest is not always best: quality costs.

● A written estimate is a *must*, peace of mind for both parties. Some contractors will not take on a 'big job' without drawings and price specifications.

But Neil goes on to say that with some small domestic jobs estimates are not always possible or required. In this case, a good relationship between client and electrician is vital. Trust is the foundation stone. It sounds as if he is contradicting himself, but I think he is making a distinction between a rush call-out job for which you get a quote on the spot, and a big wiring/re-wiring project where you need to get contractual. This might involve further costs to the client such as drawings and specifications, which would probably need to be drawn up by a professional: an architect, lighting designer or builder. A familiar situation: for peace of mind and comeback you often need to pay more.

● When electricians charge VAT it usually means that they are highly in demand and have a high turnover. Maybe too pricey for you? A smaller outfit like Neil's might be a solution. No VAT, no pack drill. But it might be wise to compare the estimates of an Electrical Contractors Association (ECA) registered electrician with the independent operator's. If the latter has 'satisfied clients' you could also call them for feedback. Having seen his work, I would trust and recommend Neil to other people.

● There is currently a shortage of skilled electricians in the UK as youngsters tend to prefer computers to building sites. The shortage has been aggravated by the construction boom.

● Installing low-voltage downlighting costs more than putting in strip lighting, but it does look better and adds to the value of the building.

● Lighting designer? For 'highly designed' homes but perhaps too costly for the average home owner.

Lighting and electrical design

Neil thinks a qualified and experienced electrician, like himself, could take on more ambitious and unusual lighting schemes if you knew exactly what you wanted. However, for really spectacular cutting edge ideas – changing coloured lights, lighting boxed in walls, under floors or other 'arty' installations – you really do need a lighting designer. Not a sparks, however skilled.

The ideal time to plan a lighting scheme is during the building stage – after plastering but before decorating. Remember that electricians can also fit telephone and TV points, intercom systems, entertainment systems and fire alarms ... so think ahead.

Working all these details through with your electrician from square one obviously saves later disruption. In a new build situation walls can be chased out and floors taken up. This also represents a final cost saving. If like most of the UK's homeowners, you are dealing with an old-going-on-antique building, it still makes sense to plan for one big blitz rather keep adding on bits and pieces as they occur to you. For instance, you might want all bedroom lights to switch on at the door but switch off from the bed? Or, you might decide you want all your low-voltage downlighters specially wired on to a suitable dimmer switch?

Light bulbs

Although I house a complete melange of lighting – tungsten, halogen, pendent lights, wall lights, etc, – I do suggest, if you can, a lighting solution that uses as few different light bulbs as possible. (Electricians confusingly call them lamps!) Stocking up

Changing a low-voltage halogen lightbulb

Changing halogen low-voltage bulbs is easy when youy know how; impossible if you don't.

- Switch off the lights.
- Remove the spring wire or plastic clip on the face of the bulb, holding it in position; keep safe.
- Draw the bulb out of the socket until it is hanging off a short length of flex. Don't keep pulling or you may get the transformer out too.
- Pull the bulb gently to unplug it from the plastic socket. You will see two tiny prongs on the back.
- Insert the prongs on the new bulb into the plastic socket. Feed the flex back into the ceiling space until the bulb is in place, then replace the wire or plastic retaining clip.

with something near a dozen different light bulbs – screw fittings, bayonets, candle bulbs, etc – adds up to one of those small but persistent headaches which can send you up the wall. It is always the one bulb you have forgotten (the fridge light?) that conks out.

Light bulbs can be ordered via mail order or online (see page 74) which can save you cash and a boring shopping trip. However, where do you store them? I find a drawer or two works best as I can find the one I'm after quickly. Stack them in a cupboard and what do you know? You will be needing a light inside to allow you to see them clearly!

GARDENERS

In a nation so passionately devoted to gardens and gardening, there is a puzzling dearth of green fingers for hire. I don't mean landscape gardeners (rapidly becoming an overcrowded profession), but what used to be called jobbing gardeners, someone sufficiently experienced to be trusted with basic maintenance: mowing, weeding, dead-heading and a little light pruning.

FINDING A GARDENER

As with all hired help, the trust element is important. It is painful to return from your hols to a moribund garden because the watering was skimped during your absence, or to discover your vague suggestion of a spot of weeding has been interpreted to mean something close to scorched earth. Wouldn't one expect a soi-disant gardener to know the difference between goosefoot and clematis, your day lilies and the common yellow buttercup?

I hate to say this but trust also has implications such as security. Your gardener must have the key to your tools and mowing machine, and so be aware when your home is empty. He/she may be as honest as the day, but prone to gossip in the local pub.

These are just some of the considerations involved in taking on a gardener, and make it all the more essential to find someone local through recommendation.

A proper annual contract, tying your gardener to a yearly plan and regular payments, provides a cash incentive and is a promising route if your gardener is semi-professional and busy enough to handle the paperwork: ie, earns enough to employ someone to deal with invoices and VAT.

However, a local 'jobbing' gardener who is fitting in your needs among a few other odd jobs, most likely prefers cash in hand. No contract here, no comeback either, but he/she could be excellent, reliable and a mine of knowledge regarding local conditions and what will and won't grow. An ever so casual visit to your prospective gardener's own garden should give an indication of whether your ideas meet.

GARDENING AT A DISTANCE

In a 'second home' situation, the country bolt hole visited sporadically, it can be difficult to tap into the local network and find a suitable person. The following avenues are worth exploring: WI produce markets, nurseries, open days for famous local gardens, a sympathetic publican, the local press and friendly neighbours. If there is an agricultural college in your neighbourhood, it might be worth putting a 'wanted' ad on their notice board, working on the reasonable assumption that most students are desperate for extra cash.

Nonetheless, your problems are not over when your researches flush out the candidate for the job. The problem – I know this from personal experience – is that unless you are a wised-up gardener yourself, it is not that easy to tell if the terms of your contract are being fulfilled: the beds weeded, roses deadheaded and the grass mown regularly and conscientiously. A scam artist can find cogent reasons for a parched lawn or puny flowering: 'there was this dry spell', 'a poxy blight,' or 'rabbits got in'. Delegating from a distance is fraught with problems.

THE URBAN GARDENER

These exist all right, otherwise how come those magnificently floriferous wisterias and climbing roses, to be seen in the posher streets of Chelsea, Knightsbridge and Notting Hill Gate? This smacks of skilled and professional maintenance. Likewise, those chic window boxes, clipped box balls alternating with a show of seasonal bulbs or cascades of ivy. Anyone who can afford a contractual window box service is only a phone call away from a skilled pruner of invasive climbers, doctor to blighted roses and so on.

Living outside these moneyed enclaves, tracking down a reliable and knowledgeable gardener is not so straightforward. This is easier in the suburbs where the majority of people have gardens but – busy commuters – lack time to maintain them properly.

Personal recommendations are important here: ask around, check out the small ads in your local paper, place cards in your local corner shop window or bulletin board or surf the net. You could also try contacting the HQ of your local park as quite a few 'green' minded young people gravitate towards part-time work in parks and their skills may be more than adequate to meet your needs.

It is preferable if you can arrange times when you are around in order to monitor progress as well as to provide cups of tea and coffee.

Terms

A sorted urban gardener will be clear about the cost per hour for their services. More than a cleaner but less than a nanny – we are perhaps talking about £15–20 per hour. Try to make it a regular date, offer cash as well as cups of tea, talk eco subjects such as composts and pesticides and you might be off to a flying start.

ACCREDITED GARDENERS

I am indebted to a well-known and very successful gardener for the following information. As he is already up to his eyes in projects, I promised not to give his name. Let's call him Jack.

The people to call, if you are searching for a qualified and experienced gardener anywhere in the UK, are the British Association of Landscape Industries (BALI). They will send you a list of associated gardeners in your part of the country. Jack says that most people find a perfectly suitable gardener through this body. Since anyone signing up with BALI 'pays a fortune to be under their wing', we are talking serious stuff and it would be sheer bad luck if you find yourself dealing with dodgy characters pretending to skills they don't possess. Jack doubts that there will be a standard hourly rate for BALI referrals, so you will have to negotiate; 'it's a bit like finding a cleaner … you play it by ear'.

I asked Jack if BALI candidates might be a bit pretentious – thinking of the word 'landscape' – for a client just looking for a knowledgeable, hands-on gardener. He himself can't be doing with all this grandiose stuff about 'landscaping' and 'garden architecture'. To Jack 'a gardener is a gardener', and no messing. According to Jack, London is now awash with pseudo outfits styling themselves as 'landscape gardeners'; 'all these people going bust in the City seem to be popping up again as landscape architects'. This may not be the scene outside the London area, but you have been warned.

Gossip footnote. Jack is not a fan of TV gardening programmes. He thinks the 'plantings are OK, if that is what you like' but he has friends involved in that scene, and their verdict is that the 'architecture' bits, the pools, the pergolas, etc, have been run up too quicky and on the cheap and 'won't be there in five years' time'.

THE TREE SURGEON

My own paved slot of a garden, nudged by buildings on all sides, is a kindly micro-climate encouraging trees to rush up towards the light and sunshine. As a result, a magnolia grandiflora is now – after 15 years – an impressive three storeys high. The downside is that its spectacular creamy white flowers are borne up out of sight and waste their overwhelming scent and beauty on the pigeons. A weeping birch – *Betula pendula* – planted as a pot-grown sapling by a friend across the road shoots up a metre a year. As for the fig tree and the wisteria, well, they are rampant. When these were accessible from a tall step-ladder, I used to tackle the pruning myself using snips and a neat little Swedish handsaw for the larger branches. However, they are now too high for me to address.

If you are in a similar situation, you will also be looking for a tree surgeon. This does not mean a boyo with a chain saw, but a trained and experienced girl or guy who appreciates that tree surgery is an art form as well as a science. It is not just about reducing the size of the tree but also shaping it for the future; cutting back breastwood and cross-growing branches while respecting its intrinsic nature.

A helpful man at the Tree Advice Trust (also called the arboricultural advice and information service – see My Directory) told me how to check on the credentials of a tree surgeon tracked down via the Yellow Pages or the internet. 'Ask to see their public liability insurance. Any reliable firm will produce it, no problem. But make sure you see it before you sign them up. Insist. If they are at all dodgy, this will scare them off.' Such precautionary measures could also save you

from finding your beloved mulberry or Kanzan cherry tree reduced, before you know it, to an unsightly arthritic claw.

Next, provide the company or individual with a detailed specification of work to be undertaken and request an estimate. As ever, it is sound policy to check out at least one other firm at the same time. Finally, arrange a time that allows you to be on hand to check progress and monitor the 'shaping' process of the tree.

When is a tree not a tree? I asked my friendly AAIS contact, having in mind a wisteria which is a tangled mass of greenery and a mere handful of racemes. 'Basically, this will depend on how much work they have on,' he said. 'However, a rampant wisteria which has been allowed to get away for a year or two really needs patient untangling from the base upward as well as expert pruning, so don't spring this on your man at the last minute.'

I phoned Treecare, the first tree surgeons (care and maintenance) that came up in my directory, and asked to see their public liability insurance. Sure enough, within an hour a page-long form was faxed through stating that Treecare was covered to a limit of £5m on any one claim. It must be said that the signature had dropped off the page and the policy was due for renewal in a fortnight, but they sounded pleasant and quickly showed willing.

LIFESTYLE MANAGEMENT

'Lifestyle management' is an idea that originated in the USA, where it has a large following among wealthy, busy people to whom time is money and spending hours chasing up a cleaner, booking foreign holidays, hiring caterers for a buffet dinner, or planning a gala wedding reception, is just a waste of that most valuable commodity. One of the more successful clones over here is ten[uk] (see My Directory), set up three years ago by a pair of young entrepreneurs, somewhat on the American model, and now employing some 20 'managers' in their Mayfair headquarters. These are young (usually late 20s, early 30s) bright, personable, energetic people of both sexes, from widely different backgrounds.

A membership fee of £1,500 per annum (ten[uk] likes to think of itself as a club) buys you into the organisation's networking facilities, backed up by a constantly updated database, and fixes you up with a 'manager' picked from their team and deemed most appropriate to your circumstances, temperament, and of course 'lifestyle'. The 'manager's' role covers all the areas not willingly undertaken by a PA, nanny, or housekeeper: anything from finding a plumber over a bank holiday to planning every detail of a slap-up showbiz wedding plus exotic honeymoon in a top trendy boutique hotel in an exclusive location.

It is tempting to see these 'managers' as super gophers, or the equivalent of a TV company's 'runners' but the company is anxious to dispel the notion that these are lowly, expendable slaveys. They may be on call during working hours, but evenings and weekends are out of bounds.

I talked to two 'managers'. She had an academic background, a degree in Chinese, followed by three years teaching in Manchuria. His work experience consisted of running clubs in London and Sydney. Both found their way into ten[uk] via word of mouth – personal recommendation – the company does not recruit via ad columns. I warmed to them both; it was easy to imagine bonding with such eager, bouncy individuals with their 'can do' attitude beaming out of them. Their clients – sorry, members – are mostly 30-somethings, they explained, City types, lawyers, showbiz personalities, run off their feet due to their various commitments and gasping for the sort of help they can give. They might each 'manage' up to 20 members at a time, which sounds a nightmare, but as they pointed out their needs tend to be spaced out, so one member might call up once a year, desperate for a cleaner, while another, moving house imminently, might need hours of assistance till the move was completed. Finding a reliable cleaner, they both agreed, came top of all members' wishlists.

Which brings me to what I feel is the nub of the operation. ten^{uk}'s database of skilled workers, right across the board from cleaners and nannies to plumbers, electricians, builders and removal firms, comes with the reassurance that these have all been thoroughly checked out, references followed up, on-the-spot inspections made and fees negotiated.

In case you were wondering how these youthful 'managers' can handle projects as demanding as, say, finding an ace cleaner, a wedding dress designer, or a cutting-edge caterer, I should explain that the 'smart heart' of the set-up is that there is a senior, specialist tier to the organisation, all experienced in their particular fields, and all responsible for updating the information provided in the company's database: details of subcontractors, plus a whole lot of information about trends, costs, whatever,

that gives the junior personnel a head start. They can also be called up when problems arise. An analogy might be that you can acess, via a bunch of feisty undergraduates, the wisdom and expertise of a whole high table of dons and fellows.

Who doesn't wistfully dream of conjuring a helpful genie of the lamp to cope with the tedious minutiae of daily life? But is this worth the £1.5K per annum membership fee?

ten^{uk} claims that its job rates are in line with the going rate, even, sometimes, due to their clout and prestige, a touch less. But reading between the lines I conclude that the whole operation is predicated on members being high-flyers, already fixed up with at least a nanny, and cleaner, and a PA or two, so this jumps the whole thing into another income bracket. Not for the likes of me, sadly, but invaluable doubtless to the stressed and frantic rich.

How come they aren't running the railways, or sorting out London Transport? The message is not for me, but I do like their style.

THE GREEN SCENE

The spectre of global warming has been with us for so long now that the scary prophecies seem to have lost their shock value. It is hard to account otherwise for the massive indifference evinced by the public towards climatic changes, already causing irreversible damage to our planet. As the polar ice caps melt and the permafrost shrinks, the people and wildlife hardest hit are those living in sub-arctic regions, such as Alaska, where lakes are drying up, roads are cracking open and houses are collapsing due to thermokarsts: dips appearing in the ground as the permafrost melts underneath. Maybe our imaginations cannot stretch as far as Alaska? Or are we, as some ecologists suggest, simply in a big denial about the whole sinister process, even while the knock-on effect – flooding, incessant rain,

gales – is being played out under our noses?

As George Marshall of environmental organisation Risingtide argues in the *Observer*'s special ecology issue (28 October 2001) the reason we are 'passive bystanders' is that we are waiting for someone else to start kicking up a fuss. 'Surely,' people reason, 'if it really is that serious someone would be doing something.'

GREEN TREES

Why shouldn't that someone be you or me? What can *we* actively do? One action we can take is to plant trees, a small thing perhaps, but as a poster I saw proclaims, 'The longest journey begins with the first step'. I am not ashamed of my own tree-planting record, getting on for one tree a year over the past

30 years – a whitebeam in Dorset, a mulberry in Islington and a whole orchard in Somerset. My paved slot of a yard in Spitalfields now has so much leafage it looks like a green tunnel.

However, Peter Thoroughgood of the Tower Hamlets local authority leaves me standing. A professed tree lover, he takes pockets full of acorns on his weekend trips to Kent where he is one of an ardent band of steam railway enthusiasts, and when he isn't greasing axles or polishing up the Pullman cars, he can be found planting acorns in suitable spots along the railway cuttings. Didn't he foresee problems one of these days with 'leaves on the line?' He explained that steam trains take this in their stride; being so much heavier they simply chomp their way through autumn leaf drop. We both revelled in the thought that at some distant date the line will be overarched by a forest of young oaks.

This reminded me that there is a mighty oak just across the road from our bolthole in Somerset; indeed tiny oaklets pop up in the flowerbeds. In future, I too will take bags of acorns on my walks, surreptitiously helping to green up a corner of the West Country which has not looked the same since Dutch Elm disease wiped out its characteristic, branchy, asymmetric elms.

GREEN POWER?

If this strikes you as whimsical and amateurish, let me suggest another practical move. Sign up, as I have just done, with Juice, 'clean, friendly electricity' (see My Directory) brought to you by Npower with

Trees as therapy

Trees do more than recycle pollutants and clean up the air. According to a Department of Health spokesperson, research shows that hospital patients who have undergone surgery recover more rapidly if they can look out on trees from the surgical wards, and the latest thinking is that ambulant patients should be conscripted into tree planting. This makes complete sense to me. Who wouldn't rather overlook a budding grove than grimy brick walls? Moreover, trees going through their seasonal cycle are an inspiring symbol of growth and recovery; from drooping saplings to sturdy trees, from spring buds to autumn leaf drop. Trees are survivors – surgical patients must find encouragement there.

Greenpeace. The power source is wind and water, which makes it irreproachably ecological. Once dismissed as a lot of idealistic tosh on the part of earnest hippies, wind power now seems to be spreading apace, siting its frail, stalky machines (which look curiously like seedlings) from the Welsh mountains to the North Sea. As a tree and wind lover myself, I found Juice's full-page ad showing a fine specimen of ash, its spring foliage madly tossed by a fierce wind, quite irresistible.

I immediately called the freephone number to enquire about transferring from LEB to elemental, ecological and frankly sexy Juice, and was greeted by a friendly female voice, whose owner was persuasive and knowledgeable. I could, she explained, enter into a verbal contract forthwith, which I did. If I didn't change my mind in two weeks, Juice would contact LEB in 28 days, and my power supply would automatically be sourced to Juice, who would then bill me via direct debit. However, she added, not all my power would be green, because Juice only aim to match other power sources, like LEB, in these early venturesome days of going national. Kilowatt for kilowatt. I must admit she lost me a bit at this point, having the haziest notion of the way power grids operate. So I would be getting 50 per cent green power, 50 per cent brown power, but only one bill, from Juice.

If this all sounds flaky, her next observation was a corrective. Due to some quirk in the Juice operations, my electricity supply, as a resident in the South East, would work out cheaper, saving £35 in every £200. But, for some reason which she could not clarify to my entire satisfaction, were I living in the North West, I might actually pay a bit more.

When I told my partner about this sporting gesture, he immediately scented a scam, or at least a marketing and PR initiative, or ploy, of which he took a pessimistic view. So I was dismayed to find a small paragraph in WHICH? (November 2001) rapping Npower (which is involved with Juice) over the knuckles for its 'Appalling track record for high-pressure sales tactics'. It looked as if I needed to do more research before signing up definitively. Are Greenpeace suckers, or is it the 10,000 – now 10,001 – people who have signed up to date?

Three months down the line plus one quarterly bill and I can report that Juice and I are getting along just fine. The big switch went without a hitch, my bill does seem a little lighter – although it is difficult to work out savings accurately without a full year's bills. Although Juice has circulated me letters to post on to my MP lobbying for more wind power, I don't see this as high-pressure sales tactics.

SAVING ENERGY/MONEY/THE PLANET

Every little helps, I guess, when it comes to husbanding and protecting the present resources and future health of our planet. While I think I have always been on the side of the angels, in the sense of disliking waste, hating built-in obsolescence, and avoiding dependency on technology where possible, I am a late starter on the eco front. We visit the bottle bank en route to the big shop, and my au pair, Fatma, has bullied me into acquiring a green bin from the council for newspapers, cardboard and junk mail, etc. Far too small, if truth were told, but a gesture in the right direction. I also use energy-efficient light bulbs.

In humble beginner mode, I checked out further energy-saving suggestions with my daughter, Tabitha, who is seriously on the case when it comes to eco friendliness; action rather than theory. It was reassuring to find her list fairly close to mine, albeit heavier on the IT side. Hence, the following suggestions are a heads-together effort. Furthermore, a lot reaches back to my childhood and my father's endless strictures about turning lights off as you leave a room, switching off appliances, etc. At the time, this seemed penny pinching but now makes sense. Energy savers, please attend:

- Use energy-efficient light bulbs (readily available via mail order – see page 74).

While costing more initially, they save both energy and money in the longer term.

- Switch off lights when leaving a room and get your family to follow suite. Kids like to get proactive here, scolding Mum and Dad.

- A brick in the toilet cistern reduces the amount of water needed to flush.

- Mend all leaky taps.

- Where possible, update fridges, washing machines, dishwashers and showers with energy-efficient alternatives.

- Encourage showering rather than bathing to save water and power.

- Always use the 'sleep' option or energy-saving mode on your computer so it rests when not in use. Ideally switch it off.

- Bulk buy eco-friendly washing-up liquid and dishwasher powder.

- Use cloth nappies, terry and gauze, rather than disposables. The latter may be handy but they take up vast landfill space. There are nappy laundering services, but it is cheaper to deal with them yourself.

- Compost kitchen waste (but not cooked leftovers), if you have a garden.

- Recycle as much household waste as you can: see page 265.

- Ensure that your hot-water tank and loft are sufficiently insulated (see page 265) You might be eligible for council grants for wall and loft insulation.

- Use your car less. Walking, cycling or public transport are cheaper and usually healthier alternatives.

- Choose washable over dry-clean clothes. Hang your washing outside to dry so you can cut down on tumble-dryer usage.

- Use 'energy saver' mode or skip the 'dry' function on your dishwasher.

- Fix motor sensors outside your house, so porch lights don't burn all night.

LOW-ENERGY LIGHTING

Not to be confused with low-voltage (halogen) lighting, low-energy lighting is a recent innovation. A range of special low-energy light bulbs last up to ten times longer than standard light bulbs and give more light for a lower wattage: ie, 10 watts in a conventional bulb equals 50 watts with a low-voltage bulb, and so on, proportionately. Thus, you could substitute a 15 watt low-energy bulb and get as much light as from a 60 watt standard bulb. Get it?

The upside is the bulbs consume less power, which is an environmental plus, while at the same time cutting your electricity bills which is a plus of a different order.

The downside is that they cost more initially, like pounds rather than pence: typically around £5.50 for a bayonet style from Lyco (see page 74), £11 for a screw style. And not all come with regular bayonet or screw fittings. Nor are they yet suitable for use with dimmer switches. Sadly, this will rule them out for most trendy-ish homes where dimmers are now the norm. Another problem is that most of the more conventional-looking bulbs are just that bit taller – say 25mm – than a standard bulb, which means you may need to check that your lampshades are lofty enough to hide the light source if we are talking about table lamps, or deep enough if we are looking at ceiling pendent shades.

I thoroughly approve of a bulb that will burn for 10,000 hours, giving 50 watt lux for a 10 watt, for a cost of around £5.50. It seems to be a move in the environmentally sorted direction, and thrifty besides, but until compatibility with dimmers is a proven fact (my information is that they are still working on it) this excellent innovation seems to have limited application. However, you need to know about it because this appears to point the way to the future of home lighting.

INSULATION

I think everyone agrees that loft insulation is altogether a Good Thing, since without it a good whack of your warmth is just escaping through the roof, thus wasting heat, energy and cash. How you set about this will depend on whether you use your loft or whether it is just a dark space, which you enter as rarely as possible to check the water tank or the state of the roof itself.

In the latter case, insulation is a possible DIY job using rolls of insulating material which are spread out to cover your entire loft floor. You need to wear a mask to prevent breathing the stuff in, rig up an extension lead to light your way, and crawl about on the joists taking care not to put your foot through the ceiling below. I know this is possible, because I did it myself many years ago in Dorset. It made a difference to the internal temperature of the house, but it was a beastly job. Still, if you are as skint as I was then, you might consider this as a DIY project. DIY sheds such as B&Q offer an advice leaflet on how to do this.

Where the loft is in use, as a home office or spare bedroom, it will have been floored, in which case (with luck) an insulating layer will have been introduced below the flooring. In addition, the roof timbers will have been clad with the insulating version of plasterboard, which has one shiny metallic side. With both of these measures in situ, you should be well snug and laughing.

RECYCLING

Most of us are into recycling to the extent of making weekly trips to the bottle bank – an entirely pleasurable exercise. It clears the decks, relieves stress (pent-up aggression) and makes one feel a worthier citizen.

Fewer of us recycle paper, tins and plastic containers with the same enthusiasm, partly because this takes more thought and effort right through the week, partly because the facilities are lacking: ie, the local council/ supermarket have not made provision for this type of trash. Many local councils run a 'green box' scheme, with regular kerbside collection – or so they proclaim in the flyer that comes through the letterbox – but while this works a treat in affluent boroughs such as High Barnet it seems not to get off the ground in poorer areas like my own Tower Hamlets. The box is delivered (oddly smaller than it looks in the flyer), you carefully fill it with newspapers, junk mail and other acceptable, recyclable rubbish, get up early so as to have it ready for collection from 7 am on Mondays, and a week later it still sits there, contents recycled into papier mâché.

It's money that makes the difference, as ever. Rich boroughs have more disposable income, fewer more urgent priorities – street crime, homeless street people, vandalism, graffiti, etc – to deal with. They can even back commercial kerbside collections: more than 30 co-operatives of this sort have sprung up in the UK (don't ask me why they are co-operatives) for which their constituents are happy to pay extra, over and above their higher rates, which is highly commendable, and makes our lot in Tower Hamlets look stingy and retrograde.

Be that as it may, the UK record on recycling initiatives is dismal compared with Germany, Holland and Scandinavia. We seem to be shaping up as the 'dirty man' of Europe, scandalising tourists with our litter-strewn streets, parks and beauty spots (even rural hedgerows); a squalid scene epitomised for me by the sad spectacle of leafless, wintry trees hung about with flapping – clearly non bio-degradable – plastic bags. Stroll through a Dutch park, or along a Berlin *strasse*, and you won't spot so much as a discarded bus ticket, never mind a used condom. It all feels so maturely civic minded and responsible. These are people,

a whole society, that see caring as taking care.

Maybe, I think, we Brits need more education, more information, to start coming good in this area? Wouldn't you like to know, for instance, what happens to those zillions of bottles we gleefully chuck into bottle banks? Are they ground to powder and then recycled into new glass bottles? Does the recycling process consume less energy than one transatlantic flight, or is it – as the sceptics argue – the other way round? Is the whole exercise a sop to middle-class consciences? Is Germaine Greer the only public-spirited individual who puts cans through her dishwasher and unstaples her glossy magazines to match up to her local collection service's requirements?

Ringing round, I seemed to meet a certain evasiveness about the nitty-gritty questions, or the broader picture. One can't help but feel that recycling is a vote-catching idea to which politicos pay lip service, flag up in their flyers and speeches, and then relegate to the back burner. Unlike Germany, we do not have an effective and popular Green Party with political clout.

My own view – which you are free to skip, no hard feelings – is that the recycling habit is a good one to get into. Waste is not only an exponentially growing and fearsome by-product of an affluent, throwaway society, but morally repugnant, a reproach to all heedless consumers. To see what Third World countries create from our discarded rubbish – wire coat hangers bent and hammered into engaging bikes, or plastic containers cut, shaped and assembled, painstakingly, into sparky, ruffled cocks and hens – is a sobering object lesson already.

Children connect readily to recycling routines and imperatives, if the family attitude reinforces what they are being taught at school. They know the planet is struggling with diverse, scary problems and that ultimately this lands them with the sticky end of the lollipop. They enjoy scolding, and putting their parents straight too, of course, pontificating about the evils of tobacco and alcohol from the lordly perch of pre-pubescent innocence. On the recycling issue, you have them over a barrel: OK, fine, splendid idea, here are three bins, one for paper, one for plastic, one for tins, and we all work together to sort and fill them. And while you are about it how about collecting up all those sweet wrappers, coke cans and plastic bags littered about the house and garden? And what if we start a compost heap behind the toolshed? So green, such fun if we all do our bit – emptying this special green bucket every morning? With notions like these, instilled and backed up actively, in childhood, I can't help but feel – I am an incurable optimist – that the coming generation must learn to respect and value

thoughtfulness about waste, about their place in the country, the world, the universe – that favourite trope of the very young?

But alongside avoiding waste, they need to discover growth. Every child should plant a tree, their own tree, as a benchmark against which to measure their own growth, year by year, and a revelation of the hunger to survive, the evolving beauty of nature, made personal, manifest. Any child who grows up alongside their own tree is surely not going to enjoy maiming and mutilating what Hopkins called 'the living green'? Or turning any green space into a litter bin? It all comes down to education, plus example, and surely this should begin at home.

Surfing the net for information about our wasteful world and what we can do about it, I came across some chewy statistics.

● The USA generates 27 million tonnes of waste every year. Of this the largest percentage consists of paper and card – 32 per cent. Four million tonnes of this is junk mail.

● Glass can be endlessly recycled either to make new bottles, or to bulk out road surfacing – 'glassphalt'. Crushed glass is known as 'cullet', and its re-use saves 25 per cent of the energy used when making glass from scratch. So now we know the trips to the bottle bank make a difference.

● Recycling tins and cans is even more worthwhile, since steel recovered from cans uses 75 per cent less energy. To check that a can is steel, not aluminium, test a fridge magnet on it: the magnet will be attracted to steel. You may have to clean off labels (GG does this in her dishwasher) but check with your recycling department first. After all running the dishwasher uses energy too.

● In theory, we should be able to recover more than 50 per cent of our household waste (a target reached by both Switzerland and Austria), whereas we scrape into this table with a measly 10 per cent. Both Australia and the USA also leave us standing, in terms of right-on initiatives. But doesn't the USA consume more energy than anywhere else via their cars, fridges and all the other appurtenances of a consumer society? It is a knotty subject to get one's head around, but it seems clear we Brits 'could do better'.

● One fact to digest is that computers tend to be replaced every three years to keep up with technology, thereby creating a problem almost as intractable as the fridge mountain, but fridges last longer, don't they – ten years or so? As zillions more people get online are we looking at a computer alp? For every 'recovered'

monitor four end up in a landfill site. Definitely not bio-degradable. I guess Mr Gates' boffins are already deeply into research about this problem, as they should be, since their gung-ho competitiveness is largely to blame. A situation fraught with ironies, surely.

Where the websites fail to deliver, in my view, is enough practical, cogent advice about what we can actually do: yes, start a compost heap (most gardeners already do this); yes, walk and cycle more, drive less; yes, buy more fresh food, less pre-packaged stuff (it's the packaging that is wasteful). But when you read that those cute throwaway chopsticks in paper sleeves that come with your sushi are gobbling up softwood plantations at a scary rate, don't you feel like throwing up your hands in despair?

Hold steady, folks, this is the first step on what will be a long and tiring journey, ambushed by corporate raiders, the bottom line, inertia and indifference. I am not a doom-sayer, nor a pessimist, but I am becoming anxious.

It is still so lovely, this teeming land of ours, where it has escaped the hard-surfacing, the developers' leaden hand, those bureaucratic edicts from Brussels, I just long to find a way to protect it from further crass despoliation. We just aren't doing enough, it seems clear.

MANIC ORGANIC

Remember when 'going organic' stamped you as an old hippy or a health freak?

Whoever would have guessed, ten years ago that we were at the sharp end of a serious shift in consumer thinking and spending that would now be looking at an annual turnover of over £1 billion per annum? Judging by the number of supermarket chains and retailers jumping on the bandwagon, this is still on the up.

There is no question that 'organic' is a selling point today even though it does cost more – on average 12–16 per cent – than non-organic foodstuffs. No one is beadier when it comes to price points than the supermarkets' management; given that they are dedicating more and more shelving to organic products we must be looking at more than a mild flutter in the foodie dovecot. Organic is now a growth sector and a buzz word, with its own restaurants, shops, mail order and literature.

Of course, it fits well with the burgeoning concern over the environment, pollution and quality of life for both humans and animals. However, a 15 per cent hike in one's weekly food spend is not to be overlooked. Anyone thinking of switching from ordinary to organic foods may want some questions answered (see page 271).

We spent most of our time in a stream under the cottonwoods, or with Old Mary the cook, watching her make butter in a great churn between her mountainous knees. She slapped it into pats and put them down in the stream where it ran hurriedly through the darkness of the butter-house. She put stone jars of cream there too, and wire baskets of eggs and lettuces, and when she drew them up, like netted fish, she would shake the cold water onto us and laugh almost as much as we did.

The Art of Eating, M F K Fisher (reminiscing about her childhood in California in 1918)
(Faber & Faber 1963; Macmillan 1983, 1991)

PROS AND CONS

First of all, if you will bear with me (possibly the most exasperating phrase to have crept into the language), I would like to record my own views, both for and against, on the organic question. Having moved from Dorset where I had a vegetable patch to Central London, I was a ready convert during the mid-'80s to the idea of a weekly 'box' delivered from a walled Suffolk garden. Although the choice was mostly seasonal, Adrian might sometimes mention tantalising 'extras': a brace of pheasant, wild duck or once a quarter of home-reared pig. When his deliveries dwindled (snapped up, alas, by the River Café ladies and suchlike) I sought organic elsewhere. To begin with I tried farmers' markets and then finally moved on to supermarket shelves. There is no getting away from the fact that the big supermarket chains account for roughly three-quarters of organic food sales in the UK. Smart or what?

Yum, yum

My reason for buying organic wherever possible is primarily a greedy one: it tastes better, more of itself, keener, fresher and livelier. Budget permitting, I am always happy to pay more for flavour. Adrian's lettuces, for instance, usually Tom Thumbs, looked exquisite once I had washed off the Suffolk mud. The flavour was at once so clean and complex, a pungent munch of all the minerals Suffolk earth is home to, that it could almost get away undressed. Like all his offerings (ah, those fir apple potatoes, that purple basil and golden tomatoes!) it was almost shockingly flavoursome to anyone accustomed to the supermarket Webbs Wonder – flavourless as crushed ice.

Perishability

However, I soon discovered that there was a downside to all these spectacular goodies; they deteriorated so *fast*. If I couldn't deal with a morning delivery of produce (picked the night before) by that evening some of it was already in trouble. Raspberries quickly became mushy or mildewy, herbs limply discoloured and saladings verging on the slimy. This doesn't happen if you grow your own as the interval between picking and eating is short. But, bought organic produce has to be dealt with urgently!

Although I didn't always have a couple of hours early in the morning, I learnt some holding tricks. In a tearing rush, I dumped the salad stuff in a sink full of cold water, the herbs in a jug of water, the box of other produce in my larder, which is cooler than the kitchen, and the soft fruit in the fridge. I then dealt with it all that evening, alongside the cook-up. I did the usual things such as blanching and freezing broad beans, making purées of vegetables or fruits on the borderline and eating salad and chopped herbs at every meal time. The rescue operation took time, concentration and large amounts of organisation.

Occasionally, my mission was overtaken by events and I had to chuck a mildewed cauliflower, limp carrots slimed at the roots or Jerusalem artichokes soft as puffballs. To do this went against the grain; it wasn't the waste of money so much as the lost opportunity to revel and wallow in flavour. The moral here is to only buy organic when you have time to cope with the produce straight away.

Due to temperature control, supermarket organic produce seems to last a day or two longer. Whether you are in sympathy or not, you begin to see why commercially driven operations use all these things we are bothered about: pesticides, sprays and waxing to name just a few.

FAQs RE. ORGANIC FOODS

● **What is the definition of organic?** Organic fruit and vegetables are grown without artificial chemical fertilisers and pesticides. Instead they rely on beneficial insects and other wildlife to deal with crop pests. Mixed crops, healthy soil full of earthworms and micro-organisms are vital to successful organic farming. It takes several years for a conventional farm to 'convert' to organic crops.

● **How does this apply to animal products?** Livestock is reared without using routine drugs, hormones, antibiotics and wormers. Animals are reared in optimal conditions, are given organic feed if necessary, are free to roam, and given clean straw and shelter.

Food hygienists' no-nos

● Airline meals

● Farmed fish and shellfish (especially imported king prawns)

● Cannelloni

● Frozen birds, fish, etc, cooked by microwave

There is a risk that the cooking process of the above three products is too brief to destroy pathogens; bacteria that have multiplied in favourable conditions. As with all mass-produced animal foods, the worry is that you are taking too many antibiotics on board with the food itself.

● **What is the consumer's guarantee that produce is organic?** Organic is a legal definition and all products must be certified by a government-approved body, registered with the UK Register of Organic Food Standards.

● **What do I look for then?** The Soil Association Symbol is the most commonly found in the UK (Scotland and Ireland have their own symbols). Where you often don't get this certification is in farmers' markets. Maybe a few stalls show it; the rest sort of snuggle in under the rubric.

● **What are the commonest reasons for going organic?** Health is a primary concern (expressed by 53 per cent of people, according to a Mori Poll), followed by Tastes Better (43 per cent), Genetic Modification free (30 per cent), and Animal/Environment Friendly accounting for 25 per cent.

● **Where does organic food come from?** Alas, more than 80 per cent of organic fruit and vegetables is imported, and with increasing demand this total is set to rise. However, the 'conversion' rate for organic livestock is increasingly rapidly and so foods such as home-raised organic meat looks like becoming more widely available.

● **Which organic foods taste most rewardingly different?** Organic milk is lovely, eggs have wonderful orange yolks and bread has 'body' as well as flavour. I am not sure that organic rice, chick peas, lentils and barley taste noticeably more

Food acronyms

It is impossible to keep track of all of these, but here are some to look out for on packaging and in the media:

● NOAEL: no observed adverse effect level
● ADI: acceptable daily intake
● TDI: tolerable daily intake
● IGR: insect growth regulators, a preferred method of controlling pests because their function is to inhibit reproduction, locking on to sites rather than human hormones, and preventing pest growth.

Battery farming

The British consume a staggering 750 million chickens annually. Sadly, most of these are battery farmed. Once a luxury meat in a poor household, chicken is now as cheap as oysters were in the eighteenth century. Chicken Tikka Marsala, an east–west concoction, is the UK's no. 1 food of choice.

Battery hens and chicken lead nasty, short, brutish lives to feed our appetite for the animal equivalent of sliced white bread. Why don't the animal rights contingent mobilise public opinion about this shameful blot on our eating habits? Foxes have at least a sporting chance; battery hens get to die before they have properly lived.

Furthermore, due to poor farming procedures, they are not a safe food. One in five contain traces of drugs that could be harmful to consumers.: Nicarbazin can lead to birth defects; Dimetridozole can also lead to birth defects and/or cancer; and Lasalocid can cause heart damage.

flavoursome. The Soil Association agreed with me that organic pasta sauces and suchlike are a touch pointless. Organic tea tastes (to me at least) pretty weird. Thus, it is really with fresh meats and green produce that the gains are most noticeable; fruit, vegetables and herbs.

● **Who benefits most from going 'organic'?** Well, veggies and vegans with their restricted diets seem the most obvious candidates. These two groups have always seemed to be ahead of the bandwagon. However, anyone must benefit from a diet that is less affected by artificial chemicals than 'ordinary' food.

DEALING WITH PERISHABLES

For suggestions on making your organic buys work for you – by preserving, cooking, puréing and freezing, etc – see page 65. If this all seems like too much work then don't buy organic! But if you can cope, your reward is flavour that can stand alone.

ORGANIC BABY FOOD

There are times when instant baby foods are a lifesaver and, given a choice, most mums would plump for the organic ranges. Baby Organix being the most popular brand, followed by Boots, Cow and Gate and Hipp.

There are sound arguments for feeding babies organically, as Lynda Brown, author a number of book on organic food, points out. The mainstays of a baby's diet – vegetables, fruit and milk – are just where chemical residues are most encountered, and because babies eat far more in relation to their body weight than adults they could be taking in up to five times as many 'residues'. Organic baby foods are pure, without any of the thickeners and added flavourings of conventional baby foods, and are produced with minimum processing. Popular with babies: pasta shapes, pear and banana purées and whole-milk yoghurt.

Prices vary very little across the organic baby-food ranges, but they all cost more than conventional foods. Lynda Brown stresses that these convenience foods should be used only to supplement home-made foods, which seems sensible both on grounds of cost, and because preparing purées of carrots, spinach, peas, pears and banana (all organic, *naturellement*) alongside the family meal is easy and quick, if you have a small food processor. (For hygiene, it's best if the baby's processor is kept only for baby foods.)

Organised mothers I know sometimes make up a batch of vegetable or fruit purée, freeze it in ice-cube trays and then store them in the freezer. One or two of these can be thawed rapidly and heated through in a saucepan at meal times. Not only is this cheaper, but you have the comfort of knowing exactly what went into your baby cubes. Though the commercial organic foods are 95 to 100 per cent pure, some mothers consider them over-flavoured with salt and/or sugar as the case may be.

Tiny pasta shapes can be cooked in a thin tomato or vegetable purée and frozen for future use in exactly the same way. Whole-milk yoghurt, flavoured with a little honey, makes a quick and wholesome second course.

Check with your health visitor, clinic or baby manual when it is appropriate to move a growing baby on to proteins – fish, chicken, eggs and cheese – the first step towards sharing in the family meals which will after all become its main diet through childhood and later. The changeover should be gradual so the baby can assimilate new flavours and consistencies, as well as the micro-organisms present in a normal household's meals. Do not think of this as scary. It is about gradual exposure to the variety of real, everyday, family food, which a healthy child will welcome but which will also be slowly developing the baby's resistance to what my mother called simply 'germs', and which its system needs to learn to cope with.

I think most mothers handle this adaptation intuitively and well. Babies today strike me as more advanced and feisty than the hugely plump infants I remember from my childhood when a 'bonny babe' was defined by pendulous cheeks, limbs like the Michelin man and an air of overstuffed hebetude.

WATER: SOFT v HARD

My parents installed a water-softening gadget in their kitchen in the '70s, as I recall a biggish ceramic cylinder with pipes coming off it in all directions and needing regular feeds with salt. It made a noticeable difference to baths and hair washing — hair did seem silkier, skin less dry — but these benefits were less noticeable than the fact the appliance gave rise to ceaseless argument about who had failed to do what, when.

It was only on a recent trip to San Francisco that I rediscovered the wonders of really soft water.

Back in the UK I discovered that there are many types of gadgets/appliances, ranging in price from under £100 to under £1,000, which will deliver water that has been purged of its 'hard salts', the calcium and magnesium which form limescale deposits in pipes and appliances, coating heating elements, consuming more electricity and leading to early retirement. It only needs a quick glance at the UK map seen in terms of hardness of water supply, to recognise that a big fat chunk of this country, slicing down from the East Coast, north of Lincoln, diagonally to Bristol and then to Southampton, is cursed with Hard to Very Hard Water. And it only takes a comparison between the results of dishwashing in San Francisco with dishwashing in London, to recognise that Hard to Very Hard Water is the

Too much iron or manganese makes water taste unpleasant; iron leaves rusty stains on your clothing; calcium and magnesium, the minerals that make water hard, turn soap into a sludgy mess,leave deposits on glasses and pots, and clog up your automatic coffeemaker. But none of these can hurt you in normal concentrations. On the other hand, many harmful or suspect chemicals can't be tasted or smelled even at dangerous levels.

The Man Who Ate Everything: and other gastronomic feats, disputes, pleasurable pursuits,
Jeffrey Steingarten (Hodder Headline, 1998)

unseen enemy, standing in the way of glasses upended to drain drying crystal clear, hair looking like those shampoo ads on the telly, skin you love to touch. I am seriously considering enlisting in the battle against Very Hard Water. Like most people, I am tempted to start small, with something like the Electrolytic Scale Inhibitor, working up to the Aquacentre, the compact update on my parents' ceramic cylinder – neat enough to fit under a sink.

The company with the longest track record in this area, Salamander (see My Directory), will send you a pack of brochures and information, with solutions to suit most purses. The main drawback to taps all gushing silky soft water is that you will need to install a separate tap for drinking water, to comply with EU regulations, but this too can be cleared of chlorine and other unwelcome traces if you get one of their special taps. Another disadvantage, if you are many and use much water, is that the Aquacentre may require topping up – salt is still the softening agent – more than once a week. So another item to add to the list.

But the upside is happier appliances, needing less maintenance and repairs, pipes clean as a whistle, and all those little cosmetic benefits, such as silky hair and soft hands.

PAMPERING YOURSELF

In my unsophisticated youth the more outré girls at my school used to get round the make-up ban in numerous and ingenious ways. For instance, they smoothed on a pink-tinted lacto-calamine lotion to tone down their infuriatingly red cheeks and give the desirable matt look. Others applied Vaseline to their brows and eyelashes claiming that this made them grow thicker, or they touched their lips up with a tiny lipstick by Tangee which looked orange in the hand but subtly emphasised the natural lip colour. Thus enhanced they then linked arms and strolled the streets of Bedford in the hopes of running into a bunch of Bedford School boys. So what's new?

Today the cosmetic industry has multiplied a thousandfold, pumping out scads of products for every inch of our bodies. Have you watched women grooming themselves after working out in the gym? They have cosmetic bags like suitcases!

However, not only are many of those innocent schoolgirl beauty aids still with us, but they are positively endorsed by professionals such as Thi Nhuyen, the late Countess Czaki's chosen successor, whose clientele includes just about every beauty of a certain age with an interest in 'maintenance'. I thought that Thi would laugh when I mentioned that I found myself turning increasingly to the babyishly simple products I first experimented with as a schoolgirl. On the contrary.

What you might call 'innocent' cosmetics are absolutely Thi's thing. Calamine with glycerine? 'So soothing and good protection under make-up,' she enthused, 'and excellent when you have caught the sun, but the best thing of all is Aloe Vera.' Sunburn, any burns: break off a leaf, apply the juice and it heals up in no time without scarring.'

Like everyone else I dimly recalled that Aloe Vera has something to do with a Mexican succulent, but it never occurred to me that you might have one growing on the window sill, thus being able to break off a leaf as needed. Thi's own plant was a present from a grateful client and she has nurtured it so carefully that it now has plantlets destined for her favourite clients. Although Aloe Vera is now obtainable from nurseries, Thi feels that these are perhaps not quite so efficacious as her own plant direct from Mexico.

Vaseline? 'Excellent protection for the skin. If you swim in a chlorinated pool smooth a little Vaseline on your face.'

Thi then tut-tutted about a client who had been in the day before with a spotty chin, a rare outbreak in this case. 'I absolutely had to find out what she had been doing to cause this rash of spots, so unexpected.' Guess what? The client had fallen for a whole slew of really pricey 'miracle' unguents by a famous cosmetic name.

'No, no,' I told her, 'these creams have upset your skin. Why aren't you using your Boots creams?' I know why not and so does she. Once in a while, most women (some men too) are suckers for copywriters' hyperbole, even when coached by Thi into

regular use of innocent and cheap products which promise nothing except to clean your skin of make-up and pollution and maybe relax it along the way. So you do your nightly clean-up fine, but you still foolishly hope for a magic potion or lotion that erases lines, smoothes out wrinkles and restores the 'muscle tone'. The latter Thi chases after with her battery of vibrators and intriguingly varied masks: one warm, one cold and all deliciously and differently fragrant.

We discussed DIY facemasks using natural ingredients. It seems you can't go wrong with a scoop of avocado, whizzed to a smooth pulp in your processor and maybe lightened with a splash of yoghurt. Egg yolk also gets Thi's approval as a skin invigorator, but she suggests a fine layer of protective cream first to guard against the 'tightening' as the egg yolk dries.

The overall bogey in Thi's skin maintenance world is the sun; boon to golden lads and lasses but a stealthy enemy over the decades. Sun does not only desiccate young complexions to the texture of lizard skin, but sows future problems and nasties: sun/age spots, scabby little solar keratoses which need to be removed with liquid nitrogen – cryotherapy. So those Victorian and Edwardian lovelies guarding their precious complexions with swooping hats and frilly parasols were not so stupid after all. What goes around, as the wiseacres tell us, comes around, or to get biblical, as you sow so shall you reap. This makes depressing stuff if you have just splurged hard-earned cash on a holiday soaking up the sun on some remote beach. You can safely do this, says Thi, if you slather on the protective lotions and settle for a golden effect rather than a dramatic bronzing. 'Sun is good for you if you take it slowly, in small doses, and wear lots of protective lotions,' says Thi, whose own face is as evenly golden, poreless and smooth as a new-laid egg.

Surfacing through our chat recurred the message that I picked up throughout all my research for this book; genetic programming is for real. Dark skins can cope with strong sun wheras light, fair skins, adapted to northern climates, eventually protest. It is a bit the same with food: your system can cope with a diet you were brought up on, but can freak out when subjected to unfamiliar foods with their own particular bacteria and micro-organisms.

I am not advocating endless stay-at-home hols for Brits, because as Thi says – and we all concur – 'sun is good for you' and so is a Greek meze nibbled under an awning with the Mediterranean slopping lazily against the harbour wall. Life is certainly made richer by new experiences. However, just savour them slowly and give your antibodies and melanin levels a chance to acclimatise.

SCHOOLGIRL 'AIDS'
Lacto-calamine

This is widely available from pharmacies. Most people keep it on hand to relieve

Cosmetic containers

Cosmetic containers are so yummy when new, unfortunately they soon look so abject that you feel like chucking them for a new lot. The cosmetic houses encourage this by egging you on with their seasonal hype. But remind yourself what they cost originally, and get tough. Clean their containers now and then (using a sponge cloth and detergent) so they don't get sticky (a real turn-off) and play with the colours a bit creatively as all the make-up artists do; mixing and layering with brushes for a customised effect. (See page 282 for making your own palette.) Whatever you do, don't let the contents get wet (pressed powder or eye shadows) or drop them so that you are left with a pile of expensive rubble.

sunburn (although plain yoghurt is another remedy to keep in mind). I find it makes a soothing moisturiser. OK, it doesn't contain Royal Jelly or Vitamin E, but it just leaves the skin feeling dewy and refreshed. It is also good under make-up.

Furthermore, it is also the best treatment I know for hives; those itchy bumps which erupt from nowhere, mostly on one's face. A good dab of calamine applied as soon as possible (handbag-sized tubes are also available) calms the itch pronto and a smear of concealer does the rest.

Vaseline

Petroleum jelly is a simple lubricant. A layer smoothed over skin helps to seal and protect it, hence its use on babies' bottoms and swimmers' faces before doing 20 lengths in a chlorinated pool.

However, it has many other useful applications as model girls – who always carry a small tub in their make-up kit – frequently remind us.

● A dab smoothed over the eye area makes eye make-up go on much more evenly on one of those days when your face feels as thirsty as the Negev desert.

● A smidgin on your brows, before applying any pencilling, keeps them tidily defined and flat.

● I doubt Vaseline can actually make eyelashes grow thicker, but it does help keep them glossy and offers some protection from mascara and curling sessions.

● I find that Vaseline also helps with dry or fragile cuticles; just rub some on after washing your hands.

● Finally, as you might expect, Vaseline also does a great job on chapped lips.

Spots

OK, we're moving on from the schoolgirl scene now since most of the products that follow were not around in that distant time. Most people who lead stressed lives get the odd spot from time to time. This is usually smack in the middle of the face and will probably appear the day you have a highly important meeting. Nothing eats away at one's confidence like the pimple burgeoning on your nose or in the middle of your chin.

I have not found anything better than tea-tree oil, which is both fiercely drying and a powerful natural antiseptic. Dab it on repeatedly with a cotton bud. If you move in there quickly, the inflammation subsides relatively rapidly and all that remains is a tiny scab which can then be disguised with foundation or concealer. However, don't pick at the scab – it will disappear in a day or two.

Home-made face mask

A fresh egg yolk (organic preferably) beaten up with a thread of olive oil, applied over face and neck and then left on for 10–15 minutes, is an effective pick-me-up for skin that feels parched and irritable. Some people stir in a spoonful of plain yoghurt too. My mother, whose skin remained remarkably sound and unlined till her 70s, was an egg/oil user.

Thi says that mashed ripe banana makes a bracing facemask, if you can deal with a pile of sludge sitting on your face; it is full of potassium.

Cucumber whizzed in a processor and spread over the face has a great astringent action. Thi recommends that you apply a thin layer of cream first before spreading the mask on your face.

Toners

Thi does not believe in toners. Plain cold water is the best thing, she says, to close pores and get the circulation going. If your tap water is very hard, try dissolving a pinch of borax in it, or keep a bottle of Evian or Vittel handy.

Face brush

Here is a thought I offer in all diffidence, because I have no scientific evidence to back it up, only common sense and personal experience. Years ago, it occurred to me that men's faces age less dramatically than women's. In their 50s and 60s their skin tends to look less papery and generally more robust. Perhaps this is due to the fact that a daily shave, rubbing a brush to a lather, has a helpful tonic effect and boosts the face's circulation?

Around the same time as I had this thought, I came across a 'face brush' at Muji, soft bristled and about the size of a 10p coin. Since then, I always start the day with a face brushing, round and round, upwards on cheeks and forehead, gently around the eyes and ending up with a whisk round my nose and mouth, jaw and neck. Although I sometimes use a face-wash cosmetic, more often than not it is just cool water.

Result? We aren't talking miracles here! My face is lined, inevitably, but not saggy and not – dreadful phase – chapfallen. It could be due to a lucky gene I have inherited, but all I can say is that this brief and simple brush massage feels beneficial and right. Once your face gets used to it, it becomes hard to start the day without this rapid wake-up call.

I read somewhere that Paul Newman starts his day by dunking his spectacularly noble head into a bucket of iced water. The same idea? I suppose to anyone under 30 Newman seems ancient, but check out the next photo you come across – it's an ageing face, but still remarkably defined and holding up well.

COSMETIC PRODUCTS

Thi is highly complimentary about the whole Nivea range; saying that Nivea contains a special ingredient no one has ever succeeded in copying. Her preferred treatment for spots is witch hazel, a proprietary brand in gel form called Witch Doctor, which has a gentle antiseptic action.

Make-up

Thi thinks we should all use a matt water-based foundation 'to keep lovely skin free' and recommends the Kiehl range; available at Liberty's and other outlets.

THE 'UR' HAND CREAM

Hand care is not an item I devote much time to, beyond wearing gloves for washing up and rubbing ointment into them when they feel dry and needy. However, I have never found a commercial hand cream, at any price range, that delivers the soothing and smoothing effect of simple lanoline (a dense, sticky ointment extracted from the natural oils in sheep's wool). Commercial, hyped-up hand creams bang on about being non-sticky, moisturising and rejuvenating (oh yeah) but their benefits vanish in seconds whereas, cheap, sticky old lanoline makes my hard-working hands feel nurtured, sleek and comfortable all day.

A few years ago, I hit a bad patch when my favourite tubes and jars of lanoline (Crookes, as I recall) vanished from the chemists' counters. Of late, 'lanoline ointment' so called, in tiny jars, is making a modest comeback, and about time, because there is nothing so effective at any price.

Rubbing lanoline on your hands will leave them feeling a bit sticky and greasy for a short while, but skin absorbs this fattiness gratefully. Not to mention nails, cuticles, etc. While moisturisers pump a momentary dampness into your skin, which rapidly evaporates, a fatty, greasy ointment really lubricates once it sinks in and gets to work.

It was my daughter Daisy, chortling about this 'ridiculous idea – rubbing mutton fat on

Lipstick recyling

Recycle squashed or otherwise deformed lipsticks into you own palette. Artists' supply shops sell little ceramic trays, with round depressions for mixing paint. If you warm a lipstick gently in the oven, then transfer the stub with a knife, it will soften enough to make a cake of colour, to be applied with brush or fingertip. Use nail polish remover to clean up the palette.

your hands' which she happened upon in an old housework manual, that brought all this to mind.

To me it wasn't ridiculous at all. Historically (read Dorothy Hartley's fascinating *Food in England*), country people always used natural fats and greases on their hands, medicinally rather than cosmetically, to relieve chapping and soreness and to forestall cracks and infection. Before lanoline was manufactured, they would have used animal fat – rendered down, strained and reasonably pure. Dairymaids, especially, needed smooth hands if they were to milk successfully. Having given the cosmetic firms a run for their money, I have found nothing to compare with lanoline for those hard-working tools, your hands.

NOTE: Lanoline may not be suitable for people who have problems with dermatitis or exzema.

PAPERWORK

Was there ever such an invasive, mind-scrambling torment as paperwork? It is bad enough in an office, but at least there you are set up to deal with it, and it can be classified under office-type heads. Domestic paperwork is a different animal altogether because you have got all that personal stuff to keep track of on top of the invoices, bank statements, credit-card statements, tax papers, service agreements and whatnot. This escalates, of course, if you work from home. You are probably short of space, and because the filing, checking and updating needed to keep ahead has to be squeezed into spare moments, around other household activities, you will certainly be pushed for time. Furthermore, you are not only dealing with it on your own, but you are not being paid.

Having delivered myself of this whinge, the fact remains that paperwork simply has to be processed otherwise you will find yourself in all sorts of trouble: threatening letters, fines, the phone cut off, and that's just the money side of things. You can't expect praise or a bonus for running your paperwork like a steel trap on legs, but once it is in hand, you will feel like a giant refreshed.

A SYSTEM

That word again. Without a system you are up the proverbial creek without a paddle. The system is where it starts, and it can be very simple indeed. The first priority is to keep it all – I mean everything from receipts to school reports – in one place, so that even if you haven't found time to sort it out, at least you know nothing has gone astray, or sneaked in among newspapers and been thrown out.

AN IDIOT'S GUIDE

While some people I know chuck all their paperwork into a kitchen drawer, I think you would be better off with a concertina, or expanding file. Rymans do a neat one, made of rigid card in fetching colours with a strong handle, for around £8. What I also like about this is that it comes with a list of printed, stick-on labels – Gas, Education, Medical, etc – which act as a useful aide-memoire.

This becomes your household receptacle or safe place. In two ticks it will be full to bursting, but you can help things along by acquiring two more props: a ring binder filled with umpteen plastic pockets, and a spike.

Ring binder and pockets

Use this to store everything that comes with the purchase of household appliances: receipts, instruction manuals, guarantees and service agreements. Each appliance has its own pocket – fridge, cooker, microwave, digital camera, etc – and their transparency allows you to rapidly flip though when some peevish bod at a call centre is hanging on while you chase up the appliance number, model name or service agreement number.

This stuff is too bulky to be accommodated in the expanding file, and having it all nicely to hand in this way is a calming exercise. Add any further correspondence to the relevant pockets.

A further refinement might be to stick a label (the sort sold in rolls for computer addressing) on to each pocket giving the date and place of purchase, model name and number, and any further guarantee or service numbers. This won't cut short the tedious rigmarole of 'you are being held in a queue and your enquiry will be dealt with as soon as one of our operators is available', but it will save time and temper thereafter and show you mean business.

Spike

In, out and pending trays are all very well for big shots in offices, with PAs in attendance, but in the home situation their presence is often an invitation to further chaos, and they can end up being treated as extra drawers. Whereas a spike, which you might keep in the kitchen, can hold a whole gallimaufry of papers in transit – recent invoices, milk bills, prescriptions, dry-cleaning dockets and mail-order statements where some items are still pending. Of course, you will still need to deal with this in one way or another, but a spike keeps this safely together. It is also too in your face to forget about!

Come to think of it, you might have a second spike for all those newspaper cuttings, recipes and sale offers that float about looking for a home. Broadly speaking, spikes are for ephemera. I get fed up with de-clutter queens telling us to start cuttings files and recipe files, as if life is really like that – tearing out the item is one thing, but transferring it, trimmed and pasted, to a proper file is the sort of activity most of us left behind as convalescent kids making scrapbooks from magazines.

Stapler

This is useful for keeping a bunch of separate items (phone bill, itemised calls and addressed envelope) from drifting apart. In my experience, you need at least three and the trick is to buy three identical ones, which all take the same size staples. I recommend you buy plenty of the latter at the same time. Nothing is more irritating than to run out of staples, only to find the size you require is not kept in stock and has to be ordered especially.

Mock not!

OK, all the above belongs to an idiot's guide to sorting and filing, and will no doubt raise a sneer among those of you with a business background, computer literate, and comfy in cyberspace. But plenty of bright people, especially 'creatives', go to pieces when the deadly paperwork intrudes upon their work and lives.

Vital documents

One separate, but pressing item, not properly covered under my Idiot's Guide, is what might be called vital documents. These would include birth certificates, marriage certificates or decrees nisi, passport, house deeds, mortgage agreements, house-loan agreements and other contracts. These are part of the household/ family archive.

Sensitive and private documents, such as wills and title deeds, are best stored with your bank or solicitor. Use photocopies for your immediate reference and store the originals in a fireproof safe. Thanks to computerisation, it is not a complete disaster when such important documents are lost, but obtaining replicas can be a long drawn out business. Keeping them safe, with copies, gives peace of mind.

Keeping receipts

Keep receipts for all home and office equipment in case you need to claim under the warranty. This means everything from installation and wiring, to furniture and electrical goods.

If you are self-employed, the costs of office equipment and supplies are tax deductible.

THE NEXT STEP: A HOME OFFICE

It is a big advantage, psychologically as well as practically, to have a destination outside mainstream household activities where you can house everything you need in the way of files, records, reference books, as well as the usual office-type necessaries: stationery, stamps, pens and pencils.

Purely domestic paperwork can easily take up a shelf or two, which could be tidily provided for in a mini-office space of the sort one finds ingeniously sketched in the glossy mags – on a landing or even under the stairs in lieu of a broom cupboard. You may even be fortunate to have enough space to devote a whole room to your home office.

The wild card in this cosy arrangement seems to be the computer set-up: PC monitor, printer and keyboard. It is not this trio which causes the problems, but the wiring involved for them to function without coils of plastic underfoot. In modern office buildings interfloor space of at least half a metre is designed in to accommodate computer wiring. Therefore, as well as one of the neat workstations offered at very reasonable prices by firms such as IKEA or Viking Direct (small desk with drawers on side and fold-out housing for monitor, keyboard, etc – see My Directory) you will need to plan the wiring provision from Day One. IKEA sells a 'snake' which bundles together most wiring fairly tidily, if not attractively, in a sort of plastic grip. But if you have – as I have – a free-standing desk light and telephone, as well as the computer set-up, you are looking at a 'spaghetti junction' coiling about on the floor. Therefore, you will need to plan for this.

Psychological

The following suggestion came from my daughter Tabitha, who lives in San Francisco. She works from home, and loves her computer unreservedly: emailing, surfing, designing websites and popping in and out of chat rooms.

But her plea comes from another mindset; 'have one nice thing to look at,' she says. This could be a plant, a picture, a photo collage or even a fish tank (though this gives rise to maintenance problems). In other words, something to anchor you back in the real world if you have been trawling cyberspace.

Lighting
This needs to cover both ambient and focused lighting, positioned so that light doesn't reflect back off the computer screen.

Secure storage
Use a fireproof safe to store valuable or vital work records: backed-up computer disks, database of contacts, financial records and contracts. It is also an idea to scan in business cards if possible.

Comfort
Comfort is straightforward: a decent, height-adjustable chair, worktops at the right height, spot (non-glary) lighting, and shelves within easy reach. Use high shelving for box files of stuff you have to hang on to (financial records going back seven years) but rarely refer to. Use the lower shelving for reference books, press cuttings, designs, plans and ongoing paperwork – legal, financial, etc.

HOME-OFFICE TIPS

● If you see clients at home, a sparky set-up inspires confidence. Aim to look lively and professional. Muji, Paperchase, IKEA and Habitat all sell chic home-office needs. If you want to be different, you could recover box files or use baskets. A comfortable chair for the client, a coffee table, a lock on the door (for privacy) all help your image along.

BT answering services

BT offers two answering services:

Callminder: £2 per month, including VAT. You can record your own message. The number of 'rings' is adjustable: short, medium or long, and messages can be picked up when you are away from home.

BT Answering Service: free. This kicks in after a fixed number of rings (seven or eight) and the call is answered by a standard recorded message, made by a BT operator. No frills otherwise.

To access messages on both services dial 1571. These calls are free. For more information or to arrange for an answering service to be installed, call 150. It takes two to three days to make these services operational.

- Cut down distractions by using a call-answering phone service.

- A speaker phone frees up your hands, or use a headset. Talking with a phone wedged into your neck/shoulder strains muscles needlessly.

- Use computer diary and accounting programs to log your day-to-day dates and activities. Otherwise, keep a big desk diary, plus a tiny handbag version or Filofax, to keep track.

- To cut costs – this is for the computer clever – use a graphics program to design and print your own stationery and business cards.

- Bulk buy paper and printer cartridges, etc, via mail order or the internet (see page 70).

- Check out internet facilities for paying bills.

- Go for the best value warranties on all electronic equipment.

INSURANCE

Have you ever paused to calculate how much you are paying out in insurance, and then multiplied that figure by, say, 60 years? And then subtracted whatever sums you may have got back through successful claims? Over a lifetime it adds up to a stonking great pile of hard-earned cash. Multiply that up by the number of householders paying out house insurance, and car owners paying out car insurance, and it is a mystery how insurance companies can go bust.

I am not arguing with the sound and prudent principle involved in car insurance, which is a legal requirement anyway, because driving is a genuinely risky activity. Over a lifetime your chances of being involved in an accident are far higher than losing your house in a fire, having the roof blown off in a hurricane, or fractures appearing in the walls due to subsidence. Like most people, I have a mortgage on my house, and taking out house insurance was a pre-condition for obtaining the mortgage. However, I do sometimes wonder whether, did I not have a mortgage, I would still be coughing up my annual premium so obediently? I would be taking a risk undoubtedly, but it is a risk I can assess quite coolly: the likelihood of my house burning down is minuscule. On the other hand, insuring against this faint possibility is costly, too costly I sometimes think.

Moreover, to judge by the cases of aggrieved householders being short changed by their insurers which turn up in the pages of *WHICH?*, or on radio programmes like Moneybox, there seems to be a real risk that the insurers find a loophole in the policy which lets them out of paying the full whack. That seems to me quite a substantial risk, in fact, almost a foregone conclusion unless you have perused and fully understood all that fine-printed jargon, with all its sneaky get-out clauses.

And then the loss adjustors enter the picture, and it becomes an interrogation where the realisation creeps up on you that far from being treated as a valued and valuable client of the insurance company in question, these bland apparatchiks, with their needling questions, seem to assume that you are guilty until proved innocent.

OK, we all know where they are coming from. Insurance frauds undoubtedly happen, mysterious fires engulf shambolic and derelict properties in up-and-coming areas like my own beloved Spitalfields, raising sceptical eyebrows in many quarters, especially when a spruce block of flats appears next on the site.

Getting into insurance, as we mostly have to, feels like a mouse lined up against a lot of hungry cats. However, you can at least be a clever mouse. Some clever mouse suggestions are:

- Get the *WHICH? Guide to Insurance*. Read it, marking the relevant passages. Phone them with further queries.

- Your mortgage company will guide you into the arms of their own favourite insurance company. However, by shopping around you get more favourable terms. Worth a try.

- You are probably lumbered with house insurance, if you have a mortgage. But – this may seem like heresy – you are not obliged to sign up for a contents policy.

My partner and I have opted out of contents insurance for the following reasons: our most cherished and valuable items (family portraits and some furniture) are irreplaceable for personal, sentimental reasons; to insure them would require a valuation, photographs to record the items, provenance, etc. To be eligible for this expensive requirement would require further expense in the way of alarm systems, which would then have to be drilled into all the people who pass through the house: our children, their friends, au pairs, etc.

Instead we upgraded the front gate defences (Yale, Chubb locks and bolts) and we now have Bella, who barks like a full grown Hound of the Baskervilles. Furthermore, the house is never empty.

● The situation is different if you live out in the country and own seriously valuable stuff. Theft here is sadly a probability. Serious thieves – by which I mean knowledgeable types with useful contacts – case the joint first, sniffing out the possibilities, then return to take snaps of the goodies, strike a deal with the fence and return to do the business.

● Another friend who owns valuable stuff and is fully alarmed, valued and insured, suggests that it pays, in the long run, if you can afford a much higher 'exclusion fee' than is generally required. This fee normally quite small – maybe between £50–250 – is what you undertake to subtract from the insurers' liability in the event of theft, fire, etc. The more you shell out in exclusion fee, the more manageable your premium, and – my guess – the more sympathetically your claims will be treated.

In my friend's case the exclusion fee is in the region of £1,000. This is a pain if you were claiming for a run-of-the-mill item; such as slates blown off in a high wind, but then – like car owners who prefer to carry the cost of a scraped wing rather than lose their no-claims bonus – you might well choose not to go through the whole hassle of putting in a claim in this instance. And, as you may know, it IS a hassle: months can elapse before your claim is dealt with – and you have to live with a leaking roof, skylight, etc.

● Whatever the basis for your claim, you need to get outside professional ratification as soon as possible. In the case of theft, report to your nearest police station, with all the evidence you can muster. In the case of damage to the building, you should call on a surveyor for a detailed report. The general view is that you will be left to pay the surveyor, whatever the claim, but he/she has provided you with vital, essential evidence to support it. You need to balance these costs against the size of your claim.

● Try to keep all receipts for costly items such as TV, mobile phone, digital camera, pearl necklace, etc.

● Take snaps of your 'good stuff' and write down full descriptions. A professional valuation will be expensive, but essential in the case of important paintings, jewellery and silver. If you have just one possible treasure, you would do well to have it properly identified. Museums such as the Victoria and Albert offer free specialist advice (see page 52) and auction houses such as Bonhams (see My Directory) often hold free valuation days.

MY DIRECTORY

The following list is not intended to be an all-encompassing directory, but is a collection of contacts that I, personally, have found particularly useful.

Aga-Rayburn
Station Road, Ketley, Telford, Shropshire TF1 5AQ
Tel: 01952 642000
Website: www.aga-rayburn.co.uk

Appliances – information
John Lewis customer service helpline
Tel: 020 7514 5323 (direct line)

Artists' suppliers
Atlantis
7–9 Plumbers Row, London EI IEQ
Tel: 020 7377 8855

A P Fitzpatrick
142 Cambridge Heath Road, London EI 5QJ
Tel: 020 7790 0884

Paintworks
99–101 Kingsland Road, London E2 8AG
Tel: 020 7729 745I

Auction houses
Bonham's
Montpelier Street, London SW7 1HH
Tel: 0207 393 3900
Website: www.bonhams.com

Christie's
8 King Street, London SW1Y 6QT
Tel: 020 7839 9060
Website: www.christies.com

Sotheby's
34–35 New Bond Street, London W1A 2AA
Tel: 020 7293 5000
Website: www.sothebys.com

Au pairs/mothers' helps/nannies
Au Pairs Unlimited
7 Donovan Avenue, London NIO 2JU
Website: www.aupairs.com

Kensington Nannies
3 Hornton Place, London W8 4LZ
Tel: 020 7937 2333
Website: www.kensington-nannies.co.uk

Camellia oil
The Tool Shop
78 High St, Needham Market, Suffolk IP6 8AW
Tel: 01449 722992
Price: £9.95 for 240 ml (approx. 8 fl oz)

Carpet cleaning
James Turtle On-site Services (free estimates)
Unit 5, 4A Manorgate Rd, Kingston-upon-Thames,
Surrey KT2 7EL
Tel: 020 8546 4222

Cleaning agencies
Betterclean (now known as Firstcall)
97A St Johns Avenue, London WIO 4EJ
Tel: 020 8965 2485

Cleaning materials
HG
Website: www.hginternational.com

Labour and Wait
18 Cheshire Street, London E1
Tel: 020 7729 6253
Eclectic mix of traditional brooms, brushes and
trendy bits and pieces, old and new.

SCP
135–139, Curtain Road, London EC2A 3BX
(also at Selfridges, Oxford Street, W1)
Tel: 0207 739 1869
Website: www.scp.co.uk
Swedish bristle washing-up brushes, plus an
extensive range of Swedish-made brushes.

Simmonds Stores
1 Godfrey Street, London SW3 3TA
Tel: 0207 352 4962

SX Wallpapers
113 Essex Rd, Islington NI 2SL
Tel: 0207 226 9056

Clock repairs
City Clocks
3I Amwell Street,
London ECIR IUN
Tel: 020 7278 1154
Website: www.cityclocks.coluk
Repair long-case clocks, etc

Consumer help
WHICH?
Members' helpline: 08453 010010
Mon-Fri 8.30am–9pm, Sat 9am–3pm
Website: www.which.net

Corn bins
IAE Ltd, Reading
For nearest dealer call: 01538 399200

Cupboard door shelf racks
These used to be common a few years ago, but
are now being replaced by chrome racks. Look
for them at:

Lakeland Plastics
Head office tel: 01539 488100
Website: www.lakelandlimited.com

MFI
Head office tel: 0208 200 8000
Website: www.mfi.co.uk/

Robert Dyas
Head office tel: 01372 361444
Website: www.robertdyas.co.uk

Drawer dividers
The Holding Company
241–5 Kings Road, London SW3 5EL
020 7352 1600
Website: www.theholdingcompany.co.uk

IKEA
11 stores, from Croydon to Edinburgh
Tel: 020 8208 5600 (Brent Cross)
Website: www.ikea.co.uk

Muji
Tel: 020 7323 2208 for nearest stockist
Website: www.mujionline.com

Eiderdown repairs
Eiderdown Studio
228 Withycombe Village Road,Exmouth,
Devon EX8 3BD
Tel: 01395 271147 (contact: Mary)
Fax: 01395 267967
Website: www.bwc@sosi.net

Electrician
Neil Roland
Tel: 020 8691 1961 Mobile: 07973 909707

Electricity
Npower Juice
Freephone: 0800 316 2610
Website: www.npower.com

Embroidered initials
Jane Adams
Chaysern, High Street, Blagdon BS40 7TQ
Tel: 01761 463655
She majors on natural-fibre fabrics, vintage
fabrics, Liberty lawn and linens.

Feather and down cleaning
Ideal Cleaners
Pound Lane, Exmouth, Devon EX8 4NP
Tel: 01395 273317 (contact: Simon)

Fridge and freezer repairs
Brian Williams
21 Berryleys, Luton, LUC CNQ
Tel: 01582 752712
Mobile: 07961 365484

Gardeners and tree surgeons
British Association of Landscape Industries (BALI).
Landscape House, Stoneleigh Park,
Warwickshire CV8 2LG
Tel: 02476 690333
Website: www.bali.org.uk

Tree Advice Trust
(Arboricultural advice and information service)
Alice Holt Lodge, Wrecclesham, Farnham,
Surrey GU10 4LH
Tel: 01420 220 22
Website: www.treeadviceservice.org uk

Arboricultural Association
Ampfield House, Ampfield. Near Romsey,
Hampshire, SO51 9PA
Tel: 01794 368717
Website: www.trees.org.uk

Horolene Concentrate
Foxell & James
See page 296, under Paint and decorating
suppliers

Horological Products
Proctor Street, Bury, Lancashire
Tel: 0161 764 2741

Joinery
Crown & Leek Workshop
11 Deal Street, London E1 5AH
Tel: 020 7377 0734

Leather suppliers
M & B Leather Ltd
121a Bethnal Green Rd, London E2 7DG
Tel: 020 7739 1369

UK Hide Co
Building D9, West Entrance, Fairoaks Airport,
Chobham, Surrey GU24 8H6
Tel: 01276 859407
The people to contact for large skins.

Lifestyle management

ten^{uk}
4th floor, 30 Market Place, London WIW 8AP
Tel: 07000 101999
Website: www.tenuk.com

Loose covers, cushions, etc.

Sally Penfold
Imasas, Middletown, Hailey, Nr Whitney,
Oxon OX28 9VB
Tel: 01993 822922

Mail-order/online companies

Cucina Direct
Phone orders: 020 8246 4300
Website: www.cucinadirect.co.uk.

Green Busines Co/ Consumablemade
Freephone: 0800 644 222
Free fax: 01983 872851
Website: www.consumablemad.co.uk

Lands End Direct Merchant UK Ltd
Freephone: 0800 220 106
Free fax: 0800 222 106
Website: www.landsend.co.uk

Lyco Direct
Freephone: 0800 525 980
Fax: 01908 143 674
Website: www.lyco.co.uk

Nicole Farhi Home
Tel: 020 7494 9051

Ocean
Orderline: 0870 24 26 28 3
Website: www.oceanuk.com

OKA
Tower Rd, Berinsfield, Nr Abingdon OXIO 7LN
Tel: 0870 160 6002
A mail-order service to die for, a brilliantly sourced collection of furniture, rugs, china (including blue and white porcelain, made in China to I7th century designs), glass, cushions, rugs etc.

Peruvian Connection
Freephone: 0800 55 00 00
Fax: 01491 875 188
Website: www.peruvianconnection.com

Tightsplease
Phone orders: Add phone no.
Website: www.Tightsplease.co.uk

Viking Direct
Freephone: 0800 424 444
Free fax: 0800 622 211
Website: www.viking-direct.co.uk

Volga Linen Co
Tel: OI728 635O2O
Website: www.volgalinen.co.uk

The White Company
Tel: 0870 900 9555
Fax: 0870 160 1611
Website: www.thewhiteco.com

Metal Repairs (zinc, stainless steel etc)

Verdigris
290 Crown St, Camberwell, London SE5 OUR
Tel: 020 7703 8373
Website: www.verdigrislondon.com

Office furniture

Habitat
Head office tel: 020 7255 2545
Website: www.habitat.co.uk

IKEA
See page 294, under Drawer Dividers

Muji
See page 294, under Drawer Dividers

Organic meat

Eastbrook Farms
Tel: 01793 790460
email: info@helenbrowningorganics.co.uk

Heal Farm
Kings Nympton, Umberleigh, Devon EX37 9TB
Tel: 01769 574341
email: enquiries@healfarm.co.uk

Paint and decorating suppliers

Leyland Paints
Numerous shops around the country.
The biggest: 6–8 Warwick Way, London SWI
Head office tel: 01924 477201
Website: www.sigmakalon.com

Foxell & James
57 Farringdon Road, London ECIM 3JB
Tel: 020 7405 0152/2487
Sell the Trip Trap floor finish, plus almost every paint varnish, stain, powder and abrasive mentioned in this book.

Pet food by mail order

PR Petfood
1283 Greenford Road, Greenford,
Middlesex UB6 OHY
Tel: 020 8723 0783

Plasterer

John le Blanc
57 St Margaret's Road, London NW10 5PY
Tel: 07776 181885

Professional and trade associations

Chartered Institute of Builders (CIB)
The White House, Engelmere, Kings Ride, Ascot, Berkshire SL5 7JR
Tel: 01344 630 810

Electrical Contractors Association (ECA)
24 Palace Court, London W2 4HY
Tel: 020 7313 4800

Federation of Master Builders (FMB)
14 Great James Street, London WCI
Tel: 020 7242 2200

Institute of Plumbing
64 Station Lane, Hornchurch, Essex RM12 6NB
Tel: 0l256 372200
email: info@plumbers.org.uk

Royal Institute of British Architecture (RIBA)
66 Portland Place, London W1B 1AD
Tel: 020 7580 5533

Propert's Hide Cream

Available at branches of John Lewis; Harrods, etc

Quickshine

Available at branches of John Lewis; Harrods, etc

Recycling information

To find out what your local council provides click on to www.recoup.org (for plastics), or for more general updates contact Valpak at www.recyclemore.co.uk.

Tesco has a scheme for recycling/redistributing old mobile phones.

Rug cleaners

Pilgrim Payne
290 Latimer Road, London W10 6QU
Tel: 020 8960 5656
Specialise in cleaning soft furnishings, curtains, wool rugs etc and will visit to give a quote.

Sheeting (and furnishing fabrics)

Givans
207 King's Road, London SW3 5ED
Tel: 020 7352 6352
Website: www.givans.co.uk

Ian Mankin
109 Regents Park Road, London NW1 8UR
Tel: 020 7722 0997

John Lewis
26 stores throughout England and Scotland
Tel: 020 7629 7711 (Oxford Street)
Website: www.johnlewis.com (sheeting N/A online)

Z Butt Textiles
24 Brick Lane, London E1 6RF
Tel: 020 7247 7776

Shoe repairs
Jeeves: ten branches in central London
Tel: 020 8809 3232
email: services@jeevesofbelgravia.co.uk
Website: www.jeevesofbelgravia.co.uk

Shout
Available at branches of John Lewis and major
supermarkets

Slack Rack
See Jeeves under shoe repairs above

Stain removal
Blossom & Browne
73a Clarendon Rd, London WII
Tel: 020 7727 2635

Stationery/office supplies
Paperchase – 34 outlets in UK
Tottenham Court Road, London W1
Tel: 020 7467 6200
St Mary's Gate, Manchester
Tel: 0161 835 9935
Website: www.paperchase.co.uk

Viking Direct
See page 295 under Mail-order/online companies

Supermarkets online
Sainsbury's
Website: www.sainsburystoyou.co.uk

Tesco
Website: www.tesco.com

Trip Trap
See Paint and decorating suppliers/Foxell & James

Victoria and Albert Museum
Opinions and Enquiry Service
First Tuesday of every month, 2.30–5pm
Main switchboard: 020 7942 2000

Washing-machine repairs
Simon Kirk
Tel: 01279 860563

Washsaver
Aquavator Ltd
Orderline: 0870 900 2011

Water softeners
Salamander (Eng) Ltd
Unit 24, The Reddicap Trading Estate,
Sutton Coldfield, West Midlands B75 7BY
Tel: 0l2l 378 0952
Website: www.salamander-engineering co.uk

Wood-burning and solid-fuel stoves
Robeys Heating
Green Lane, Belper, Derbyshire D56 1BY
Tel: 01773 820940
Website: www.robeys-heating.co.uk

Upholstery
Association of Master Upholsterers
Website: www.upholsterers.co.uk

Ted Jones
8 Market Street, Chipping Norton, Oxon OX7 5NQ
Tel: 01608 643255

A V Fowlds & Sons Ltd,
Progress Works, 3 Addington Square,
Camberwell, London SE5 7JZ
Tel: 020 7703 2686

INDEX

Acknowledgements

Whew, bear with me (insider joke – see page 71) while I get my breath back! What I thought of as a sharp sprint turned into a considerable marathon. Innumerable people helped me along the way with advice, information, encouragement, curiosity.

On the publishing side my thanks are due to Denise Bates, whose idea it was, and to Margot Richardson, who tidied my manuscript like an editing Mrs Wonderful.

Without Fatma Kilic and Karim Tali, rescuing lost documents and overseeing my panicky first steps on computer, I might never have made it to the finish. I can't thank them enough. Maggie Duke and Ann French, experts in their different fields, provided invaluable blue-chip information and expertise. Thanks too to Frances, the velvet glove behind Bruern Stable Cottages, and Jenny, (more rubber than velvet glove?) for their generous help on essential details. WHICH? editorial staff were regularly helpful, indeed brilliant, faxing me archival information in abundance. Thanks in spades to my interviewees, both interesting and interested – their contributions appear as 'Doing it Their Way'. My daughter, Tabitha, snatched moments between breastfeeds to update me on ecological issues, surfing the net and much else, toujours present and empathetic. The MD of Karchers Ltd lent me a steam cleaner, which I can hardly bear to return, so useful it has proved. And then there were all those alert, charming, funny, 'anons', who picked up a phone and made a random call both useful and entertaining.

Two things revived my flagging energies over the course: one was Doing It myself, all that sweeping, mopping, ironing routine that writes more easily from immediate experience, and the other was the selfish thought that in future I would be spared the endless spiel to my au pairs. A copy of Home Time says it all. My family won't read it: they think they know it all, would you believe? Nevertheless, they demand and get a pat on the back for forbearance, fortitude, those 'family' qualities sweetened by a reliably decent meal at the end of the day.